shelter

of the

monument

A Provincetown Love Story

Yvonne deSousa

Black Rose Writing | Texas

Cover photo by Russell Dutra

Author photo by DL Quiroz

ISBN: 978-1-68513-316-0
PUBLISHED BY BLACK ROSE WRITING
www.blackrosewriting.com

Printed in the United States of America
Suggested Retail Price (SRP) $22.95

Shelter of the Monument is printed in Sabon

*As a planet-friendly publisher, Black Rose Writing does its best to eliminate unnecessary waste to reduce paper usage and energy costs, while never compromising the reading experience. As a result, the final word count vs. page count may not meet common expectations.

Praise for
Shelter of the Monument
A Provincetown Love Story

Intertwining her coming-of-age story with the dark side of addiction, "*Shelter of the Monument*" perfectly illuminates the sadness, anger, hope, and affection experienced by those who watch a loved one struggle with addiction. Yvonne deSousa blends her gentle wit and compelling levity in this tale of innocence lost, never abandoning the compassion and tenderness she will always hold for her first love. Shining a light on the deep effects of addiction on those around them, Yvonne gives the reader a glimpse of a world that is sometimes dark, sometimes heartbreaking, but always filled with the unbending belief that love can fix the unfixable.
–**Lisa Febre, author of** ***Round the Twist: Facing the Abdominable***

The power of love is astonishing in its ability to both break and heal. Richard and Yvonne more than loved each other, they liked each other and respected each other. Richard's support at a pivotal moment forged the base for Yvonne's future and it is heartbreaking that addiction destroyed what could have been a monumental love story. While reading this raw and honest life history, I recalled moments in my past where one person's opinion could make or break me. Every reader will recognize a piece of themselves in this memoir about love, loss, and family.
–**Cheri Krueger, author of** ***The Abduction of Adrienne Berg***

Yvonne captures young love from its first buzz, to the lessons learned - and losses endured - along the way. *Shelter of the Monument* shows young readers - and reinforces for older, nostalgic readers - that first loves never really leave, even if they go away.
–**Courtney K. Hurst, author of** ***My Ride. My Rules***

Grab the tissues.

What is it about good girls that attracts them to bad boys? I spent the firbst half or so of *Shelter of the Monument* wondering why a smart, talented girl like Yvonne was as addicted to Richard as he was to cocaine. I kept rooting for her to move on, to leave him in the past, but that's true love for you. Even once she did, she really didn't. As I read on, I began to get it. Her story is so well-written, compelling, and true to life, it would be impossible not to.

The memoir begins when Yvonne first meets Richard, a tall, ruggedly handsome guy 11 years her senior, while she is still in high school. Other than the difference in age, and, of course, his addition to cocaine, he's perfect—smart, funny, kind, and somehow attracted to her, she is instantly smitten. The book tells their love story, of their on-again, off-again relationship. And it's beautiful and heart-rending in the telling. My father, who I often quote, would have called this a "tear-jerker," and it's that, but so much more. I confess that I still don't know the answer to my question, but I'm probably as close as it's possible to be, thanks to this sensitively and incredibly bravely told story. Five stars to this one.

–Bill Schweitzer, author of *Doves in a Tempest-Valley of Horror*

Painful lessons of love's failures and of a woman's strength—

"What's reality when it comes to your heart?" Ms. deSousa poses this question in her remarkable memoir, *Shelter of the Monument*. Written in a straight-forward style, deSousa bares her soul and heart as she tells a story that primarily centers on one relationship that lasts more than twenty years.

The narrative begins with an intelligent but tentative seventeen-year-old Yvonne deSousa. Then she meets Richard and her world changes. Richard is older, charming, and handsome, so it's easy to see why Yvonne is drawn to him. But aside from his outward features, Richard possesses a nurturing and caring nature. Not surprisingly, he is the first person to recognize the depth of Yvonne's good qualities. Before she sets off for college, Richard tells Yvonne that she is equal to anyone, perhaps exceeding others. His words alter her self-perception and gives her the strength and confidence needed to face whatever trials the world has to offer.

For decades, Yvonne's lodestar is Richard; however, tragically, Richard's lodestar is drugs. Many times he tries to cease his dependency, but unfortunately he finds himself caught within the snares of an insidious existence. Ms. deSousa helps Richard battle his demons, and for a time things appear as if she will have the beautiful life she has imagined with the man she loves. But the power of illicit substances is too great for Richard to break his dependency. Ms. deSousa documents her years with Richard and her years apart from him. Because Richard is the person she loves deeply, he is never far from her thoughts. We are taken—absolutely drawn—into a private world that anyone will recognize.

Ms. deSousa shares her ups and downs with family members, friends, lovers, and jobs. She also provides a perfect view of the hardscrabble life for year-round residents of the famous Provincetown community. More importantly, she reflects and accepts a world that is seldom orderly, which allows her to confront her darkest moments with courage. She prevails.

Although this story happened years ago, many people living today can relate to the central situation: to follow your heart instead of your sense; to reach your hand to someone who cannot keep himself from drowning; to be willing to give your life to someone who recklessly destroys his own. Empathy, desire, and compassion are strong emotions, and Yvonne deSousa reveals her feelings upon every page. *Shelter of the Monument* will stay with every reader who has "loved not wisely but too well."

–Thomas DeConna, author of *Accustomed to the Dark*

For those who struggle with their own overwhelming demons, and for those who love the person underneath the demon.

shelter
of the
monument

contents

prologue

part I – learning

part II – living

Someone I loved once gave me
a box full of darkness.
It took me years to understand
that this, too, was a gift.

–Mary Oliver, *The Uses of Sorrow*

prologue

It wasn't the first time I wanted to puke in this stifling room, but this afternoon's dread had nothing to do with math. These were just my teachers, teachers I had known for years. Provincetown High School was so small that my classmates and I knew their stories, their family histories, their gossip. And they knew ours. We were all part of the extended, family-like atmosphere of our quirky little town.

But today they frightened me, looking formal and serious as they did. Why were they asking me questions about my character and my goals? They were the ones who had shaped them. Or at least, had told me what my character was, and what my goals should be.

Following the 2:10 bell, the six of them had gathered here and rearranged the desk chairs in a U formation. Now I was sitting in a single seat at the open end of the U, shifting uncomfortably as they decided if they should admit me into the National Honor Society.

Minutes before, I had been among 14 of us waiting in the humid third-floor hallway that September afternoon; three seniors, 10 sophomores and me.

The seniors admitted they were only waiting for the inquisition to boost their college applications. The sophomores actually cared about this stuff. Their class, a large one of 38 students, were all brilliant and dedicated to all things teachers valued. My class of

30 was just the opposite: a bunch of unruly, casual party goers who were too indifferent to care. When we first entered this building in the seventh grade, the principal made a point of telling us we were the sorriest bunch of students he'd ever seen. Rather than motivating us, it made us proud. We found out later he gave the same "sorry students" speech to each incoming class. We bragged that he eventually would take it back. With us, he never did.

But how could any school induct a new batch of National Honor Society members without at least interviewing one junior? And that one was me. The token "good girl" who did what was expected of her, a reverse rebel among my crew of sharp witted but unmotivated teenagers.

I wasn't motivated either. I just wasn't brave enough to show it.

The reordering of the room didn't provide the usual comforting landscape of my world. From the usual position of my desk, I could see the working harbor, an ever-changing landscape depending on the tides, the wind, and the time of year. My tiny hometown, with a year-round population of 2700, was an eclectic mix of Portuguese fishing families, artists, a thriving gay and lesbian community, seasonal tourists, and washashores still looking for the freedom of the sixties. And it fit. Amid all the different lifestyles, we sought comfort from the beautiful sea that surrounded us in three directions. But now, with my desk turned around, all I could see were some of the dull granite stones of the 252-foot Pilgrim Monument next to the school; the landmark that noted Provincetown's pilgrim history and kept watch over all of us. No wonder Costello was always grouchy; there wasn't much to appreciate from her view.

My teachers, now operating as the NHS committee, were defining the Society and its members as a distinct group who "demonstrated character, leadership, scholarship and service," values that did not define me. My character was boring at best, my leadership skills non-existent, and any service skills I had basically sucked. They amounted to helping our librarian during elementary school visits, as I enjoyed both kids and books. And scholarship? Well, unless you counted doing homework because your parents made you, I didn't have much of that either.

But when I was invited to interview, there was no way any adult was going to let me walk away from it.

My mother: "Of course you'll interview; why wouldn't you?"

My father: "Don't be foolish; you're going."

My history teacher: "See you after school; don't be late or we may have to take that into consideration."

My gym teacher who had also been my 8th grade science teacher: "See you at three."

And, of course, Costello herself, the unpopular teacher of all thing's math-related: "I'll expect you to be sharp and well-prepared this afternoon."

"You don't look so good. You're not nervous, are you?" Lenny had asked me before I was summoned into the room. He was a senior and full of a swagger I would never possess. He was another townie, just like me, so I was used to his confidence. It was hard to be timid around people you had fought with over crayons in Aunt Franny's nursery school.

"No," I lied. "It's just too nice to be inside. And seriously, like I have a shot. They had to bring in someone from the class of '87. But I'm ruining our reputation being stuck here with all you bright futures."

The sophomores laughed.

"Maybe," Lenny replied, "you guys *are* a bunch of deadbeats. But they're just our teachers. Go show them what you're made of."

Problem was, I wasn't made of anything...

part I

learning

chapter 1
roommate

He was gorgeous. Everyone thought so. I thought so. My taste ran to blonde, scrawny guys, but what did I know? I'd had many crushes but never really dated. Unless you counted my buddy Glen and I telling people we were dating when we were 13. Since we did the same things on "dates" as we did when we were just hanging out, it didn't really count.

Richard was anything but blonde and scrawny. His dark brown hair and brown eyes perfectly matched his medium complexion. He wasn't built in the way of the huge weightlifter types who grossed me out. His body was that of someone who worked hard for a living, with strong arms that I imagined could wrap you up and hold you forever. With thoughts like these, it was amazing I could even exist in his presence. I did everything I could not to be noticed by him. Which, of course, was so obvious I wound up looking like a fool; a silly 17-year-old fool trying desperately not to be noticed by the mysterious man in the room. Luckily, no one was paying attention. I had only recently gotten comfortable talking to Andy, and he had been in my life for years. No wonder I could barely breathe when I was in the same room with Richard.

The room was the living room in the apartment my sister Laurie shared with her boyfriend, Andy. Laurie and I were close, and I hung out with them often. At their place, I could deal with whatever teen angst I was succumbing to. It didn't hurt that one of my friends (whose parents traveled all the time, leaving her with the ultimate party spot) lived in the same complex. I would hang at my sister's for a bit, and then head to the party at Sue's place. Visiting at Laurie's made me feel grown up. Until Andy's best friend Richard moved into their spare bedroom, turning me back again into the lame kid I believed I was.

Richard was 11 years older than me, and despite his dark features, he was anything but dark. He was funny and mischievous, yet never mean. He was handsome, and, as far as I could tell, kind. Once Richard moved in, I continued to hang out at Laurie's. But on these visits, I would sit quietly, trying to make myself invisible, which was the way I felt most comfortable when my insecurities set in. Then one time I couldn't help myself.

I was sitting cross legged on the floor, alongside the speakers, when the song *Must of Got Lost* came on the radio. I started swaying to the chorus. When Laurie looked my way, I immediately stopped and stammered that I really liked the J. Geils Band. The seventies song was from their generation, not mine.

Andy told me I had the band wrong. I said I didn't.

Laurie spoke up, "Andy, I wouldn't argue with Yvonne when it comes to music. She really knows her stuff."

"Eighties music maybe. But this is my era and there's no way the J. Geils Band sings this. Give me a second and I'll come up with the right group."

Andy was a bit of a know-it-all, and it could get annoying. "Take all the time you want, but it's J. Geils," I responded. "Lead singer, Peter Wolf."

"Yvonne, no offense, but you're wrong. I'd put money on it. Wolf though, that's familiar. Maybe it's Steppenwolf, or something like that," he said. "Bad Company possibly?"

"It's J. Geils," I said as the deejay came on the radio and read back the playlist. "And finishing up this last set were our local boys from Worcester, the J. Geils Band."

Andy said nothing but turned a particular shade of red that clashed with his strawberry blonde hair. I smiled but didn't say anything either. I did not want to seem like a show-off, and it was not a big deal. It was just a good song I happened to like.

But I felt eyes on me. I turned, and it was the first time I was the focus of Richard's grin. Some people call the famous expression 'the cat who ate the canary' grin or, in crude circles, a 'shit-eating grin.' It was a look Richard was known for, but neither of those sayings fit. Not quite a smirk, his half-smile was direct, teasing, and a little roguish. And his eyes sparkled. If he was flashing you his grin, he was radiating delight directly at you. So why flash it at me, at that moment of me showing up his cocky friend over the name of a band? In the past few visits, all he had ever seen of Laurie's little sister was shyness. Did my silly debate with Andy show him a glimpse of something more?

After that, I could not stop thinking about Richard. And evenings at Laurie's were different. Richard made a point of including me in conversations, and he appeared interested in what I had to say. His attention was both exhilarating and horrifying. It was all I could do to respond. That is why I surprised myself two weeks after the J. Geils conversation when I reached out to him, egged on by my far more brazen friends. True, I needed a favor. Still, calling him seemed fitting, even if it was crazy.

The Christmas holiday break had just ended, and my friends and I were ready to celebrate with a small party. We were seniors, officially counting down the days to graduation and excited to celebrate our future freedom. Sue's parents had just escaped the dreary winter by heading south again. Their latest departure was fine with us. Now we had a place to party, but a party wasn't a party without alcohol, and we weren't 21 yet. For one reason or another, we could not get in touch with the folks who usually helped us in this particular dilemma. The start of the weekend looked bleak unless we could figure out this problem.

Laurie and Andy weren't home, and it was questionable how much Laurie would approve. She had begrudgingly bought for us in the past, but made it clear she did not enjoy supporting our drinking. As a result, I only asked her to buy for us in dire party emergencies. Richard's work truck was parked in their visitor spot. I thought he was cool enough that he might not care about the legality/illegality of underage drinking. Asking him was an appropriate (ok, technically inappropriate) excuse for contacting him. Before I had thought it through, I voiced this option out loud. Of course, my friends encouraged, pressured, and dared me into trying it.

Terrified at the idea of talking to Richard without the guise of hanging with my sister as a safety net, my finger shook as I punched in the number and held my breath. My voice cracked when he answered, and I stumbled over the reason for my call.

"I, um, really just need something at the liquor store and thought maybe if you needed something too and if um, I gave you money, then, um, maybe you could pick up something for me?"

"So basically, you need me to buy booze for you?" he asked.

"Um, I guess so, kind of...."

Heather and Sue could hear his laughter on the other end of the line. It wasn't condescending; it was just laughter.

"Alright," he said, still sounding amused. "Come on over."

I shivered on the short walk across the parking lot. I had thrown on my coat but refused to wear a hat or gloves; gloves seemed childish, and I dreaded what a hat would do to my already wavy and uncontrollable hair. Richard met me outside and I noticed his hair was damp. I must have caught him just out of the shower. I tried to erase the image of him in the shower by telling him I liked his truck. He laughed as the truck was just a truck. It was an aging, metallic blue pickup with his employer's construction logo on the sides, and dents and scratches over the rest of it. He asked me what I liked about it. I told him I liked the faint smell of sawdust that I noticed when I hopped into the cab. He shook his head and started the engine.

On the drive through the empty winter streets, we talked a little, but it was a different sort of talk. I expected to feel awkward, and I did, but only somewhat. I was nervous that I, so uncool, was alone with this handsome, very cool guy. Yet, I was also relaxed. Naïve as I was, I recognized a current between us, a sort of energy that had nothing to do with being his roommate's baby sister. I didn't understand it, but I knew it was there.

Like all direct drives in the off season, this drive was a quick one, just 2 miles down Bradford and ½ a mile down Conwell to the year-round liquor store. It was too quick for me. I stayed in the warmth of the running vehicle while he ran in. Back at the complex, I figured he would drop me off and I would thank him and then get buzzed with my friends. Instead, he helped carry our peppermint schnapps, light beers, and sickeningly sweet wine coolers into Sue's place and, to my pleasant but anxious surprise, he stayed for a bit. After a couple of drinks, the silliness and drama of teen life was raging among my friends and he wasn't impressed.

Heather, already buzzed yet way more experienced in the ways of the world, sensed the energy, too. She put her hand on Richard's shoulder and told him to be good to me, her best friend, and that if she heard otherwise, she would kick his ass. Richard and I escaped to the spare bedroom then and talked some more while sitting close together. We talked about my sister and Andy, his job, what I wanted to do when I graduated and growing up in Ptown. We flirted too. At least, I think I was flirting. I'd never done it before.

He must have known that he should leave before the feelings between us got out of hand. I walked outside with him, and he kissed me. It was the most incredible high I had ever felt in my life. I'd only been kissed a couple of times before, and each were awkward and meaningless. But this felt sweet and affectionate, and a little dangerous, too. It was exciting and romantic in ways I'd never imagined. It was quick, but it was real. Richard kissed me. Me!

We pulled apart and said goodbye. I thanked him for buying for us. Then, as I turned to go back into Sue's, I slipped on some ice and fell right on my butt. Falling at all, let alone after such a kiss, would have been total, end of the world humiliation for any teenager. But for me, it was unbearable. I wanted to run away before I burst into tears but knew I would probably slip again. I looked at him, shattered. His only response was that famous grin — a grin that giggled only slightly and eyes that asked if I was ok and silently telling me not to be embarrassed.

chapter 2
date

I didn't see him for a couple of days after the icy slip and fall. Sometime early in the next week, I went to Laurie's, bringing her some mail my mom had asked me to take over. Our Mom was not a big fan of Andy, so she tried to avoid their apartment as much as possible. Richard wasn't there that afternoon, and though disappointed, I was also relieved. As much as I wanted to see him, I was also anxious about seeing him.

These emotions were new to me. I was used to being self-conscious and downright frightened of various social interactions, especially if those interactions included someone as handsome as Richard. That he had kissed me and then I promptly embarrassed myself, made the thought of being near him again staggering to comprehend. What if I did something even more ridiculous? Would he realize I wasn't worth his attention and decide that there was someone, anyone, better he could spend those precious moments with? Yet, I remembered how natural our conversation had felt and was even more confused.

None of this made any sense. Here I was wanting to get close to someone who downright intimidated me. The situation was both lovely and horrifying at the same time. Avoidance was the way I would usually proceed in a similar situation; a crush on a senior when I was a freshman, speaking quietly within a group, looking down and not saying much when meeting someone new. But being near Richard was nothing like those other scenarios.

Somehow, despite my vulnerability, avoiding Richard was the last thing I intended.

The next few days were dreary, and I had no excuse to take a ride in the evenings. I did my best to look for him and his truck at various construction sites as I went back and forth to school, but I didn't see him until the Friday after he bought for us. I showed up at Laurie's and she was a little grouchy and not as welcoming as usual. It didn't take long to see that her mood had more to do with an argument she had with Andy than it did with me.

She let me know they were all leaving soon to go to meet some friends. She sat for a bit, as did Richard and Andy. I tried not looking at Richard, not sure if I could handle it if he looked back. But the impish Richard wouldn't let me off that easily, practically flirting with me in front of my sister. Mercifully, she was too annoyed with her own boyfriend to notice. She said goodbye to me and headed down the hall to touch up her makeup. I said a generic goodbye to the room, intending it for both Andy and Richard. But Richard told me to wait, he would walk me out. Andy looked away, declared, "I'm not seeing this," and downed the rest of his beer.

At my car, Richard asked for my number. He knew I had my own phone. My mother worked at the unemployment office where she helped lines upon lines of people every day in between fielding hundreds of calls. She quickly tired of answering our home phone, only to have it be for me, her third daughter, and the only one still living at home. With Laurie in an apartment with her boyfriend, and Audrey having married young and moved out of town, my mom wanted some peace and quiet in the evenings. She bought me a phone and had a private line installed in my bedroom. And now Richard had the number and promised to call.

Since Sue's parents were back, and I hadn't made other plans not knowing what the evening might bring at my sister's, I went home. I lay on the sofa and waited for midnight when *Friday Night Videos* came on, hoping to get lost in the cheesy romance of eighties music. I was having trouble believing Richard would really call me. Why would he want to? Didn't he know amazing guys like him didn't call chubby, mousy girls like me? Sure, he was nice to me, but he was a nice guy. There must have been many other women he would rather call. Still, he'd asked for my number. What was that about?

Saturday arrived and there were social things I could have done. I could have driven around town with Serena and Lynn. I could have driven around town with Glen, Shannon, and Kristin. Or I could have driven around town with Heather and Sue. Nothing appealed to me. I stayed home by the phone with a good book I pretended to read.

I was in my room Sunday afternoon, finishing up an English paper on the life of Eugene O'Neil and his connection to my hometown, when the phone rang. I had let my guard down as the phone had been ringing all day with friends complaining about this assignment that was due the next day. But this time it was Richard, calling to ask if he could make me dinner the following Friday. My heart skipped, and I said yes before I could talk myself out of it. Was this real? If I hadn't recognized the distinct way he said hello, "HEL-lo," I would think my friends were playing a trick on me. I heard crowds and music in the background and guessed that he was calling from the payphone at the Governor Bradford, the popular local dive bar.

As soon as I said yes, he started talking about menu options, as if I would care what he made. He asked if I liked Skully Joes and, trying to be cool, I said, "Of course." But he got me to admit I had no idea what he was talking about, which made him laugh. Being the granddaughter of Portuguese fishermen, I should have known what they were. Instead, I was surprised when he explained that Skully Joes were haddock dried out and then patted into cakes, and definitely an acquired taste. He said he might make scallops instead.

I stayed away from Laurie's all that week because I knew I could not keep the news of our date away from her or keep it together if Richard was home. But he called me on Wednesday to confirm and then again on Friday afternoon. He told me where to park my car and that he would meet me on the street. We were having dinner at his friend Ronny's place. Ronny and Richard had been as close as brothers growing up, and Richard had a key to his small apartment, which he was welcome to use when Ronny and his wife were out of town.

He met me on the street and led me up the stairs into the small one-bedroom. He took my coat and offered me wine, which I happily accepted. Wine felt familiar to me. When I was twelve, I had gone to Portugal with my dad. At our first dinner out, I thought I would be allowed to have a soda with dinner, something my mom would never let me get away. My dad, always easy going, was surprised at my request and said, "Soda?! You're in Portugal now and you'll drink what the Portuguese kids drink. You're having wine." Since then, I had come to appreciate it even more than the sugary wine coolers I drank with my friends. But it felt ridiculous to add bottles of cheap chardonnay to our packie store runs.

From the counter, I watched him cook. It seemed natural for him, as he chopped, stirred, and added spices to our meal. Cooking being one of the many talents I didn't possess, I didn't offer to help. I sipped and fiddled with the glass as I listened to the sizzling sounds coming from the frying pan. I turned away from him for a bit as I tried to sort through being a nervous wreck and totally comfortable. The tension broke when I felt him come up behind me, put his arms around me and lightly graze the back of my neck with his lips, a most passionate kiss I didn't realize existed. I could feel the sensuous tingling roam from the top of my head to the very tip of each one of my toes.

After dinner we sat on Ronny's couch and kissed, a lot, in between making jokes about how much garlic he used in the scallops. In the middle of this, he stopped kissing me, excused himself, walked over to an end table, and turned over a picture.

"What are you doing?" I asked him.

"I can't kiss you like that while they are looking at me."

They were Ronny's parents who had watched us all night from a formal anniversary picture. Ronny's mother's portrait was especially disquieting as she had been my school nurse, Richard's school nurse and maybe even my parents' school nurse as well.

"Aren't they freaking you out?" he asked.

"Well, a little. But I'm surprised they're bothering *you* that much."

"You just knew her from school. I practically grew up in her house and it's weird having her watch us."

Then he took my hand and pulled me up.

"Come here, I need you to help me with something," he said, pulling me towards the bedroom.

I panicked. Was this it? Could I handle it? I was crazy about him and trusted him completely, but I was a little overwhelmed. The kissing Richard and I had been doing was way further than I had ever been before. Still, I followed him into the bedroom. He took off his shirt and then lay on his stomach across the double bed.

"Ok, I need you to walk on my back."

"What?" I wondered if this was some slang more experienced people used for sex.

"Seriously. I pulled my back the other day, and it's killing me. Having you walk on it will feel like a massage."

"You know that's weird, right?"

"Why, is there something else you want to do in here????"

"Cute," I said.

"Please."

"I'm not on *Candid Camera* or anything, am I?" Sexual tension and nerves seemed to drift away when we were teasing each other.

"Trust me."

I took off my shoes and socks and then climbed on the bed. I stood on his back, and using the wall for support, stepped where he told me to. He said it helped. Afterwards, I laid in his arms for quite a while. At the end of the date, he walked me to my car and kissed me goodnight. This time, I managed to stay upright after we pulled apart.

I drove home but could have danced all the way back to my house. I was so happy. This was real. Richard, funny, kind, handsome Richard, had made me dinner and wanted to be with me! We had spent hours together and there was no pressure to go places I wasn't ready to go. Since he'd moved into my sister's, I'd heard rumors about his hard-partying lifestyle, some likely true and some likely false; rumors that involved alcohol, women, and cocaine, the drug of choice for twenty-somethings. But I'd seen none of that. Tonight, he only wanted to be with me, and it was sweet and awesome and there was no question about it- I definitely wanted to be with him.

chapter 3
firebird

After that first date, we spent as much time together as we could. It was winter in Provincetown and his construction work was sporadic. I was in school during the early part of the day. But if Richard was not working, we sometimes spent afternoons together. One afternoon he was at my house but was nervous about being there. I called my mom at work to confirm that she wasn't coming home soon. I used some ridiculous excuse — "is it ok if I call my friend long distance, the one who moved away last year? I feel like talking to her and could use her opinion on this homework I'm doing." After hanging up, I realized how silly this all was. Richard was 28 years old, a grown man, and I thought I was so clever, calling my mommy to make sure we had privacy.

It's not as if anything outrageous was going on. We were moving beyond kissing, but not by much, especially not at my house. I was too wimpy for that. And as for Richard? Well, he respected my mom — at least the little he knew about her. It's not as though he was afraid of being caught. The mischievous side of him would have gotten a kick out of that. But he knew our situation was unusual and taking things too far in my mother's house didn't seem right. So, we hung out in my teenage room, complete with all my teen angst books and rock star posters. At least I was mature enough to not worship the teeny bopper stars — no Duran Duran or heart-shaped Rick Springfield posters for me. Mick Jagger, in a total classic rock pose, was who was hanging on my wall.

Those afternoons were rare, however. Mostly, we drove around in the evenings. That's what Ptown teens with cars did in the off season, navigating the narrow and deserted streets with a carefree ease impossible from May through October. In January 1987, there were not that many places worth a drive. Most of the businesses were closed for the season and the ones that were open were not conducive to a teenager's wallet. The exception was a lone pizza place on the main street that featured crispy crust pizza and still had a jukebox. But it got old fast. And then there were the two convenience stores, the bars, and friends' houses to check out. There was also the pier, a drive which might provide something interesting to look at within the bay. And, of course, the ocean beach. Even with temperatures in the low teens, the beach was always beautiful enough to be part of the drive, especially at sunset, where we often met up with others just to be out of the house. Who cared if it was 22 degrees with a wind chill? It was a place to go. Even better, if there were people parked there, it was only townies in the winter; no tourists mucking up the scenery.

And that was the route my friends and I circled endlessly when there was no other place to hang out. The only movie theater open that time of year was small and over 20 minutes away, and often its offerings weren't worth the trip. If we had money in our pockets and needed anything but food or cigarettes, we might venture to the nearest department store, 30 minutes away. Not only was it the place to buy clothes, shoes, makeup and cassettes, it had a Papa Gino's in the same parking lot. A trip to Bradlees was a bit of excitement in the frostier months.

However, random drives weren't what 28-year-olds, who could get into bars and didn't have to worry about parents, did. Maybe that's why our time together often ended early. I couldn't be out late on school nights, and my curfew on the weekends was midnight. Richard never seemed to mind. I never thought to ask him what he did after we said good night. I pictured him going back to Laurie and Andy's and watching TV if they were already asleep.

We usually took my car to do the driving loop around town. Richard had his work truck, but it wasn't great on gas, and he wasn't supposed to be using it for his own purposes.

It was fine, though. My car was a classic red Firebird I had inherited from my dad when he bought something more sensible for the impending birth of my younger half-sister. The sporty car had been my dad's bachelor wheels when he and my mom divorced. Lucky for me, the beauty came to me when he remarried and was starting a new family. It was considered prime back then, but it had its tackiness. A huge, regal Firebird was painted on the hood. And if that wasn't flashy enough, my dad had his name highlighted in gold lettering on the sides of the driver and passenger doors.

The car was known. Since Provincetown in the winter was a boring place, gossip was about the only thing of interest going on. One of my mom's friends was approached by a local woman once, saying how happy she was to see that my parents had worked out their differences and were getting back together. "But what about his new wife and the baby?" the woman questioned.

My mom's friend asked, "What are you talking about? What makes you say that?"

"I couldn't sleep one morning, so I decided to go for a ride. I saw his car parked at her house. I admit, I got curious, so I started driving up Johnson Street and peeking through the Salvador's yard to check out 11 Arch in the early hours and it's always there."

"You damn fool," replied my mom's friend. "Freddy gave Yvonne the car!"

It did not help that not only was the car conspicuous, but that my dad was also a very popular guy with everyone, especially his fellow police officers. One day, my friends and I decided to take a road trip to the closest mall, an hour away, making this a very big deal for us. On the way back, I was driving faster on the highway than I should have been. We didn't notice the three state police cars pulled over until we were right on them. There was no time to slow down without breaking too hard. I thought we were done for as we fled past. But they only beeped and started waving, "Hey Freddy!"

The thing was, I was a lousy driver. My lack of confidence in this area was completely valid. Though a pretty good student, I did so poorly in drivers ed that I'm certain I am the only kid in the history of the program to have ever been held back. When the science/drivers ed teacher (it figures as science was my next worst subject) finally passed me, he told me to get *a lot* of practice before I took the official test.

It was only because my dad was the parent who went with me to the registry that I got my license on the first try. I was not even close to ready, but my dad was. My friends had licenses; his kid should have her license too. At the registry I chatted with a girl whose test was just before mine. She said she had been driving for a while and wasn't worried. When she returned, defeated, in tears, and without a license, I told my dad we should leave. I feigned a headache, stomachache, earache, and backache, all to no avail.

"Don't be ridiculous," he said impatiently.

The same trooper that had failed the first girl called my name, shook my dad's hand and said, "Hey Freddy, how've you been? I saw the name and was wondering if this was your kid."

In my dad's car, the trooper told me to drive five miles down the road, do a three-point turn, and come back. He then turned around in his seat and chatted with my dad about police stuff, blind to the fact that my three-point turn took me about ten points, and I only just missed hitting a bicyclist on the side of the road. And, like that, I had my license.

I begged my dad to take the wheel for the drive home. He insisted I drive. I came close to taking out two cars while going around a rotary. My dad yelled at me. I had a license — didn't I know how to drive?

But I was fortunate: I never had a serious accident. So a few months later, my dad, realizing a pink car seat with stuffed animals around it ruined the cool factor of the Firebird, passed it on to me.

I preferred Richard driving and had no problem giving him my keys but couldn't ask him to do it often. I had to make sure it was when my dad was off and there was no way he was likely to see us. Even seeing his fellow officers while Richard was driving was a risk, but one where I figured I could delay the confrontation and maybe make up an excuse, claim the cop was wrong or I wasn't feeling well. If my dad saw Richard driving my car, it would have been very tough to explain. But if he just saw him in the passenger seat, well then, I could just be giving Laurie's roommate a ride to his girlfriend's. It would be easy to leave out the fact that I was the girlfriend.

On one of those 'driving all around town just to be together' nights, I was behind the wheel when we pulled up to a stop sign. I waited patiently for the approaching car, more than 100 yards away. I felt the car shaking. I looked over to the passenger side and found Richard softly, yet enthusiastically, laughing at me.

"What?" I asked, very confused.

When he caught his breath, he gave me some driving instructions.

"A stop sign means you have to stop, but it doesn't mean you have to hang out forever. A whole parade could pass by the time that car gets here!"

That was Richard, teasing me, teaching me, without once, ever, letting the insecure girl I was feel insecure.

As we got to know each other better, I understood him more. Despite his playful side, he was one of the most mature people I knew. And he made me feel mature when he asked my opinions on things and actually listened to my answers. He seemed to care about what I had to say. I didn't know much outside of my little world, but Provincetown was a topic for unending conversation;

its history, the interesting characters, the fishing industry, the extreme differences between summer and winter, the dynamics of such a small town with a gay population and a straight population that worked so well together. We shared a bit about growing up and we were both proud of how progressive our childhoods had been. We talked about how cool it was that our little town was filled with so many artists, even though neither of us appreciated art that much. The exception for me was literature, as I always loved to read. I told him what I had learned about Eugene O'Neill and Tennessee Williams writing some of their plays in our town. Richard always listened and was patient when my usual quiet shyness turned to rambling on about a topic I enjoyed.

Richard was also honest, almost to a fault. I learned quickly not to ask him a question I didn't actually want an answer to. He was always kind with his answer, but he was going to tell it like it was, whether I liked it or not. He was never fake either — always honest about himself as well as his opinions of the world around him. He didn't volunteer the things about his life he wasn't proud of, but if you asked him, he would state the basics. No elaboration necessary.

When I asked him where he had been over the last few years, why he had only just recently returned to town, he told me he had been married and he and his wife lived in her hometown, somewhere near Boston. He said that his ex-wife was a nice person, but he had married too young. He also admitted that he hadn't been ready to stop partying while she was more serious, so their goals weren't in sync.

His honesty made me feel like he respected me and trusted me with these adult issues, like his divorce and his part in it. It did not make me want to ask about the details, though. I was having too much fun. It was enough to know about a former wife. I didn't need to know if she was pretty or thin or if she had an impressive job. I also didn't need to know what type of partying he was talking about. When we were together, he drank a bit — not much more than I did. And if he drank more than me, he definitely handled it better. I had never seen him drunk or even buzzed. He would smoke a joint or two at my sister's, but so did my sister. Pot didn't seem like a big deal. I had even taken a hit here and there. I didn't get the high everyone else talked about, so it wasn't anything I enjoyed or that we did together. If he did any other partying, I wasn't ready to know about it.

I preferred the fun stories, the ones I could relate to. During one of our rides, Richard told me a story about a connection we had years before. Even though Provincetown was so small that everyone knew everyone, and he grew up just a few streets away from my house, we had only just met. He was a couple of years older than Laurie and as kids, that made a difference. Audrey was even younger than that. It was possible my older sisters knew him and his siblings, but not well.

In the early '70s my cool dad had a speed boat. Small and basic, it was white with red trim. He would moor it in the harbor and row out to it in high tide or simply swim. At dead low tide, he just walked up to it as it sat peacefully on a sand bar, push it through the muck and seaweed a few inches until he had enough water to jump on, start it and take off. Often, no matter the tide or how my dad got to it, it wouldn't start, and he would curse at it in his native Portuguese to get the engine going. I thought that was the proper way to start a boat until my teens.

My dad wanted a son. I never doubted that he loved me and my sisters, his stepdaughters, but he had hoped I would be a boy. Luckily, he would have one much later. But for many years, his home was all female. Richard grew up on the same quaint neighborhood beach that we had. Short of males to take under his wing, my dad befriended him. Richard told me that when he was about 12, my dad would take him out on the boat. He would see Richard hanging around and looking for trouble on the shore and ask if he wanted to take a ride. It became a regular thing that thrilled the young Richard.

"He would let me take the wheel sometimes. I would ask to take over as soon as we cleared the breakwater but he would say no. It took me a while, but eventually I figured it out. He would let me steer when we were passing the nude beach. Then he would pull out his binoculars and scope out the scene. Once I asked him what he was doing, and he said it was official police business. Ya, right. I was a kid, but I wasn't stupid!"

Richard was laughing as he told the story. I could have done without the nude beach detail, but it was funny. This got me thinking about how we might have crossed paths back then. I would have been one, maybe toddling around the beach in just a diaper. Did he accidentally splash me with water as he was running to jump into my dad's boat? Did my fat baby fist throw sand at him just because that is what babies did? I thought about how I would love to go back in time and see that scene. Him as a kid, hanging with my dad in his boat, and me watching from the tidal pools, reaching out and crying to go with them. I could see the scene so clearly it was like it was my own memory, not just Richard's.

chapter 4
mom

It was getting harder to keep our secret. The first sign for my mom was innocuous. Every year, our small high school staged a musical that was eagerly anticipated by the whole town. Our history teacher had a drama background and was incredibly talented. The music department also did an awesome job. In such a modest school, teachers could focus on each kid's individual talents, making the production a definite hit.

Ours wasn't your typical high school musical. Our entire community, even people without kids, looked forward to the spring production. The artistic history of the town was rich in theater and that tradition continued. With the bleakness of winter doldrums continuing for months, everyone felt the high school musical was the event that ushered in a new season of warmth and excitement. Many people without students at home, but who were bored, volunteered to help with costumes, set design and make up. In one way or another, pretty much every student took part, even if in just a small way, including me. I could dance ok, but my singing and acting weren't that great. Except for a fancy dance number I got to perform in *Grease* the year before, I was always relegated to the chorus. That wasn't a bad thing. Being a small part of something wonderful was still wonderful.

That year's production was *The Pajama Game*. Just as the four-nights-a-week rehearsal schedule was about to start, I decided not to participate. This wasn't a huge rebellion, but it was unusual, and my mom didn't understand it.

"I'm still going to go, and I will help them, maybe do programs or something. I just don't want to put in all that work my last year of school," I explained to her.

"But you always love doing it and it's the last time you and your friends will all be in a production together. Is this because of Heather?" she asked.

My friend, Heather, was going through a tough time and struggling with school. After leaving her parents' house, she stayed with us for a week before officially moving in with Sue. Heather had a lot of talent, but problems in her life which started the year before, made her lose a key role in *Grease*. Even if her grades had been up to par, she wouldn't have been able to keep up with rehearsals this year. Soon she would stop going to school all together.

"No, it has nothing to do with that. I'm just sorting through college stuff and doing other things. They don't need me and this way I can have fun and enjoy it when I see it, like everyone else in the audience."

The real reason, of course, was that I would have more time with Richard, and he was well worth giving up a part in the chorus to fill those long rehearsal hours hanging out with him.

Where to hang out was getting tricky, though. Some nights we would hang out at Sue's, but he didn't really like it. Richard liked my friends well enough but being there only reminded him of our age difference. He was long over the 'parents are away' teen scene. We would still see each other at Laurie and Andy's, but that was also difficult. Richard didn't come right out and admit we were seeing each other, but he didn't go overboard trying to hide it, either. And I was going so far overboard trying to hide it, I might as well have been wearing a life preserver.

Not at all approving, Laurie tried to ignore what was obvious. Soon she gave up, told us she knew, and that she would give me till the next morning to tell our mother. If I didn't, she would. Richard and I went into his room to talk. Laurie didn't like it and made her opinions known through the closed door.

"Calm down," he hollered back at her. "Do you really think I'm going to ravage your little sister with you right in the hallway?"

No, he wouldn't do that. But the thing was, while he never pressured me, it was clear to both of us we were moving in the sex direction. Richard knew I didn't have any experience, but the more we were together, the more eager I became. Most of the hesitating on my part was from my lack of confidence. But when I was with Richard, I wasn't insecure. When I was with him, I was surer of myself than I had ever been. He made me feel that way. For so long, I was afraid of my own shadow and felt unworthy of my limited space in the world. And old habits die hard. Especially when an older, handsome, more experienced man wants to kiss me and wrap his arms around me. But my apprehension was diminishing and each time we were alone, we were growing closer, emotionally and physically.

Clearly Laurie wasn't happy, but she gave us some privacy, anyway. Funny how she sometimes bought beer for me and my friends and smoked pot in front of me, but the idea of her little sister dating her older friend was too much. Richard and I knew we only had two choices: tell my mother or break up. Neither of us wanted to break up. Laurie telling my mother wasn't the only threat. Eventually, enough people would see us together that it would get back to one of my parents. It was incredible that it hadn't happened already. I kissed Richard goodbye and told him I would tell my mother in the morning.

"Ok. I'll call you by noon. If your phone is disconnected, I'll know it didn't go well," he said, grinning his classic grin.

* * *

With my mom being tired from work in the evenings and my being tied up with homework, activities, or friends, she and I had gotten into the habit of catching up on weekend mornings. She was an early riser and liked to get some chores done first thing. By the time I woke up she was ready for her second cup of coffee, and we would chat. This habit kept us close.

Still, of course, I was nervous when I told her about Richard. But she took it amazingly well. Shockingly well, actually.

"Well, I'm not surprised. I could tell something was going on. You have been quite smiley lately. And say what you want, but quitting the play told me something was up."

She only knew Richard in passing, but she liked him. He had always been friendly to her the few times she was at Laurie's. Since my mom wasn't fond of Andy, Richard was like a breath of fresh air. It was also possible that she didn't know how old he was. I am sure she didn't know he had been married and recently divorced. While I knew about his brief marriage, it was a topic that barely registered. Richard being a divorced older man was something I chose not to think about too much.

I worried my mom was going to order me to stop seeing him, but she didn't. "I'm happy that you're happy, and he seems like a nice guy. Let me just sit with this a bit. And take it slow, very, very slow...."

"I knew I liked your mother," Richard said when he called later that morning. "I'll have to bring her some fresh seafood. What does she like better, lobster or scallops?"

"I like scallops — the smell of lobsters boiling is nasty. And watching them fight the boiling water is just cruel. Go with scallops."

"I'm not bringing them for you," he laughed.

chapter 5
cop

I was kidding myself. Richard and I wouldn't last as a happy, normal couple. Accepting the fact that I had been seeing someone older than me was a lot to ask of my mom, especially since my dating was new territory for her. I was her dependable daughter, a senior in high school and off to college in the fall. I was the daughter who never gave her any trouble, and I'd been honest about the relationship. She wanted to be supportive, but she had a lot to think about in the week following my disclosure. Still, her handling the news so well convinced me that all was well. Having conquered telling my mom felt like enough of an accomplishment for now, so I decided to hold off a bit longer before telling my dad.

It had been a month since the night Richard took me to the liquor store and our feelings for each other became obvious. That upcoming Saturday would be Valentine's Day, a holiday that had never meant much to me before now. Silly elementary school cards and candy hearts could never compare to having a boyfriend on the day dedicated to love. As the cold, dark week passed between my talk with her and the romantic holiday, my mom kept her thoughts to herself. She smiled and teased me when I would run to my room every time my phone rang. But unbeknownst to me, her thoughts wavered between being happy for her youngest daughter and imagining worst-case scenarios. Laurie didn't help the situation. Still not approving, it was likely she told my mom her own opinions about Richard, doing nothing to ease my mom's worries. Laurie was also eager to share the plans Andy had made for their own Valentine's date; plans that meant Richard would have the apartment to himself.

Richard and I had plans as well. He was making me dinner again; a nice, fancy dinner. This time we could enjoy ourselves without the awkwardness or the secrecy of our first date. Valentine's Day was the most passionate day of the year. Who knew where the night would lead from there? While we never specifically talked about it, it would be fitting if that was the night we took things to the next level. I couldn't imagine my first time being with anyone else but the tender, kind Richard I was so crazy about. How much more romantic could my first time be if it took place on the night dedicated to romance? It was exciting to think about. I wondered if he was thinking about it, too.

We only saw each other once or twice during the week. Because Laurie was not thrilled about our relationship, I had stopped spending time at their apartment. The Friday night before Valentine's Day, I hung out at Sue's and Richard joined me there for a little while. We took a ride together and said goodbye before 10. I wanted to be home early, while my mom was still awake even, to further emphasize that I was her responsible daughter, and she didn't need to stress about this new guy in my life.

The next morning, I did not mention what my evening plans were; I never had to before. But as I started getting ready later in the afternoon, she asked me what I was doing. I told her Richard was making me dinner.

"At Laurie's?" she asked.

"Yes.

"And Laurie and Andy won't be home? You'll be there alone?"

"Yes."

What my mom's specific worries were that evening, I could only guess. Her youngest becoming a woman, phrasing more suited to her teen years? Or her baby being taken advantage of by an older man? Perhaps she worried that by falling in love with a fellow townie, I would skip college altogether, something she knew I was on the brink of doing anyway? Was she worried about me drinking? Doing drugs?

"I'm not sure I'm comfortable with you being alone with him. Maybe you shouldn't go out tonight," she declared.

"What? Why?"

"I don't need a reason. I just don't want you going out."

"That makes no sense. I was out last night, and it was fine," I protested.

I couldn't believe it. Why should she force me to stay home when I had done nothing wrong? She refused to budge or explain. We argued, calmly at first, as I raised different dating scenarios. Instead of dinner at the apartment, Richard and I could go out somewhere, the pizza joint or some other public place. We could spend time at Sue's, where there were always several of my friends hanging out. We could just ride around like we had been doing or even (and I wasn't sure how he would feel about this) watch a movie at our house. But the more suggestions I listed and the higher my voice raised, the more she appreciated how important he was to me. My desperation seemed to further convince her that my being with him was a mistake.

Her decisiveness jolted me out of my naivete and I knew it was over. Not just our evening plans, but our whole relationship. Maybe it was the firmness in her tone. Or maybe it was the reality of the situation. Either way, I knew at that moment that Richard and I were done. My mother's approval was gone. Without her approval, there was no way we could continue to see each other. I was shattered.

He called in the middle of our heated discussion, asking what time I was getting there. While my mother listened, I stumbled over what to say. "Um, I'm not sure."

His voice changed. I think he knew we were through at that moment, too. We both had been waiting for the axe to fall.

"What do you mean? What's up?" he asked.

"Let me call you back in a minute," I said and hung up the phone.

"Mom, please..." I tried one last time.

"You're not going out tonight and that's the end of it. And this relationship is over before it gets out of hand."

I felt betrayed. I thought she was on my side. Sure, Richard wasn't the boy next door, I knew that. But in the week since I had told her about him, nothing had happened that should have alarmed her. Maybe she had heard some things she didn't like, but she saw how happy I was. Suddenly, in this very moment, she changes her mind about the whole thing? I had dared to hope that she might see this relationship as something real, at least more than a simple cliché. But I had more to think about than my own misery. I had left Richard hanging, and it wasn't fair to him. He deserved to know what was going on and to hear it from me directly.

"If that's the case, I have to go tell him. It wouldn't be right to just end things without talking to him," I stated.

"You have a perfectly good phone you can use to call and tell Richard you're through. You don't need to go there to do that."

"You're kidding me, right? We have plans tonight and now not only are they not happening, but we're over and you want me to tell him that over the phone? That's unbelievable! I just need to go over there and talk to him. I'll be quick. What can happen in a few minutes? If I am not back in half an hour, you can call the cavalry."

"You're not going out tonight, and that's the end of the discussion."

Betrayal turned to anger. I thought of the unfairness of Richard getting a quick call from me while my mother listened nearby and my anger turned to fury. White hot fury. I almost never disobeyed my mom. I was the easy daughter, the one who was afraid of her own shadow and terrified of disappointing anyone. I picked up my car keys and met my mom's eyes straight on.

"I'm going to go over there and tell him to his face that we need to end this. He deserves that much. I will be home in half an hour. Do what you have to do, but I wish you would wait just 30 minutes." I walked out, but not before noticing the shock on her face.

* * *

I don't know what Richard told Laurie and Andy about our brief phone call, but no one was in a good mood at their apartment. Andy was very quiet, and Laurie seemed a little righteous, even a little caustic. I ignored her. Richard was the only person I cared about just then, and it was Richard I was there to see. He seemed mad, an emotion I was not used to seeing on him. Was he mad at me? At my mother? At the situation? He was at the counter chopping vegetables for the dinner we were supposed to be sharing in just a little while.

"Why do I have the feeling you're not going to be able to stay?" he asked.

"I'm not."

"You can't be surprised, Yvonne," Laurie interrupted. "This whole situation is a little ridiculous, don't you think?"

"You want to give me a break?" Richard snapped at her before I could think of anything to say. She continued to get ready for her own fun night.

"Can we talk in the bedroom?" I asked.

"Yeah, I guess we need to," he said.

He turned off the stove and motioned me down the hall. But before we could walk out of the kitchen, the phone rang. He was closest to it and could have ignored it, but he sensed the caller had something to do with what was going on with us and he wanted to be the one to deal with it.

It was not my mother. The second I had left the house, she called my bluff and notified the cavalry — my father. A big deal since she wasn't speaking to my dad at that time.

Richard said hello with a bit of an attitude, and immediately recognized my dad by his heavy Portuguese accent. "This is Freddy, let me talk to my daughter."

Richard was pissed off enough to use some sarcasm, even if that was all he could think of to do.

"Which one?" he asked with scorn.

"You know which one. Yvonne. Get her on the phone!"

Here is why my dad was a good cop. He had an innate ability to diffuse any difficult situation by making you think he was your best buddy. It worked with drunk guys on the street, and criminal suspects. It worked with troubled kids blowing off a little too much steam and it worked with their irate parents. I knew better. But I fell for it as my mom was the target of my anger at that moment.

"Yvonne, your mother just called me all upset about something, saying all kinds of crazy stuff. What's this foolishness? Why's she bugging me?"

My dad is annoyed at my mom too, I thought. I couldn't stay too much longer, and I couldn't think of too many places I could go where I would be hard to find. But I definitely didn't want to go home.

"Dad, why don't I come over to talk about it?"

"Yeah, that's good. Come over and tell me what your mother's yammering on about."

I hung up the phone and walked past Richard down the hall to his room. He followed me silently.

"I'm so sorry. I don't know why she changed her mind."

I started to cry, not hysterically, just soft, quiet tears. Richard was angry, but I still wasn't sure who with. It was agony thinking it might be me. I was that insecure, foolish, 'no right to take up space in the world,' kid all over again; the woman I felt I was when

I was with him was now weak and useless. He had cared for me and planned this whole wonderful night for us and now I had to break up with him because my mommy said so.

Whomever he was mad at, he still wrapped me in his arms.

"I guess we shouldn't be surprised, huh?" he said, kissing me. "We thought this might happen last week."

We stayed like that for a while, just holding each other, trying to ignore Laurie's loud banging around in the apartment and arguing with Andy, purposely it seemed, just outside the bedroom door.

"Seriously, aren't they supposed to be gone already?" Richard muttered. "Hey, I got you a card. I know it's not a big deal, but here. I made a great dinner too. I was hoping to spoil you a little tonight. For what it's worth, here's your card, at least."

It was a simple card, but to me it was beautiful, the best card I would ever receive.

"I'm so sorry," I said again.

I was in his arms once more. He kissed me deeply, a kiss we held for several heartbeats. A long kiss, but not long enough. He squeezed me then and told me I should go, before it was too late, and he wasn't able to control himself or did or said something stupid to one of my parents. I walked out of his room and out of the apartment in complete silence, ignoring my sister. Richard stayed in the bedroom.

* * *

Arriving at my father's house, I was barely in the door before he started. *So much for him just wanting me to explain to him why my mother was hysterical.* My stepmother, Kathy, and I got along very well. She half hugged me while holding my beloved baby sister, Suzanne, 20 months old and sound asleep, in her arms.

"Freddy, calm down. Sit and talk to your daughter. Yvonne, I'm going to put Suzanne to bed, and I'll be right back."

I wanted to put Suzanne to bed myself. My little sister was a safe escape, and I wanted to take her from her mom, carry her into her room and stay there with her, listening to her sleep. But likely my dad would have just followed me into her room. His 'resolve the situation' speech was turning into a 'talking at me' speech. But he didn't yell and was just using his position as my dad to state his case — Richard was not the guy for me. My mom might have annoyed him with her call, but she was right to get him involved. This could not continue. Blah, blah, blah.

Kathy put a glass of merlot in front of me and joined us at the table. It wasn't the first time she and I had chatted over a glass of wine. *That* was something my police officer dad didn't have a problem with. In our Portuguese culture, kids drank wine all the time. Apparently, they couldn't date people they cared about, but they could drink illegally in front of a police officer.

Kathy tried to help by backing up my parents but in a gentler way. She was 10 years younger than my father and Richard was 11 years older than me. I got a little freaked when she tried to be sympathetic by telling me that Richard hung out with one of her brothers and yes, he was a good-looking, nice guy; and yes, she had thought about dating him before she met my dad. But Richard was just too into drugs and that was a dangerous thing. I almost choked on the wine.

"He never does drugs with me. Maybe he's over all that," I offered, pathetically.

"I doubt it," my dad said. "You don't just give up that kind of thing. You need to stop dating him. Once a druggie, always a druggie."

"Don't say that! He's not like that!" I shouted in my frustration, not caring about waking the baby. Breaking us up was one thing but bad-mouthing him during the process was uncalled for. The least I could do was defend him. I took a deep breath and lowered my voice.

"Besides, I've already broken up with him. You and Mom have made that clear."

"So, it's settled," my dad announced.

In the end, my fury at my mother conspired with my adoration of my baby sister to convince me to stay there. I even thought that I might move in with them. I'm sure my dad called my mother so she would know where I was. And without a change of clothes, or a toothbrush, I stayed at my dad's, waking early to play with Suzanne and chat with Kathy. On Monday, I waited until my mom went to work and then went to my house to get some clothes. Since it was school vacation, I only needed a few things. So much for thinking how awesome school break would be. I had never played the divorced kids' game of when-one-parent-says-no-run-to-the-other before, but in this situation, I felt justified. Incredibly immature but justified.

I wish I could say I had some awakening that led me to take the high road and go home. Or that my mom apologized and begged me to come back. Truth was, I missed my room. I missed my phone and my stuff. I went home one afternoon a couple of days later, so when my mother returned from work, there I was. I don't think we talked that first night. But little by little, we got over the Valentine's Day incident. I was still heartbroken. But I was no longer furious. And heartbreak is a little easier to take in your own world with your own sad love songs to accompany your tears.

chapter 6
senior

It was real; we were through. There would not be a last minute, surprise happy ending. This was my first romantic break up, the first of many in my adult years. But the first always stings the longest and sharpest. I survived, of course; you always do.

Back at home, my mom and I put our most serious argument behind us and moved on, slowly growing close again. One reason things had calmed between us was because I refused to share my sadness with her. I refused to hear her minimize my feelings and so would go into my room whenever I felt a fresh round of tears coming on. Alternating between sappy and angry rock music over and over helped. Because we were talking again, and I was hiding most of my feelings, my mom thought she was in safe territory telling me of a phone call she had just received. Maybe she wanted to help me see that she and my father were right to put a stop to our relationship. But her story backfired.

The call came from Richard's older sister, Elaine. Ironic though it was, now that we had broken up, news of our relationship was getting around. While they weren't what anyone would consider close friends, my mom had advised and supported Elaine when she sought to join the school committee, a board on which my political mom had previously served for several years. Elaine was still grateful and now returned the favor by sharing details of why Richard was bad for me.

"She told me he's not a great guy and definitely not a match for you. She said he's always in trouble, drinks, takes drugs, just not a good person."

I did not know Elaine, but I knew her husband, as he had been one of my teachers at school. I also knew she had kids of her own who were much younger than me. Looking at it now, she was likely trying to be helpful, one mom to another. But she had no right, and I was furious all over again. And I let my mother know. This was the second of many times I would defend Richard and my loudest argument to date. Louder than when she had told me I could not leave the house, and the relationship was over. My sorrow contained both fight and righteousness.

"I can't believe she called you and said that stuff! She must be really cruel to sell out her own brother like that. She doesn't even know me — maybe I'm a bad influence on him. How does she know that I'm not into drugs myself? What a horrible bitch!"

"I think she was just trying to warn me, Yvonne," she demurred, something my proud and strong mother never did, especially with her daughters. She did not want to lose what we had just salvaged of our relationship since this all began. "I shouldn't have said anything."

"No," I yelled. "*She* shouldn't have said anything. I don't know what her problem is, but Richard was nothing but kind to me. I'm sick of people making him out to be a bad guy when he's not. We can't be together and he's too old for me, ok, I get that. We aren't seeing each other anymore because of that and it sucks, but I'm dealing with it. So what the hell does she want to bad-mouth her brother for? If she believed he was all those things, what is she doing about it? Is she helping him? Or does she just like to call up random people and talk crap about her family?"

My mother didn't respond to that and we let it go. I stayed angry and vindicated. No wonder Richard had such a bad reputation when his own sister assumed the worst about him. How could Elaine not see in him all the great things I saw?

* * *

The fact that it was senior year helped a bit while the winter days passed. My mother and I went to the high school musical together, the one I had quit to spend more time hanging out with Richard. I thought that watching it now would be hard. Here was the glory of all the hard work my friends and classmates had put in, and now I was not a part of it. I did not have my first love, or the excitement of being in a great show. How was I supposed to handle that? But it turned out that it was not hard at all. It was a relief to just watch and enjoy, to be happy and proud of my friends, and entertained instead of worrying about makeup, costume changes, and stage fright.

There were parties too and a funny thing happened in the aftermath of the rumors of my relationship with an older guy. I was neither popular nor unpopular, and I hadn't dated much. I was the girl you invited to parties, but only if you remembered to. Only one of my classmates had ever expressed an interest in dating me, and that was Glen in the seventh grade. Our "dating" was no different than the hanging out we did when we weren't dating. We'd only kissed once, and that was because a friend dared us to. We were buddies now.

But suddenly, guys seemed attentive. It was confusing. At one party, we were drunk and playing some silly alcohol game. A couple of guys were flirting and vying to get my attention. But that could not be. It had never been before. It was a kid named Scott who put an end to the games. Amid the talking, laughing, and general party noise, he took my hand and lead me to another room to make out. I don't think the guys assumed that since I had more experience now, they could take advantage of me. Scott's kisses were sweet and none of the others had acted inappropriately. But maybe, since Richard had been interested, other guys started noticing that I could be interesting? Or maybe Richard's attraction had given me a confidence they could see even though I did not? Could I believe that other guys might be attracted to me as well? Maybe they had flirted before, but I'd been too shy and self-conscious to notice?

Not much ever happened with Scott beyond that night. I remember riding around with him a few times, but I don't remember where or why. We did not date, although he seemed to like me. I'm guessing it was clear I only wanted to hang out in a group with our other friends. I liked Scott well enough, and he was cute. But I was pining for someone else.

* * *

In March, I received my first college acceptance letter. It came from my safety school, Salem State. I found the letter in the mailbox one afternoon and it felt like something big enough that I should share it right away. It was a busy time of day for my mom at work and so I would surprise her with it when she got home. Still, I was eager to tell somebody. Laurie had the day off and so I called her apartment. I was caught off guard when Richard answered the phone. Usually, he would be working that time of day.

"HEL-lo," he said with the regular, goofy inflection he used on the phone. Yet, it sounded flat.

"Hey," I stumbled. "How, how are you?"

He was quiet after the greeting. I didn't know what to say and so I blurted, "I got my first college acceptance letter. I was calling to tell Laurie."

Immediately, his tone changed. "That's awesome! Good for you! That's really great news! I knew you could do it."

His excitement embarrassed me. "Ya, it's cool. But it's just a safety school, no big deal."

"It's a *huge* deal. I'm so happy for you. Hey, guys, it's Yvonne. She got her first college letter. She got in!"

Laurie immediately grabbed the phone. "That's great. What school?"

In the background, I could hear Richard filling Andy in. I smiled, thinking about how happy he was for me. If he was this happy, maybe I should be, too? All of my college applications had been filled out and turned in before we started dating. We had talked about it some. But since it was not a big deal to me, I did not go on and on about it. Now here he was, so excited and proud. I had not thought I could miss him more than I already did.

Laurie said all the right things but certainly was not as excited as Richard.

"How come Andy's home? I thought he'd still be working."

Andy and Richard worked for the same company and we both knew I was asking about Richard, not her boyfriend. It almost felt like I should apologize for calling when there was a chance Richard might answer the phone, as if I was using Salem State as an excuse to talk to him. I wanted to make it clear that his voice answering the phone at that time of day had surprised me.

"They finished the job early and there wasn't enough time this afternoon to do much on the next one."

That made sense and we said goodbye. I was smiling when I hung up, but my smile had nothing to do with the mail.

The year progressed, and more college acceptance letters came in. Any excitement I had when I received them came from thinking how happy Richard would be to hear about them. If he had danced around Laurie's living room over my acceptance into my safety school, how would he have reacted when I got into what should have been my dream school? Emerson College was my dream school only because it was the most prestigious. But I just did not care. I hadn't cared when I applied, and I did not care now. I had no interest in going to college and was just going through the motions as I was expected to do. I did my homework and got good grades because when people told me that's what I should do, I did it. I stopped seeing Richard because that was what people said I had to do, so I did. I was going to college because that's what people said I had to. To do differently didn't even seem like an option.

* * *

We did not see each other at all. No one had ever said that we shouldn't even talk to each other, but somehow, that was how we took it. I didn't feel welcome at Laurie's while he was still living there, probably because Laurie and Andy did not want to get on my mom's bad side. It didn't matter. Soon, Richard was hardly ever there. Eventually, he moved out. I did not know where. When I started going to Laurie's again, I found the courage to ask her if she had seen him. She said she hadn't. She dropped a name.

"I don't think he's at Patty's, but who knows? Andy hasn't really seen him either. They've been at different job sites."

I had heard Patty's name before. I did not know her, but I knew she was about my sister's age, not originally from our town, was into the drug scene, and was someone Richard sometimes hung out with. I had never asked him, never thought it was important to ask. Or more likely, I did not ask because I was afraid of the answer.

"I don't think he'd move in with her," I said. "I guess I shouldn't be surprised if he starts seeing her again, but I don't think he would live there." I was trying to sound mature and indifferent.

"You're probably right," Laurie said. I was, but I would not learn that until later.

"I wonder what he sees in her."

There were rumors of her reputation, and I did not know any differently. It wasn't fair to assume they were true when I was so eager to dispel rumors of Richard being a bad guy.

"We asked him once when he was living here, before you. He would spend the night with her and then they would fight, and he would be back here. When Andy asked him why he kept going back when they fought so much, he said it was because 'they had the best sex known to man.'"

It was painful to hear, because it was something I could never compete with. I had voiced the question because I thought I wanted to know the answer. But the answer only made me feel much worse.

* * *

The weather grew warmer, and spring arrived. The crowds had not, however, and so summer jobs were still a few weeks away. But no one wanted to be stuck inside any longer than they had to be. In the immediate hours after school, but before the evening hours when we were forced to do homework, all my friends and I did was drive the pre-destined loop of our town; down Commercial Street, detour at the pier, back on Commercial to the breakwater, and then follow the entire length of Bradford Street and start again. Every fifth or sixth ride we would turn down Shankpainter Road to drive past Piggy's, the nickname of the popular straight dance bar we couldn't enter, a quick look in the parking lot of the local VFW, and then head out to the highway and on to Herring Cove Beach. We'd just drive over and over, looking for something to do, someone to see. With the promise of the summer season looming ever closer, there was the potential of more interesting sights than what the gray gloom of March and early April had offered.

Serena was the most boy-crazy of my friends and the most brazen. She had also perfected the skill of identifying desirable men and their vehicles at an extreme distance.

"Look, turning down the pier—it's a Roderick truck." Roderick was the company that her crush worked for.

"Damn, that looks like an Ambrose truck. What should I do?" I would say spotting a pickup almost a mile down the highway. Ambrose was the company Richard worked for.

"Don't worry, it's not an Ambrose truck."

"It's the exact color! How can you tell?"

"The headlights are different; the fender is a little off and..."

And she would be right. Once in a great while, I might pass Richard and we would wave and look away. It broke my heart. But I couldn't help but notice, maybe hope, that the fleeting look on his face seemed to say he was hurting too.

Serena and I discovered on one of our many drives that he had picked up a second job. We saw him in the windowed office of the Mobil station right in the center of town, clearly there as an employee and the only one on duty.

"How convenient," the bold Serena said. "I need gas."

"No, you don't!" I shouted. I was afraid to see him even as much as I wanted to see him. I don't know what I was afraid of, but pulling up to the pumps and talking to him seemed more than I could handle.

"You're right, I don't," she said. "And I don't have any money, anyway. So, we'll be boring and just ride around."

As the Mobil station was on Bradford, we would pass it every 20 minutes or. I tried not to look at him. Serena was bored and, for a little excitement, honked the horn every time we passed. I was mortified. On our likely tenth pass, I begged her, "Serena, when we go by the Mobil station this time, please don't beep the horn. It's humiliating and makes me look like such a kid. As my friend, please, please don't do that."

"Ok, I won't," she promised. Instead, as we passed, she slammed on her brakes and yelled out the window, "hey Richard!" I glared at her.

"What?" she asked, acting all innocent. "I didn't beep!"

I dared to look over. He was standing in the window, flashing me his grin.

chapter 7
graduation

The core group of my 30-member class first met when we all started at Aunt Franny's nursery school. Beginning with those early days of toys, naps, snacks, and figuring out who in our group would be our closest buddies, we'd grown up together. Apart from a new kid here and there, and the slight shift in friendships that occurred in seventh grade, when the kids from Truro entered our school system, we were more than just a class. We knew each other's strengths, weaknesses, secrets, embarrassing moments, dramas, and pet peeves. We weren't family exactly, but we were so familiar that school sometimes felt like home. Those ties would loosen soon. Graduation was approaching, and we would be heading out on separate paths, away from the things that helped us feel secure.

The last few weeks of high school were a blend of emotions. There was a seriousness about that time in life. Major decisions needed to be made, paperwork to coincide with those decisions had to be done, exams had to be studied for, preparations for the future started, summer jobs to confirm, and rehearsals staged for the graduation ceremonies. We were a wild group, though, and always made sure to take advantage of the parties, freedoms, and senior privileges. We worried less about final exams than we did about escaping school during study halls and lunch time. We made the most of our senior skip day by throwing a huge beach party.

While the underclassmen squirmed at their desks in the sunny May breeze, we were drinking beer by the water we loved so much.

I enjoyed the fun times and made it through the not-so-fun times well enough, again, by doing what I was supposed to do. Based on a couple of decent poems and well-written essays I was proud of, I thought maybe I would become a writer. Or not. Who knew? I didn't understand that even though I could write when I had to, I didn't enjoy the process at all. With no commitment or sense of anything outside of Provincetown, writing seemed as good a job as any, so I had applied to Emerson College.

Emerson College was a communications school that focused on the arts, with an emphasis on media, writing, publishing, journalism, and visual and performing arts, and its curriculum was designed to bring each student into the spotlight. For me to consider going there in the first place was beyond ironic. Being an anxious kid who desperately wanted to blend into my own comfortable background, the spotlight was the last thing I wanted. But there I was, deciding to go to that particular college anyway. When you get into a school like that, you accept. I still didn't care. It was not the best choice for me to make, but I had made it and that was that.

The future career goals I was supposed to have were vague. All I really wanted to do was get a year-round job in my town, get married, and raise a family in the beautiful place where I grew up. The only other career that somewhat appealed to me, was working in the court system. I wanted to stand up for the underdog, to support people for whom the rest of the world had no time or patience. Already struggling with the idea of going to a four-year school, I couldn't imagine going to law school, too. I thought about becoming a social worker. But my parents worried that with my quiet temperament and sensitive ways, every sad case that came across my desk would run me over and I would never survive the onslaught. I thought about kids I knew who had gotten into trouble, so I also considered being a parole officer. Andy had a few minor encounters with the law and had friends who'd had many criminal offenses. He told me I had the wrong idea about parole officers wanting to help people.

"Everybody hates their parole officer. It's not a job about helping people."

Besides missing Richard, I was feeling the absence of another friend who was being left out of all the senior year functions. I was fortunate to have many friends, but Heather and I went back the furthest. And now her life was spiraling out of control. After a major fight with her parents involving her boyfriend, she had left home, staying briefly at my house and then at Sue's party house. We didn't know it then, but her boyfriend Sean was not the answer to her prayers as she hoped. Eventually Heather moved in with him, and in March, so far behind in her classes, she quit school altogether. He promised her the world and claimed to have connections in Los Angeles. His plan was for them to work like crazy that spring and summer, saving as much money as they could. They would head to L.A. in the fall where Heather could get work as an actress, the ultimate fulfillment of her dreams.

During this time, I saw Heather work a lot and mostly saw Sean hanging around. They shared a small apartment with Jerry, a guy who seemed to be interested in me. He was new to town and older, though his exact age was hard to determine. He was handsome, pleasant and flattering, but I did not return his interest. Even if I weren't still dreaming about some resolution to my split with Richard, I'd heard Jerry had a temper and could be a violent drunk. It didn't take long to see that for myself. Still, with the unknown quality that came from not knowing much about him before he arrived in Provincetown, and the speed in which he showed his swift anger, there was a crazy part of me who thought if my parents found out I was dating this jerk, Richard would seem like Prince Charming. I enjoyed hanging out with Heather at the apartment, but I did not want to give Jerry a false impression. Especially since Sean had decided me dating his roommate would be a great idea and relentlessly pursued the issue. After a few drinks, Jerry got a little aggressive about it as well, grabbing at me when Heather wasn't looking. When I told him to back off, he was shocked. How was it possible I did not want to be with him? He got furious and kicked me out. I left, gladly, and relieved I hadn't gotten pulled into that particular nightmare.

As I walked home alone late that night, I had an image of Richard driving up, rescuing me, taking me in his arms, and telling me not to worry about Jerry. Then taking me home and telling my mother how he had saved me and only had my best interests at heart. Clearly, this was the fantasy of the teenage girl I still was, the girl who thought she needed to be rescued. I didn't realize that by telling Jerry to fuck off, I had rescued myself.

Wherever he was that night, Richard was not on my route home. Not long after, Heather and her boyfriend moved out of that situation and into a worse one. They rented a tiny room above the sleaziest hotel in town, an inn with a popular gay bar on the ground floor. A place where the staff and regular guests slept in the rooms above the bar all day while noise blasted from the first floor all night. A place where Heather, the only one working during the day and working a second job at night, never got to sleep, not really. She was living there when graduation rolled around.

It was tradition for graduation to be held in the amphitheater of the National Seashore, a gorgeous outdoor location with a backdrop of sand dunes and the Atlantic Ocean. It made the ceremony even more momentous. The only downsides to this were that the amphitheater was on the outskirts of town and thus not easy to get to without a car, and it was a haven for bees. Everyone knew this; the seniors, underclassmen, faculty, families, and friends all knew not to arrive wearing any type of scent on them, lest they become the center of the bees' attention.

The morning of our commencement dawned with torrential rain. The predictions were that it would stop early, and the day would be beautiful. By 11 a.m., the rain was still coming down, and they made the decision to hold graduation at the town hall. No where near as beautiful as the amphitheater, the town hall offered a historic location, and because it was in the center of town, it was easily accessible. No sooner had our principal announced the move, the rain stopped. Still, flowers were on their way to the hall, so that was where our graduation would be.

I hoped Heather would come. I knew it would be difficult for her to watch us get our diplomas when she would not receive hers, but now that the ceremony was downtown, it would be easier for her to stop in, even briefly. But with the sun out, Heather assumed graduation was still at the amphitheater, and, between her two waitressing shifts, she had no way to get there. Only blocks from us, she sat in the dingy room in the crappy inn shedding tear after tear....

I was not the smartest kid in my class, not even close. But I was the most responsible with schoolwork. I was the one with the best grades, not because the work came naturally to me, but because I did my homework and studied, just like I was supposed to. This led to a high-grade point average, making me the valedictorian of our small class. I had to give a speech and the tiny, emotional rebel in me wrote one based on a desk in Spanish class. Whichever underclassman used the desk before me wrote beautiful poetry, poetry that was speaking directly to my broken-hearted soul. I wondered who this student was, and while it would not have been too hard to figure out, I also liked the mystery of not knowing and of hoping they were saving their words somewhere else. Every Monday, when I got to Spanish class, the desks would have been scrubbed over the weekend, the words disappeared. It seemed a shame, such a waste, to just dissolve this gentle art with chemical cleaning fluid every week. I took this stance and wrote my speech about how sometimes graffiti could be a good thing. Our class advisor was also our English teacher, and he made me rewrite the speech several times until it became more appropriate for the occasion and commented on the importance of creativity in education.

With my grade point average, and my reputation for helping others, I was also the only one in our class invited to become a member of the National Honor Society, a fact noted by what I called a gold curtain cord around my neck, hanging over my graduation gown. One of my classmates teased me about it, using the very words I had.

"Hey Yvonne, what's up with the curtain cord around your neck? Are you decorating or something?"

I laughed, but Mike, one kid I had known forever and who I sometimes had a crush on, spoke up.

"Knock it off, Chris. Yvonne worked hard for that curtain cord, and we should be glad that at least one of us is wearing it today."

It wasn't lost on me how great all of it was. And after Mike stood up for me, I felt a little proud. I smiled and gave my slightly rebellious speech on behalf of classmates I had grown up with. My family and friends were there, and it felt good to have them rooting for me. Right after receiving their diplomas, all the girls in the class were given flowers. It was Laurie and two-year-old Suzanne who walked up to the podium to hand me my lovely bouquet. Relatives from Boston had driven two hours to share this day with me. Our small town was very supportive of its students and there were many scholarships available, increased by an incredibly generous bequest from the estate of a local woman who'd passed only 4 years before.

When the ceremony was over, my 12-year-old cousin ran up to me and said, "Do you know you made over $10,000?" He'd been busy adding up my scholarships as they were announced. I smiled, thinking about what he must be imagining and wondering what he would do with the money if he didn't need to use it for school.

My mom threw a party at a restaurant run by some dear family friends, and it was all very special. And I felt special and grateful. But something was missing. It was all so huge that it seemed strange not to be sharing it with two people who were so important to me. I was sad Heather was not among us and devastated that Richard wasn't one of those faces packed in the hot, crowded auditorium. As proud as my family and friends were, I knew he would be prouder. Yet, when I was giving my speech, I felt he was there. I felt the focus of his special grin amid the hundreds of people in the auditorium. It was impossible to scan the whole room to see if my sense was correct. With all the eyes that were on me at that moment, could his have been on me too?

Many weeks later, I learned he was there, just as I thought. Finishing work on what had turned out to be a gorgeous Friday afternoon, and drinking his after-work drink with his buddies at the Bradford, Richard learned graduation was moved and would start at 3 p.m. He heard it from another bar patron complaining about all the unexpected traffic in the center of town. He hadn't even known graduation was that day. He looked up at the grimy Miller Lite clock high on the wall behind the bar. It was 2:50. He downed the last of his Southern Comfort and said no to the bartender's offer of another. He left the bar and shook off the sawdust from his workday while walking to Town Hall, timing his arrival for just after the ceremony began. By then, my parents would have found seats up close to take plenty of pictures, and not seen him come in. Entering the auditorium of the old hall, he positioned himself in the doorway of the standing-room-only crowd. He watched me give my speech and joined in the applause that followed. It hadn't been my imagination. He had been there. And he was proud.

chapter 8
summer

Graduation weekend coincided with my 18th birthday, so I gave myself two days off. On the following Monday, I jumped headlong into my summer job. My desire to avoid college had nothing to do with laziness. I knew if I stayed in town, I would need to work one, even two, jobs. Working wasn't a problem. Kids who grew up in Provincetown started working the summer season at young ages and I'd seen my share of interesting jobs since entering the workforce as a kid. At ages 10 and 11, I was a mother's helper, a storefront sweeper, and ran my own high-end shell-selling business. I can say it was 'high end' as my shells were not the casual magic marker shell scribblings of my fellow shell sellers. Upon his retirement, my great uncle discovered his artistic talent and began painting beautiful nautical scenes on clam and quahog shells. He made an attractive wooden display case for them and set the prices. I could keep the money; he didn't need or want it. But he wanted to make sure that I was not letting his work go too easily. It was important to him that the purchaser value the time he put into creating these beach masterpieces. At between $5 and $10 a pop in the mid '70s, they sold well. Some tourists gushed over the designs and were thrilled to purchase them. Others, in a hurry, likely bought them assuming my young self-had painted them. When asked, I told my customers that the work was not my own. Some cared, some didn't.

During the summers I was 12 and 13, I was an innkeeper. It was up to me to hold down the fort at the *Casa deSousa*, my family's guesthouse. My parents purchased our home from my mom's family. It had been her grandparents' home. It was huge and designed to be run as a guesthouse, something many fishing families did for money since fishing was hardly a steady income. We lived on the first floor of the house, and in the summer, rented out the rooms and the two apartments on the second floor, as well as a little cottage off our driveway. After my parents divorced, my mother needed a year-round 9-to-5 job. When the tourist season came, Laurie and Audrey were old enough to hit the busy retail district of Commercial Street for regular jobs. Thus, it was up to me to run the family business. Luckily, I didn't have to clean rooms; my mom did that on her lunch breaks, after her regular workday ended, and on her days off. But I had to answer the phone, take reservations, and check in and check out our guests. Checking in guests meant taking them, often young, single men, most likely gay but not always, up to the rooms they would stay in and leaving them their keys. Despite my father being a police officer, we didn't think then how dangerous that could be, and it was never a problem. In the late '70s, our happy little town still had the luxury of being naïve to the dangers of the outside world.

When I was 14, I could get a work permit and lobbied against running the guesthouse in favor of making real money at a minimum wage job. My mom converted the units into full-season rentals, and I went to work in a candy shop that made its own fudge and taffy. Each day I would come home tired and sticky but pleased that I was working for a real paycheck, even chipping into Uncle Sam with taxes. Heather worked at the candy store too, and it was nice to work together. Our school gossip changing to work gossip, complaints, and stories. Hanging out on one of those summer nights, we watched *Psycho* together for the first time, challenging each other with how truly scared we were. Only a few days later, a part time Wellfleet resident and frequent visitor to our hometown, Tony Perkins himself came in looking for fudge. Though much older than he had been when he starred in the movie, he still resembled Norman Bates. Heather ran into the cramped stock room to hide amongst the boxes of taffy, and I gifted Mr. Perkins an extra half pound of penuche fudge so he wouldn't bring out his Bates knife and start swinging.

When I turned 16, the candy business got old, and my next summer employment was at a gift shop. The owner was a nice older man named Kurt who paid more than minimum wage, with increases each year and generous bonuses when Labor Day came around. Laurie had worked for him for years and put in a good word for me. I was grateful to be hired, as it was a cute shop and an easy job.

That was the job I returned to after graduation. Heather did not have a phone, so we stayed in touch by stopping by each other's work to make our plans to hang out. She stopped by the gift shop more than I stopped by one of the two restaurants where she was waitressing, as she was always busy, no matter the shift. Summer visitors had big appetites to fill, they needed energy for all they planned to see and do, keeping the waitstaff very busy. Heather also had to walk by the gift shop to get to the miserable room she was sharing with her boyfriend, where she would go to try to get some rest in between her exhausting shifts. Sometimes after her long hours, we would meet around 11 p.m. when the restaurants closed, and she was finally done for the day.

Our favorite thing to do was to take cheap wine, disguised in a thermos, and cigarettes to the bulkhead at the end of the public parking lot. I don't remember who was buying for us then. Probably Sean. It seemed the least he could do as he didn't do much else. The bulkhead was a cement wall that separated the parking lot from Provincetown harbor and connected the two main piers in town. We would take our shoes off and dangle our feet over the edge, just a few feet from the bay water at high tide, but over 15 feet from the sandbars at low. We smoked and drank and discussed our dreams, our futures, our problems; hers more intense than mine, as there was already trouble in her relationship. I think by then she knew her boyfriend was not all he promised to be, but she stayed in the hopes that she was wrong. And perhaps (though she wouldn't admit it, even to me), she felt she had nowhere else to go.

This quiet place was where we were when I told her how desperately I did not want to go to college. It was also where we were when she told me she was pregnant.

As August rolled around, my mom and I would have been packing for my dorm, but I remember little of it. When I think about that summer and school, I think mostly of dread. No one could quite put their finger on why I wasn't more excited. I didn't get it myself.

There must have been some sort of emergency, because the tenants in one of our apartments unexpectedly left. A very unusual thing for people to up and leave in the middle of the summer. It would be tricky, but not impossible for my mom to find another tenant. She'd always had a soft spot for Heather, and while she had no use for Sean, she wanted to help her out. And maybe my mom thought I would be more eager to leave for school if I felt that Heather's life was stable. Heather and Sean could not afford my mom's summer rent and my mom could not afford to let them move in for free. So, they struck a deal and soon Heather and I were living under the same roof. She still planned to head to Hollywood in the late fall. With her great figure, she thought she could hide her pregnancy for several more months. If Sean's claimed connections got her screen tests right away, the delivery and the raising of the baby would just have to overlap her movie career.

I had not talked to Richard all summer. Because the gift shop was on the main street, I would often see him drive by. I got even better than Serena at spotting his truck from a distance, eagerly waiting for a glimpse of him as he approached. Sometimes he would look in and smile, other times not. I was busy with customers most of the time and would only see the blue of his pickup as it passed. But I still felt that little lift just knowing he had been nearby.

Laurie realized that her little sister would not be home much longer, and she wanted some special time together before I left. One night we went to dinner and to see the just-released movie, *Dirty Dancing*. I loved it. Laurie loved it also and, for days, talked about how much she loved it. I felt cheated. As much as I enjoyed the movie, I noticed things about it that no one was talking about. How come Baby's parents didn't object to Johnny's age as much as they objected to his working-class status and his assumed relationship with Penny? Clearly Johnny was a lot older than Baby; in fact, he looked about 11 years older to me. Yet, no one seemed to care. My sister, who had freaked out and been unsupportive about my dating a man 11 years older than me, never brought it up. And how come all the parents' groups who were putting warning labels on rock music didn't object to the sex scene? Baby and Johnny dance together, get close and then kiss for the first time. Seconds later, in the next scene, it's obvious they've had sex. One could argue that Johnny took advantage of the situation and took advantage of a much younger girl. Richard would never, had never, done that to me. He purposefully took things slowly, yet my sister seemed to think that Johnny's speed was fine because it happened in a movie she loved. It really pissed me off. I did not want to be dramatic by comparing my relationship with Richard to a sappy movie, but the parallels would not stop nagging at me; especially when I saw Laurie gushing about how romantic it was. And then there was that ridiculous, famous line, "Nobody puts Baby in a corner." *Richard would never say something that cheesy,* I thought.

Little did I know that within two weeks, Richard would use better words to say pretty much the same thing. He would say them to the person who needed to hear them the most, and it would be the most important thing anyone had ever said to me.

* * *

In the last week of summer, actual panic set in. One night, while waiting for Heather to cash out her tips, I sat alone on our wall at low tide. The exposed sandbars below me were covered with rocks and broken shells. It was a long way down. Not for the first time did I wonder if I would get out of going to college if I got hurt. I would never have killed myself. I didn't want to lose my whole life. I just had no use for the life I was being directed towards. It didn't seem likely that the somewhat soft sand would kill me, but from this height it could cause damage. If I just broke a leg, or a collarbone, would I still have to go to college? If I just fell, and got seriously injured, wouldn't that be excuse enough to stay? It seemed so easy for it to happen; everyone knew I was a klutz. Even as I pondered these thoughts, I berated myself. Some of my class-mates had signed up for the military and had already left. There were rumors of tensions heating up in the Middle East and who knew where these friends of mine would wind up? How ridiculous and selfish to think about hurting myself so I didn't have to go to college! It was not like I was being sent to a war zone.

These thoughts only made things worse. I still wanted to get hurt but being such a wimp only solidified feelings I had fought forever; basically, I was a total loser. In the end, I did nothing drastic, mainly because I was still the responsible person I had been taught to be my whole life. Responsible people did not let themselves fall off high walls to get out of doing something they did not want to do.

While both of my parents had pushed me to college, my mother was realizing how much she would miss me. She tried to cheer me up with words of encouragement, but with me the only one of her daughters still living at home, I could tell she was hav-ing a hard time. Heather was under her roof, but Heather was not her daughter and Heather's boyfriend was a wall between any extra closeness that might develop between them when I was gone. Still, the person who seemed to dread my leaving the most was Heather. The only people who knew about her pregnancy were me and Sean, and Sean was anything but a support system. I think our friendship was the only sanity in her life at that time and she feared a future without me nearby to confide in. I felt the same way about confiding in her. My leaving was making us both ill.

Four days before Emerson's orientation, Heather had the night off and we were driving around town. She was behind the wheel of my car. Because of the baby, she wasn't drinking. I wanted nothing but to drink. I'd brought with me several bottles of disgustingly sweet wine coolers but was too sad to actually be drunk.

"I can't describe it. It's like this huge rock in my stomach that is weighing me down, making it impossible to move or do anything. It hurts a lot too. I don't see it getting any better. It just gets worse as it gets closer," I told her on our drive.

"You don't think it's just nervousness about going somewhere new?" she asked.

"That's what my parents say. That's what everybody says. But I don't think so. I think this is different. I wish I could talk to Richard."

"Do you think you don't want to leave because of him? Is it that simple?"

"No, I don't think so. But I feel like if I could talk to him, I might feel better. It would cheer me up. Or maybe I'm just looking for an excuse to talk to him. I don't know. It's just the way things ended was so lame, you know? This is so weird and so huge, and I don't know. I guess I want to talk to him about it, or say goodbye, which is dumb because it's not like I'm not coming back. Damn, I'll probably be on the bus back the very first weekend."

Heather drove down Shankpainter Road. Richard's truck was in the Piggy's parking lot. She saw it just as I did.

"Well, this could be your chance. What do you want to do?"

I panicked. Everyone knew the bouncers there were strict. I'd heard this many, many times from both of my older sisters and from Richard himself. There was no way I could get in. And he was likely in the bar with a girl, Patty even. Could I handle that? Did I want the one daring thing I ever did in my life to be making a fool out of myself?

"I don't know. I mean, how could I even get in? What if he's with someone?"

"We could just park across the street," Heather said. "Wait to see what things look like when he comes out."

"That could be hours. Like that's not totally pathetic. Dammit!"

Heather had continued driving, but now she turned the car around in the VFW parking lot.

"What are you doing?"

"You said it yourself; you think talking to him might make you feel better. You won't know if you don't try. If you're worried about seeing him with another girl, then I'll go in for you."

She parked next to his truck and quickly turned off the car and got out, taking my keys, and leaving me feeling like the biggest loser in the world. I didn't even have the guts to go look for him. After all we'd been through, I would think I could at least manage that.

I watched her summon all her acting skills to appear as though she belonged in the bar. She strode by the bouncer and ignored him as he called to her. I watched him follow her inside, and within seconds she was out again. But Richard was right behind her. She told me later that luckily, she had seen him just by the door. Before the bouncer could stop her, she quickly told Richard I was outside and needed to talk to him. He put down his drink and followed her out. Leaving the bouncer in the doorway, they walked to the car. Heather got into the driver's side again and Richard came to my window.

"Hey," I said weakly.

"How've you been?"

"I don't know, good, I guess. Things kind of suck, but ok."

Heather broke in. "I think you guys need to talk. Richard, if you're not doing anything, do you feel like giving Yvonne a ride home?"

I held my breath. If he was on a date, the answer would be no.

"Yeah, that's a good idea. Feel like going for a ride?" he asked me.

I nodded and opened the car door. Before I could get out, Heather grabbed my arm and whispered in my ear.

"Come upstairs when you get home, no matter what time. I'll be waiting."

I followed him to his truck, and he drove us to the beach. He shut off the engine.

"So, you're leaving soon?"

"Yeah, in a few days."

"And you're not looking forward to it. Look at you — you're scared to death, aren't you?"

"I guess. Everyone's saying that it's just nerves."

"Wow! You're terrified! I can tell. And I bet I know why."

I looked at him. I didn't know why. How could he?

"You're terrified that when you get there, every person you meet is going to be smarter than you, or richer than you, or prettier than you, or have more of a reason to be there than you. And I am telling you that you're wrong. You're as smart and pretty as anyone and you have as much right to be there as everyone else, maybe even more. You have to remember that."

That was it. That was exactly what I had been afraid of. My mousey little self didn't think I had any right to breathe any air except the air that made up my beloved hometown. No one else had figured it out. Richard knew exactly what was going on with me. He knew that, for some reason, I felt less than those around me. And he was telling me it was time to stop. I smiled, and he leaned against me and hugged me.

"That was some speech, by the way."

It took me a second to understand what he was talking about. I couldn't believe it when I got it.

"You were at graduation?"

"Ya, for a bit. Your speech was really good."

"It was no big deal. Mr. Seeley was really the one who wrote it."

"Really? Paul Seeley wrote that, huh? I know him pretty well and wouldn't have thought he would come up with something like that." He was grinning at me. He knew me so well. I laughed.

"I'm glad you were there. I had hoped you were, but I didn't think so."

"I found out about graduation and that it was downtown just before everything started. I'm glad I was there too." He kissed me. It felt so good to be in his arms again. The worries about school disappeared. All I could think about was how happy I was when I was with him.

We kissed for a while and then he started the truck.

"Let's go for a ride."

I worried he was taking me home. I didn't want this night to end. This time with him was exactly what I needed.

He didn't take me home. He drove past my street, turning down another several blocks away. He parked in front of an old, rundown sea captain's house known for the ship figurehead of a maiden positioned over the entryway of the main door. I had walked by this house hundreds, maybe thousands of times.

"I'm renting a place here. I thought I would invite you in. That is, if you want to."

I nodded. So this was where he'd been living when he moved out of Laurie's. He hadn't been living with Patty at all. He took my hand as we walked to a door in the back of the building.

"Damn, Berto's home. My roommate. Do you know him?"

I did, just from around town. I remembered him taking pity on me when I was about nine and struggling in roller skates on Commercial Street. Berto was a great skater and had taken it upon himself to give the nerdy kid some skating tips. His age was somewhere between mine and Richard's. He was walking out as Richard and I were walking in. He seemed surprised to see me. He did not say hello but only mumbled something to Richard about garbage or rent or some other roommate type of thing, and then he left. We were alone.

The details of what followed that evening are hazy. I had always thought I would remember everything about my first sexual encounter. But for some reason, my brain didn't retain the details. I wasn't drunk. In fact, I don't know of a time when I was more sober. And I was so thrilled to be with him. Richard was a guy I loved. How could I not remember every second of that experience?

What I cherish about that night and what stands out most in my memory, is that I felt treasured. And safe. And precious. Those memories are so strong that they overwhelm the others. If there was any awkwardness, the sweetness of the night eliminated it. And while it was the first time I had sex, it wasn't about sex. It was about Richard wanting me to know that no matter what, I was loved. A big part of his decision to take me back to his place might likely have been about protecting me. I think that deep down, as proud as he was about my future, Richard worried that my first time would be with some drunk frat boy he had no respect for and who had no respect for me. Richard cared for me enough to want to make sure that my first time was special. Even if feeling special was the only specific memory I kept of that night, what more could someone ask of their first time?

It was late when he drove me home. He kissed me long and hard, parked right there on my street, not worrying if my mother woke up and saw us. I told him how much I would miss him. He promised me I would hear from him before I left. He kissed me again and smiled as I got out of his truck.

Heather was already at the bottom of her apartment stairs. She had two cigarettes lit before he even drove off. We said nothing as she handed one to me. We just leaned back in the Adirondack chairs on my patio, smoking our cigarettes while we looked at the stars.

chapter 9
college

Very early, three mornings later, Heather and I stood by my dad's car. She was still in her nightgown, and she was in tears. I thought I would vomit. It was time to go.

My mom was not much of a city driver, so my dad would be the one behind the wheel on this trip. But my mom wasn't about to miss this big moment, dropping her baby off for her first year of college. My parents had been getting along better since the spring. And so, even though divorced, with my dad having a new wife and baby at home, they would take me to my college together.

People thought this was weird. I wasn't thinking of anything except how I wished that instead of getting into the back seat of my dad's car, squeezed next to my pillows and suitcases, I wanted to head down the street and walk to my gift shop job. I wanted to tell them they didn't need to be short-staffed. I was back and could cover all the shifts until they closed for the season. But, of course, I couldn't do that. Even my boss had said goodbye and prepared for my leaving; evidenced by a wad of cash stuffed in my pocket, my yearend bonus.

Everything packed, it was time to start the two-hour drive to Boston. I hugged Heather and glanced at my house. I looked both ways down my little street. Richard had promised I would hear from him before I left. I hadn't heard from him and now I was leaving. My last inspection of my neighborhood was to see if he was nearby, waving. Maybe, like in the movies, he would suddenly appear and pull me away with him, and we would ride off into the sunset to live happily ever after. But that didn't happen.

As we turned onto the highway, my parents talked about the police station and town politics. With my dad a police officer, and my mom a respected member of the town's Board of Selectmen, this was a conversation that enthralled them both. I sat in the back seat and wondered why he hadn't fulfilled his promise. Why promise me that I would hear from him, and then not follow through? It was a disappointment and a question, but I refused to let it change anything about the last time we saw each other. That night had been perfect, and I was so happy for that time with him. I honestly didn't expect our relationship to start up again. Yet, I was convinced that his feelings were real. Whatever had kept him away, I refused to believe that it changed anything that had happened between us. He cared for me and that was enough. Halfway into the trip, I tried my best to put him out of my mind. Richard or no, I was still terrified about where we were going. But the time had come to suck it up and just get through it.

On Beacon Street in downtown Boston, my dad, like all the other parents, triple-parked and started unloading the car. My mom stepped up onto the sidewalk and took in the surroundings, smiling broadly. I didn't smile. Reluctantly, I did what I guessed the responsible college student was supposed to do; I went into the building and tried to figure out what came next.

There was a registration desk with older-looking students with clipboards behind it and a line of students in front. I got in line. Stepping in behind me was a tall, pretty, black girl. When I was up next, I told the guy at the desk my name and that I was in room 418. The girl tapped my shoulder and when I looked at her, she seemed to sneer at me.

"You're in room 418? I'm in room 418. *I'm your roommate!*"

She said it with such an attitude it was all I could do not to go running to the car. My unworthy thoughts took hold.

This girl only just met me, and she already hates me.

Am I that much of a loser that she could hate me just by look-ing at me?

Maybe I should apologize for being her roommate, tell her I'll try to get a new room or something?

Then I heard Richard's voice in my ear. "You are as smart and pretty as anyone and you have as much right to be there as every-one else, maybe even more."

It was as clear as if he was standing beside me. *Richard thinks I'm good enough to be here, so whatever this girl's problem with me is, it's her problem and her problem only.*

What I said was, "Nice to meet you. I'm Yvonne."

She softened and told me her name was Tracy. Later, I learned she was from the Midwest and had to fly out to school by herself. She was as frightened as I was and had what was even more cause for concern. She had heard rumors that Boston was a racist town.

We checked in and my dad, ever the gentlemen and flirt, helped pile her bags onto the elevator with my own. We got to the fourth floor, where we found our room and met our third roommate, Raquel. Richard could say what he wanted about my being as pretty as anyone, but even he would have stammered looking at Raquel. She was model-gorgeous. In fact, she had done some mod-eling. She'd arrived with her mother and stepfather, who were both shocked when they learned my parents were divorced but had taken the long trip together. Raquel's mother couldn't imag-ine spending even a minute in a car with her ex-husband without trying to kill him.

Because they had gotten to the dorm so early, Raquel had staked her claim on the lone single bed, moved it to a corner, and begun decorating. But even though she had already taken over and was even more beautiful than the posters going up in the boys' rooms next to ours, she was nice.

I let Tracy pick the top or bottom bunk. It wasn't that old habits die hard; I simply did not care. Even though there would be three of us in one room, the room was a decent size and nicer than others by comparison. There was one odd exception, however. There was a door in one wall that appeared out of place. When we opened it, we saw another room not much more than the size of a closet with two beds stuffed in and barely room to walk around them. It was an odd set up — the school couldn't possibly be planning to fill that room, could they?

As we unpacked, first one, and then a second girl, arrived and discovered their bummer of a room assignment. The more brazen of the two singled me out. Everything about her screamed money; her clothes, her shoes, her jewelry, her luggage. She'd arrived by herself but had been driven to the school in a chauffeured town car.

"This your room?" she asked. "This is *our* room. I can't believe it!" She was practically spitting she was so furious. "We don't even have our own door into the hall! We have to use yours."

My instinct was to offer to change with her. I was a nice person and really, I didn't want to be there at all. What did I care about the size of my room? But then I got offended, not for my own sake, but on Richard's behalf. It was like he was beside me again and pissed off that this girl thought she could bully me into switching with her. It was only my wanting to please him that made me say to the girl, "Oh, that's ok. Don't worry about it. We don't mind if you use our door."

She walked off in a huff. She was rich. And she was a snob. But soon we became friends.

Raquel, her mother, and stepfather left to explore the city. My parents invited Tracy to join us for lunch. She did and then we came back to the dorm. My mom and dad took one last look around, hugged me, and left. I think I saw a tear in my usually stoic mom's eye, which did not help. If she was sad to leave me, then why couldn't I go back with her? Later that night Tracy, Raquel and I sat around our room getting to know each other. We had passed other kids in our small suite of 13 here and there but getting to know one another started with the actual roommates.

The next day, we each had various orientation events scheduled depending on our area of study. At lunch time I found myself alone in my room and hungry. I had my meal card but was not sure I could handle the stress of going to the dining hall by myself. Walking to the nearest bathroom of the only two we thirteen students had to share, I noticed that the door of another room was open, and a girl named Lisa, whom I had briefly met the night before, was inside reading. I thought of Richard's words. I knocked.

"Hi Lisa. Are you hungry? I'm thinking of going to get lunch. Do you want to come?"

She did. We also became friends. And before long, I had settled into the routine. When I talked to my mother later that week, I told her about the friends I had made and how classes were not that bad.

"So, are you coming home this Friday?" my mom teased, clearly happy that I was settling in.

"No, that doesn't make sense. And the suite mates are thinking of checking out the city on Saturday."

"Wow, if this keeps up, I won't see you until Thanksgiving break," she said.

"Oh no, I'll be home Columbus Day Weekend. I don't have classes on Fridays, so I will get four whole days."

I might have adjusted to school better than expected, but Provincetown was still my first love. I had already found the bus station and picked up the Cape Cod schedule.

chapter 10
flowers

When the Friday of the three-day weekend arrived, I took a bus back to the Cape. It felt so good to be back on that side of the Sagamore Bridge, the official gateway to Cape Cod. Was it my imagination, or did the air seem fresher? Both my older sisters, Laurie and Audrey, picked me up at the station. During our 60-minute drive down the Cape, I told them stories about school, stories I would repeat several times later in the weekend. With only about 6 minutes left to the front door of my childhood home, we rounded the last hill before town. I gasped at the view. My little town splayed out before me under the striking Pilgrim Monument. This view was not a new one. I saw it from the highway every time I entered Provincetown, but it was always beautiful. After five weeks at school, the longest I'd ever been away, this sight was what made me feel most at home.

I spent the weekend visiting and catching up with friends and family. While at my dad's, I filled Kathy and him in on school and played with little Suzanne, who seemed to have grown years rather than weeks. I didn't get to see Heather much those first two days since it was the last big tourist hurrah of the season, and she was working nonstop. Sunday afternoon, Laurie and I took a leisurely ride around town in my car. At one point, we passed Richard. He smiled and waved, and we waved back, but I didn't smile. Nor did I stop. He looked surprised. I was still confused about him breaking his promise to me.

My mom made a family dinner that night. During the meal, Laurie casually said, "Don't let Yvonne go out tonight. We saw Richard downtown."

Was she serious? It was like he was some big, evil monster that would devour me, and that we had bumped into him earlier meant that he was prowling the streets looking for me. My mom said, "Well, you do go back early tomorrow. Maybe you should stay in and rest up. You have been running around all weekend."

I couldn't believe it. An attitude came upon me, and I lost my obedient little girl ways. I scowled and said, "You sent me off to the crime-ridden city of Boston where I'm keeping my own hours, getting myself off to classes no matter how late I stay up or what I'm doing while I'm up late, walking the streets or whatever, and now that I'm in town, you want to keep me home so I can rest? You're kidding me, right? If I'm responsible enough to take care of myself in Boston, I'm definitely capable of taking care of myself in Ptown!"

What could my mom say to that? Nothing. After dinner, I helped her clean the kitchen, and we watched TV for a bit. It wasn't much later that I grabbed my car keys and headed out. This time, I did go looking for Richard. And as if it was meant to be, I found him walking down Commercial Street. He got into my car when I called out and I drove to the far end of the town parking lot, where we could watch the boats on the pier while we talked.

"So, how's college life?" he asked, smiling.

"Not as bad as I thought it would be. My roommates are nice, and I've made some friends. Classes aren't horrible."

"Then why do you look grouchy?"

"I don't know. I don't mean to look that way. I'm just surprised that I didn't see you before I left."

"Ya, I know. It just would have been too hard, I think, for both of us."

"I guess. But you promised I would hear from you and then I didn't. And after that night, I guess it just bummed me out."

"I promised I would say goodbye. That's what I meant."

"But you didn't."

"Not in person," he said. "But I said goodbye in the card."

"What card?"

"Ah, the card that was with the flowers. The card with the letter in it. That card."

At my puzzled look, his face became puzzled too. "Yvonne, I left a card with a letter in it and some flowers in your car the night before you left. Please tell me you got them."

I hadn't and told him so.

"I can't believe this! That would have meant so much to me. I can't believe I didn't get them," I cried.

"It meant a lot to me that you have them," he said. "There were things I couldn't tell you that I had to write. And I wanted to wish you well."

"What things?" I asked.

"Things that were easier to write than say. Can you get them? Where'd they go?"

We tried to figure out what happened. He had left them in my car, so I would be sure to get them when I drove off to school. But, he had gotten confused by the date I was leaving, putting them in my car on the evening that I had actually left. I could picture it. Late, maybe even after the bars closed and most of the town was asleep, he had parked near my house. Then, quietly, crept up my street, carrying flowers, and placed them in my car. Was my car locked? It didn't matter. He would have easily jimmied the door. The effort it took to do such a special thing for me filled me with intense longing. It was all I could do not to burst into happy, frustrating tears.

"But your car was still there."

"We can't take cars to Emerson. There's no parking. Laurie! I told her she could use my car while I was gone. Hers is about to die any day."

"I'm surprised Andy hasn't fixed it yet; it wouldn't take that much. I saw her driving yours a couple of times, but I thought maybe you were home, and she was just borrowing it."

"This is the first time I've been home. I'm so sorry that I didn't get your gift. Please tell me what you wrote."

He shook his head. "You have to get it. Make her give it to you. She must have saved it."

He changed the subject then and asked me about school. He also asked if I was dating anyone.

"Just my luck. With the huge theater department at my school, there are a ton of gay guys. It's like a mini-Provincetown in downtown Boston."

He laughed. "They can't all be gay, can they?"

I confirmed that there were many nice straight guys, but that I was still getting used to things. I asked about him.

"Patty and I have been back and forth; you know how that goes."

My honest Richard. I knew I should never ask him a question unless I wanted an honest answer, but I had asked anyway. His answer was not what I wanted to hear. Yet, I was not surprised. Of course a guy as fabulous as him was seeing someone. Did I really expect him to miss me as much as I missed him?

I didn't know the specifics of how "that" went. That, I chose not to ask.

"Well, I hope things are going good. I hope you're doing ok," I said.

He shrugged, hugged me tight, then said, "You're going to do great." And then he got out of the car and walked away.

I drove around for a while and sat at the beach for a bit. Back at my house, I was pleased to see that Heather was home. But so was Sean. I didn't hate him, I just wanted to talk to my friend without him butting in. He was in the mood for a visit, though. I got the feeling that if I asked Heather to come outside, he would come with her. So I told them both what happened.

"Man, that sucks. I wish I'd thought to check the car for you," she told me.

"I wish I had thought to ask you. It never occurred to me he would confuse the date or think I was taking my car. Do you believe this? I let her use my car, and this is the thanks I get."

"What are you going to do?"

"Make her give them to me. I have to pick her up tomorrow, so she can give me a ride to the bus and then use my car! Isn't that rich? I'll get them back."

The next morning, I said goodbye to my mom and drove to Laurie's. Instead of waiting for her to come downstairs, I went up and demanded that she give me my card and letter. She said she had no idea what I was talking about. I told her about my conversation with Richard.

"Oh, please. He's lying. I don't think he has that in him."

I knew he wasn't. "Damn it Laurie, I am sick of you bad-mouthing him all the time! Especially since you thought he was just fine until he took an interest in me. What is that about?"

"He's just not the angel you think he is."

"And I have yet to see him be the villain you keep claiming he is! He's been nothing but sweet to me."

"He's just not for you."

"Obviously, since we're not together. But damn it, if someone gives me a gift, or leaves something for me in MY car, I think the least you could do is give it to me! Especially since I'm letting you use MY car."

"I don't have it. I never saw it."

I believed her. But I also believed him. So, what happened? Who else had access to my car? I thought of how I had to leave my keys in case my mom needed to move it in an emergency. My mother!

Back at the dorm that evening, I skipped dinner in the dining hall and waited until my suite mates left, all of them, including my pseudo-roommates in the tiny, attached room, and called my mother. I wanted to be alone when I used the hall pay phone to confront her. I called and demanded to know if she found anything in my car after I left.

"I guess that means you saw Richard before you left town," which meant she was admitting to finding and keeping my surprise.

"I can't believe you didn't tell me about it, Mom. It was a special gift for me! Where is it? You need to send them to me right away."

"Well, the flowers are dead."

"No kidding! I meant the card and the letter. I can't believe you haven't sent them to me already!"

My mom didn't send care packages of homemade cookies like some of the other moms. But each week, she mailed me the local newspaper, the Advocate, so I could keep up on all the news from home. She could have easily slipped Richard's notes in the envelope.

"I threw those away, too."

"*What?!* How could you? What did they say?" I screamed, practically hysterical.

"Calm down, nothing. Just good luck with school and that kind of thing. I don't remember a letter."

"Richard said there was a letter too! How can you not remember? Do you really not have them?"

She said again that she had thrown them away.

"I can't believe this. What were you even *doing* in my car, anyway?"

This was a low blow. The car had been my dad's bachelor car when they divorced. There clearly had not been any emergency; she had not needed to move it. But, she'd had some weird emotional impulse that led her to get behind the wheel of the cool car that had been her ex-husband's. Maybe she did it just because she could. She certainly hadn't had the opportunity to drive his sports car before. And when she opened the driver's side door, she had found my gifts from Richard and had tossed them into the trash like they didn't even matter, like they weren't the entire universe to me.

She said nothing about being in the car. She only said, "I didn't think they were anything you needed to see. You were already gone, and you didn't need any distractions from the foolishness with this guy. It was nothing important."

"It was to me," I cried. And then I hung up.

We went much longer than usual before talking again. She still sent me the weekly paper, and I ripped open the envelope each week, hoping there was a surprise inside; maybe she hadn't thrown Richard's notes away. But they were never in there. Of course, she never apologized. It just wasn't her way.

After a while we started talking again, although our conversations were chilly at first. Eventually I got over it. She was my mom, after all.

In calmer conversations, I asked her many times over if she had kept the card with the letter inside and if so, to please, please give them to me. Each time, she swore she threw them away and didn't remember what they said. And that must have been the truth. I never did learn what Richard had written to me when I went off to school.

chapter 11
freshman

Back at school, I focused on classes, my new friends, and exploring Boston. Despite enjoying my first year, there was that part of me that got most excited when college and Provincetown merged. Two of my PHS classmates were also in school in the city and we met up a couple of times to reconnect. What new part of the city had one of us discovered that the other two hadn't? Who had they talked to from back home? How were our former classmates doing?

By the end of late October, Heather and Sean were ready to head out west. They stopped to say goodbye. I wondered what my new friends would think of the obnoxious Sean, but I needn't have worried. He was a master of turning on the charm; it was what made Heather fall for him in the first place. My dorm mates didn't think too much of him either way. Heather was a different story, however. My usually confident, funny, dear friend was not herself at the visit. She wasn't impressed by the school or my roommates. Heather walked into the suite full of drama, flare, and downright snobbishness. She was loud and bossy and acting as if she were already famous and the school should bow to her. This was not my friend, and it was embarrassing.

She was herself at lunch, when it was just the three of us. Back at the dorm, I saw yet another side of her I did not recognize. She became meek and quiet and couldn't wait to leave. I'd hoped they would spend more time with me; when would I see my best friend

again? On Beacon Street she hugged me goodbye, and I was surprised by her tears. Saying goodbye was heartbreaking, but still,
what was her hurry to get on the road? It wasn't until they left
that I realized the problem. As terrified as I was about coming to
school, Heather was terrified about her future. All she would have
to rely on from here on out was Sean, and that wasn't a consoling
thought. She was very smart, attractive, and talented. And now
she was pregnant, her belly just starting to show, and was desperately trying to find her place and overcome her own fears and
insecurities. The attitudes she brought to Emerson were acts she
was testing to tell herself that she was in control. She knew she
wasn't.

Small town and big city fused perfectly in my fantasy life.
Thoughts of Richard were still front and center and most of my
dreams involved him coming up to see me and us exploring the
city together, or him getting his own apartment in Ptown and me
spending every weekend with him. Richard would have absolutely
hated the city, but that fact didn't fit into the daydream. Neither
did the fact that I wouldn't be able to help him with rent, and it
wasn't likely that Richard had enough money to afford a rental of
his own. In the back of my mind, I probably knew that this was
because some of his money went to drugs, but in my perfect little
world, he was drug free, and we were a happy couple.

Despite thinking about Richard, I was starting to look at the
guys around me. One would think that since I was away from my
hometown and, finally feeling confident, I would have been interested in all types of guys. But the first guy I even had a remote
interest in was not a gorgeous actor wannabe, or a dramatic, passionate playwright. Nor was it one of the frat boys or brainiacs or
rich kids.

No, the first guy I was interested in was the shuttle bus driver.
Emerson's campus was spread out along Beacon Street, placing
my small dorm on one end and the major dorm and cafeteria at
the other, about a mile apart. The classrooms were mixed in

between. One mile was not a long walk, but it could be a drag in the rain. Thus, the college offered a shuttle. I liked to walk and didn't take the bus often. But when I did, I felt a kinship with the friendly, blue-collar driver. He was a little rough looking, but cute in a tough guy kind of way, though not nearly as handsome as Richard. Still, something about him struck me. Maybe it was that his clothes and attitude were familiar to me; perhaps reminding me of people I knew from home more than these new friends of mine did. And it might have been my imagination, but he seemed to be a little more sociable to me than to the other kids and smiled a lot more when I got on the bus. It could have simply been because I made a point of saying hello. Other students, many used to being chauffeured around, ignored him. He was just the bus driver, the worker paid to take them where they planned on going. I started taking the bus more often, which didn't help me fight the 15 pounds college kids are famous for gaining in their freshman year. Just as I got the courage to flirt with him a bit, he was gone. We were told that he was fired, but the administration refused to say why. There was a rumor that he drove a bunch of students to a party off the assigned route, which would have fit with the rebellious nature I thought I saw in him, but I never knew for sure.

I assumed they fired him because he didn't fit with the artsy, elite campus. It was just like me to believe he'd been wronged without knowing any of the facts. I channeled that emotion into a fiery creative writing project; one that was based on another doomed relationship I developed at Emerson, although not a romantic one.

Despite my scholarships, college was expensive. To help pay tuition, I had a work-study job. My job was to monitor the front desk of the dorm building to make sure no one snuck anyone up to their room without signing them in or tried to bring in alcohol. It was pretty silly as no one would walk by carrying obvious cases or bottles and I had no permission or interest in searching my fellow students. I guess my job was to be on guard for emergencies, although all I had to help with that was a phone with campus security and the resident assistant's numbers written on a card on the wall behind me.

I worked the night shift—11 p.m. to 2 a.m. or 4 a.m. to 8 a.m. Often visiting me was the dorm custodian, an elderly, dark-skinned Hispanic man named Lopez. His hours were as bizarre as mine and we would often chat. I was not afraid on this job as the front doors to the building were locked, but it still helped to hear him moving around in the basement and getting his early chores done. One day, I came down to the desk and found out that Lopez had been replaced. When I asked why, I was told they fired him because a supervisor caught him asleep on the job. I was incensed because I knew he didn't have much money. How would he and his family survive? He was old and tired; maybe he was just resting during one of his breaks? I balked and argued, but only to the RA who was my supervisor. There was nothing I could do. I was a work-study student with no clout or clue how these things worked. I wrote a story about Lopez and while my professor thought it was good, it didn't occur to him that maybe it was something he could speak out on. Pathos is great for creative writing, but in the end, doesn't always accomplish very much.

At times, my hometown connections and Boston life intersected in ways that were pretty funny and felt like a breath of fresh air. Lisa was even more shy and timid than I was. She'd had a sheltered childhood, having been raised in a lovely but strict, family. The two of us were walking along a shabbier part of Commonwealth Avenue and came to an area where the real off-the-grid 19-and 20-year-olds lived. These were the street performers and musicians barely getting by, living on Ramen noodles and pot. Not so much college kids, but heavy partiers and punk rockers. We could tell by the art posters advertising nondescript bars with live music plastered along the apartment buildings and light poles in the neighborhood. As we walked, we saw a strung-out-looking guy sitting on a stoop in front of a particularly derelict dwelling. As I approached, he seemed familiar. Soon we were both smiling and before Lisa knew what hit her, he was on me in a big bear hug and Lisa was freaking out.

"Yvonne, do you know this guy? What the hell?? Come on, what's going on? We've got to go!"

"Lisa, it's ok, this is Nate Bennett — we went to school together."

Nate was wild-looking with a punk haircut, several piercings, and multiple tattoos. Not surprising, as he had always been an edgy classmate. It was so good to bump into someone from my little corner of the world that I felt like I was instantly back on the 'meet rack,' the Ptown benches in front of town hall. I wanted to reminisce with him and share the wonders of my hometown with Lisa, but she looked suspicious and eager to get out of the area. Nate invited us to a party that night and I wanted to go. I knew I would never convince Lisa; she couldn't get away from Nate fast enough. But I thought I could get some other friends to go. It didn't happen. No one was interested or available, and I wasn't brave enough to go alone. Both because it would mean walking in the city by myself late at night and also because if I walked in without my new friends and didn't see Nate right away, where would I find my safety net?

* * *

By the time I went home for Thanksgiving, things had gone back to normal between my mom and me. I didn't see Richard in town anywhere that long holiday weekend, although I certainly tried, driving my own loop between the Bradford, the last apartment I knew he had, and work sites I thought might be his company's. Since this was before cell phones, there was no way to call him. Not that it mattered; he never got one even after they were popular and affordable. I couldn't help thinking he must know I was home. Why wasn't he out, making himself available so I could say hi?

The unfortunate conclusion was likely in the words he said to me the last time I saw him, "Patty and I have been back and forth...." If he wasn't out, then it was most likely because he was at her place. It wasn't easy to think about, but it was what it was. Somehow, I accepted it. What choice did I have?

I didn't see him on Christmas break either, although I didn't have a lot of time to look. Shortly after the holiday, I had my impacted wisdom teeth pulled during day surgery at the local hospital. My dad took me to the appointment. When I woke up in the recovery room, I just wanted to leave as soon as possible. A nurse kept bargaining with me.

"You can leave after you drink this cup of water."

I drank the water.

"You can leave after you drink this Ginger Ale."

I drank the Ginger Ale.

"You can leave after you eat this Jell-O."

The last thing I wanted to do was eat or drink anything, but I wanted to go home, so I did what she said. Finally, she told me I was ready to be discharged, and she sent my dad in to help me get my things. The minute I saw my dad, I puked. It was like the scene from the *Exorcist*. I spewed horrible purple vomit over my hospital bed, over my clothes, over everything.... There was a ton of this disgusting mess, all amazingly coming from me. My dad ran away and the nurse grinned. She wasn't grossed out at all. I guess the plan was to see what would happen when the liquids and Jell-O mixed in my stomach, and if I would have any effects from the anesthesia.

"Do you always have that reaction when you see your father?" she smiled.

She helped me clean up and let me leave—my dad walking several feet in front of me and making me lay on the backseat with paper bags he grabbed in the gift shop surrounding me in case I repeated the horror movie scene. Before taking me home, he stopped at his house and picked up Suzanne. She was two and a half and very smart for her age. My dad told her I had been to the doctor and needed taking care of. She walked with me into my house and stood by as I lay on the sofa. Then she pulled a blanket up over me and patted my arm over and over. It was good to be home.

chapter 12
baby

Back at school after the holiday vacation, my suite mates and I discovered that 7 of the 13 of us had just had our wisdom teeth pulled. Seems that with the long break, it was a good time to get the surgery done. Some of us still had puffy cheeks. We discussed our procedures and tales of recovery. While my hospital vomit story got the most laughs, I noticed that my fellow students moved far away from me if they thought I'd consumed too much from the Jack Daniels bottle we were passing around.

The winter showed us a new version of Boston. The city was not easy in the snow, and we got by as best we could, slipping across the icy sidewalks and spending more time in the dorms. CD players were the new thing and two of the wealthier students had received players as a Christmas gift. They enjoyed showing off this new way of listening to music to the rest of us. We did our best to balance parties with studying when we were stuck inside, but it wasn't easy. Beer bongs, nip bottles and laziness often beat out the various assignments, but somehow, we were all still passing. There was a lot of whining too, especially from the students who had come to Emerson from the warmer climates; they were not enjoying New England weather. We locals teased them about their complaints of being cold and loved to share our own exaggerated winter adventures, bragging about the Blizzard of '78 even though we had just been little kids when the historic storm took place.

It was no wonder then that we all went a little stir crazy and counted down the days until March. While my dorm mates were making their spring break plans, there was never any question what I would be doing. It wasn't a matter of not having the money to travel. I just didn't want to go anywhere. Unlike a few of my other financially strapped friends who would have to work on their break, I would not be able to do so. The vacation was too early in the season for me to return to my summer job. I would spend my days sleeping late in the bed that had been mine since childhood and blasting loud music of my choice while my mom was at work. I would also visit with friends and family, making a special effort to spend time with Suzanne. Kathy was expecting again and while I was excited for a new sibling, I decided playing with my little sister as much as possible was important before a new baby took up residence in her home. Mostly though, after sharing close quarters and only two bathrooms with 12 others in my suite, I was looking forward to having my own space for a bit.

During that spring break, I saw Richard again, the first time since Columbus Day weekend. This time I was walking, savoring the still chilly, salty air, when he pulled up beside me in his work truck.

He smiled, but his eyes didn't light up as completely as I was used to. And he looked worn out. He was saying hello, but something told me he didn't intend to chat.

I didn't want to let him get away. Without thinking too much about it, I opened the passenger side door and hopped in. It would have been an embarrassing failure if the door was locked, but luckily townies rarely locked their vehicles.

"Ahhhh, Richard, you don't write, you don't call," I said, trying to kid with him. He didn't react. "Got time for a ride?" I asked.

He paused and didn't seem thrilled, which did nothing to help the sudden burst of confidence that led me to jump into his truck in the first place. But he stepped on the gas and continued down-town, turning after a few blocks to head to the beach.

"How've you been?" he asked. I told him I was home on spring break.

"What, no Cancun or Ft. Lauderdale for you?"

"Please, what would I do in Ft. Lauderdale? I'm just enjoying sleeping in and hanging with people."

I chattered away about school stuff. He stayed quiet. My inse-curities raged. Was he just being polite, agreeing to go for a ride? Had I become inconsequential, someone he could no longer be bothered with? Inside, I turned back into that insecure little girl; the one who felt that what I should do was get out of his truck and walk the now several miles home in the afternoon cold.

But he was the one who'd taught me not to be that cowering girl and so I stayed where I was and asked what was going on with him.

"Patty's pregnant."

My heart broke. Selfishly, it broke for me. It should be me. If he was going to have a baby, it should be mine. That was the life I wanted, to stay in town and start a family. Younger than I planned, but with Richard, it would be worth it. We could marry and make it work. I did not care about any of the other stuff I was supposed to be planning for my life. Kids were great, and I wanted to be a mom. We had only been together one time. What if I had gotten pregnant then? I would be more than six months along. We would have already been starting our future. Now Richard would be a father but was having a baby with someone else. A woman he had a rocky relationship with. A woman who couldn't possibly love him as much as I loved him. A woman who wasn't me. With his usual playfulness gone, Richard looked intense, unhappy, and maybe even a little frightened. He had been there for me during a rough time. I wanted to be there for him. If this was bad news, then I wanted to be supportive. If it wasn't bad news, well then, I would have to be supportive anyway, despite my own misery.

"So, you're not happy about it?" I asked cautiously.

"I don't know. I guess so. It's just that we don't have the best relationship or lifestyle. We definitely don't live in the best set of circumstances for raising a kid."

We had never actually talked about his drug use. Not entirely clueless, I'd begun to accept that there was truth to parts of the rumors. While I never saw it, cocaine was a big part of his life. And I'd heard that coke was a big part of Patty's life, too. I knew that when he said "lifestyle," drugs were what he meant. In addition to the huge news of the baby, the drugs were also likely why he looked so bad.

I wanted to cry but knowing that I was at least partially crying for myself, I refused to do it. I had to be a help to him, not a burden.

"Do you mean the partying?" Partying seemed a safer term to use than snorting lines. "Do you think the baby's health could be at risk?"

Patty was a mother already. She had a twelve-year-old son and, as far as I knew, he was healthy. But he had been several years old when she had moved to town. She might have been clean when she was pregnant with him.

"There's that. I think, or I hope, that Patty's toning it down while she's pregnant. You'd think so anyway. But let's face it— we're kind of a mess together. I'm not sure that's great for a kid. And she says it's mine, but what if it's not? We're always back and forth, and I know she's been with at least one other guy a few times."

This was all beyond me. I didn't know what the right thing to say, or the right thing to do, was.

"Richard, listen to me. I know I don't know much about any of this stuff, but the one thing I think is that if you have doubts, you have to figure it out early on. You can get a blood test. Maybe you can even get one before the baby is born. If not, you can do it at the hospital or as soon as possible. You can't make decisions about how you're going to handle this if you have doubts about being the baby's father. If it's going to matter to you, you have to know right from the beginning. You can't fall in love with this child and then, a few years later, get into a fight with Patty and have her say something that makes you wonder. You can't tell yourself you don't care, and that you will be the baby's father no matter what, and then have her mess with you by hinting that you may not be. You can't put a kid through that. Will she get a blood test?"

"I don't know. She swears we don't need it and that I shouldn't have any doubts, but that could be because she's happy about it. And she's lied to me before about other important stuff, so why not this? I'm just not sure. I guess I can insist on it, but if she freaks, it'll make things worse."

"Richard, please seriously consider this. It won't be good for any of you if you're trying to raise a child with this unease hanging over your head. It just won't help the situation."

I bit my cheek before I continued. I had to tell myself that this wasn't about me. It was about an innocent baby and this man I loved.

"If you decide it doesn't matter, then don't get the test. But it seems like it does. And if you find out that the baby's not yours, and you and Patty work things out, it will still need a father figure. You can be that. You'll just be that without wondering all the time."

I didn't want him and Patty to work things out. If Richard was the father, then I wanted to help him with the baby. I loved children, was told I was smart (although I doubted that) and was responsible. The one thing I knew was that I was responsible. My mind drifted to custody arrangements and the thought that together, Richard and I could give this child a normal, healthy home. This child could grow up with my new sibling. Yes, it would be awkward having Richard's child and my new brother or sister the same age, but it would also be really great. Then maybe we could give his baby a little brother or sister, too. A baby didn't have to be the end. Richard would be a great dad. But not like this. Not with this weariness and confusion in his eyes. I didn't know if my advice was good advice or not. But it was all I had.

I hugged him then. I held him tight, and he buried his face into my neck. We stayed like that for several minutes, me just holding him. He pulled away from me and started the truck, drove to the corner of my street and kissed me without a word. I wanted to say some brilliant words, to give him something helpful before I left. But I had nothing. Everything, even goodbye or good luck, seemed useless and pathetic, the words of a ridiculously clueless college student. I got out of the truck and watched him drive away. He did not look back at me as he drove off....

chapter 13
patty

I went back to school overwhelmed and depressed. I had little time to ponder Richard's circumstances, however, as the end of my first year in college kept me busy. I did what I knew how to do. I worked hard to get good grades that I didn't really care about. If college was what I was supposed to do, then far be it from me to do it half-assed. And so, I passed my finals, packed my bags and said goodbye to my new friends, thrilled year one was over.

Once home for the summer, I immediately went back to my gift shop job. Before long, other friends returned from wherever they had been in the off-season and the parties began.

I liked to drink, and for the most part, could handle my alcohol. And it was fun to stay out until crazy hours, knowing it was safe to walk home alone (unlike in Boston where it definitely wasn't,) sneak into my house, sleep for an hour or two and go to work, not only hung over but often still a little buzzed from the night before. It was never a problem. I knew my job well, so my responsible reputation was never tarnished.

I didn't get to talk to Richard at all that summer. But he was never too far away, so brief glimpses of his handsome face were all I could hope for. One afternoon I was alone at work, which was unusual, even in late May. It was slow, however, so maybe my fellow worker, (perhaps Laurie as we had a few shifts together,) was on her break. I was at the cash register, which sat on a counter at the front of the store. Behind the counter was a window looking out on Commercial Street on one side of the building. The wall opposite had several windows as well, which continued the view with the front door to the shop in between. The door and windows allowed for great people and traffic watching when it wasn't busy, which was rare. I happened to look out the window and saw Richard's truck approaching. I positioned myself where I could best watch it advance and then pass. Seeing him at a distance wasn't much, but if it was all I could get, I would take it. I thought that maybe I could run out to say hi, leaving the store, the cash register and the few customers unattended. Of course, I would never do that.

It was a moot point, anyway. As it got closer, I saw he had a passenger. I prayed no one would come to the counter until after he'd driven by. I wanted to see who his passenger was and study as much as I could of Richard for a second or two, hoping to find out how he was doing.

As his truck passed the open door, I saw his passenger very clearly. She was resting her head on the open window frame. Her long blonde hair gleamed in the sun. It was her I was able to study. I didn't remember ever meeting or even seeing Patty before, but somehow, I knew this was her. Since the seat was reclined slightly, I couldn't see her belly. But with her flowing hair and relaxed posture, she seemed beautiful to me.

It was a devastating feeling. She was the mother of Richard's child, and she was striking. And she was with him. I didn't have a chance.

I lifted my eyes to look at Richard and saw his profile. He was completely focused on the road ahead of him. He didn't need to be. The throngs of walkers, bikers and baby carriages had yet to arrive at our touristy main street. It was way too early in the season for a townie to need such caution. Unless that townie was trying not to look at a salesclerk, who was likely looking at him.

As they drove on, another thought hit me. As much as I was looking at her, Patty was looking at me. She was checking out every inch of me as well as I was checking out every inch of her. While I had positioned myself to look out the store, she had positioned herself to look in. Somehow, she knew about me and knew where I worked. And if she knew and cared, it must be because she knew something else. Something I had only suspected and desperately wished. She knew I was important to Richard. As much as I thought I needed to be aware of her, she thought she needed to be aware of me.

And that made me feel just a bit better.

chapter 14
weddings

Laurie and Andy were getting married in Provincetown, as were Shannon and her boyfriend Michael. The weddings were within 24 hours of each other on the same weekend in April.

I was in both.

Ten months had passed since I had seen Richard and even longer since we had talked. It was my sophomore year in college and finals were looming. But first I had marital responsibilities calling my name.

Laurie would tie the knot at 6 p.m. on a Friday and Shannon would say her vows at 10 a.m. the following morning. Both couples complained about the insensitivity of the other couple for choosing the same weekend for their wedding and refusing to change the day. I did not have a date for either and both weddings were stressful in different ways. Shannon's was very formal, with actual gowns for the six bridesmaids; gowns complete with crinoline and long-sleeved gloves. Her wedding was to be a large extravaganza, and there were fittings, planning meetings, hair appointments, and a bridal shower.

Laurie's wedding was smaller and a lot less formal. Audrey and I were the only bridesmaids, and we found our dresses off the rack at the local mall — miraculously in our sizes, as though the dresses were meant for us. Easy. But Laurie's wedding was emotionally taxing. That February, my mom had taken in a foster

child. Apparently, she missed having a teenager in the house because when she heard of a local fourteen-year-old girl who had
been removed from her home on an emergency basis, my mom
decided to give foster parenting a try. Though she was younger, I
knew the girl from our small high school. Samantha was in eighth
grade when I was a senior, and we both had been in chorus. I knew
her to be a nice kid with a beautiful singing voice.

And then there was Richard. Or, should I say, there wasn't
Richard. I had heard months before that Patty had given birth to
a healthy baby boy and his name was Jesse. The news about Jesse's
parents seemed to be that they were together and separated, almost on a daily basis. That was all I could find out about
Richard's life. Andy was still in contact with him but refused to
talk to me about it. Andy wasn't well-liked by either of my parents, and my family still seemed to think that Richard was some
dangerous criminal. Because of this, Andy had no interest in upsetting my parents further, especially since they were paying for
most of the wedding. And so Richard, Andy's best friend, was *not*
invited, with the understanding that there would be a scene if he
showed up. My mom and dad, though divorced, were on the same
page with this firm decision. They believed Richard held the power
to corrupt and completely ruin me just by breathing the same air.
Ridiculous. He had stayed away from me as they had insisted. I
was holding my own at school, and yet they still saw me as weak
and easily manipulated.

It did not help that I had yet to bring home a medical or law
student, a boyfriend that they would approve of. They kept waiting, and I found it amusing, as Emerson was not a school that bred
lawyers or doctors. Its graduates were more likely to be starving
artists and theater folks with, perhaps, a future famous newscaster
appearing every once in a while.

School was another issue. My roommate that year was a wild, hard-partying girl with a heart of gold. If there was such a thing as a "bad boy" among friends, Jeanine was it. New to Emerson though a sophomore, she had moved into our room for orientation and then returned to her hometown near Boston for a few days before classes started. When I arrived with the other returning students, she had left me a note saying she was sorry she wasn't there to greet me, but I should help myself to the beer in her mini fridge. It was clear we would get along great. Each weekend became an adventure, and I never knew what to expect from her or from the strange parties she invited me too off campus. Still, my grades held steady. Even so, it was clear to me that Emerson was not the ideal school for me. It was designed for specific career goals and almost two years in, I still did not have any. And despite the generous first year scholarships I'd received, the expenses were outrageous. So in between assignments, studying for finals, somewhat scary adventures with my roommate, pre-wedding events and doing my part to welcome a frightened young girl into the family, I was also applying to other colleges.

I was happy for my sister but didn't need to be all over every wedding detail to show it. I was also annoyed with her for supporting my parents in the whole "Richard should not attend" thing. It seemed hypocritical since Richard had been her friend, too. During wedding preparations, I would often tune out, pondering how silly Laurie and my parents were being and how unfair it was to the groom. I hoped Richard would defy my parents and come, anyway. My 19-year-old brain visualized the scene in a way most favorable to me. He would arrive and, seeing me all dressed up, become overwhelmed with his love for me and whisk me away from my controlling parents, aka Johnny/Baby *Dirty Dancing* style, but not as cheesy. Of course, my fantasies assumed Richard was not with Patty and would thus show up alone.

Poor Samantha was lost among Laurie's wedding plans. While Laurie, Audrey and my mom were talking flowers and menus, I used the time to get to know this shy, frightened kid who had suddenly landed in the middle of all this wedding craziness. Selfishly, I confided to her about my hope and my lost love visions and how Richard was a hero wrongly accused. She agreed to be my backup if he showed at the wedding and would help me any way she could. In the end, what these secret talks did was to help her feel like she had a role at this ceremony and established a permanent friendship between us.

But it was silly. All of my righteous indignation had nothing to do with Richard himself. I had not yet realized that most guys care little about weddings, and Richard had likely already celebrated with Andy with a shot for luck at the Bradford. He probably didn't even remember their wedding date.

Laurie and her groom would need luck on their marriage if for no other reason than the awkwardness of their rehearsal. Ours was not a religious upbringing, but we were Catholic and our parents made sure we received our sacraments, if only to appease our grandparents. When we entered the church, Audrey dipped two fingers into the holy water font. I was impressed, assuming she was about to bless herself. Instead, she used the water to straighten an annoying cowlick on top of her head. When the well-known strict priest arrived late and with his leg in a cast, my dad thought it would be fun to tease him, asking if he was late because he stopped for a cocktail and then had a little accident on the way to meet us. Father Burns was not amused.

Fortunately, the actual ceremony proceeded without incident. And the reception went off without a hitch as well. Richard didn't crash the event and so, instead of a dramatic, romantic reunion with the love of my life, Audrey and I competed with each other by flirting with the DJ, who clearly had no interest in either of us.

I went home and went straight to bed. The next morning, I put on the bridesmaid dress layers and got the scoop from my fellow maids as to what I was supposed to do, and when to do it, during Shannon's wedding. Their rehearsal had taken place the night before while I was entering Laurie and Andy's reception. The shock on Fr. Burns' face when he happened to look up from the altar and see the same bridesmaid from the evening before, again dressed up and sitting in the front pew, was downright priceless. The priest's surprised look is the only thing I remember from that day.

chapter 15
fireworks

Before I knew it, my education at Emerson was over. I came home for the summer with a fall enrollment scheduled at U-Mass/Boston and a cherished memento from Emerson College, something special that I was able to share with my friends at home. It was an official fake ID. It had my picture and said I was a girl from New Jersey named Gina Romani. It was poorly done and, ironically, had been useless at school. Since Boston was a college town, all the liquor store clerks knew what to look for and laughed me out of their businesses the few times I tried to use it. It should have been useless in Provincetown too, but not for the same reason. Since everyone in town knew everyone else, there was no way I was getting away with buying alcohol from a local shop. The clerks might not have recognized a fake ID, and maybe they didn't know my name, but they definitely knew I wasn't from New Jersey.

My ace in the hole, however, was a tiny gourmet grocery owned by two elderly gay men, fairly new to town. The shop was their retirement plan, and it likely came with a liquor license when they bought it. Since liquor licenses were hard to come by, they knew not to give it up and, while not very interested in beer themselves, they stocked a small supply. They didn't seem to know the first thing about fake IDs or townies and, fortunately, they didn't know me.

Hence, it was that I became the buyer for our town's underage police department. Here my dad was a senior officer, and I was the alcohol supplier for the younger crew. Each summer, the town hired additional police officers (mostly criminal justice majors who had gone to a brief, amended academy) and put them on the streets to handle traffic duties. Shannon's husband had been one of those summer cops and was now a rookie on the force. My friend Glen hoped to be in the department one day. Several summer officers rented one of my mom's second floor apartments, so we all tended to party together. It's probably not fair to call my friends Shannon, Glen, Kristin, and Chris police groupies, but they did get a kick out of hanging with them. I definitely did not see myself as a groupie. I didn't hang out because I thought it was cool they were cops. I just liked to hang out.

Many nights, Kristin would let her car idle a block away from the Antique Inn Market, the little shop where Gina Romani was of legal age to buy. I would casually walk in and purchase our supplies for the night. We would then drive to where whatever officer who hosted that evening's party happened to have his traffic detail and would pick up his car keys. We would shove the alcohol in the trunk and then go do our own thing until the 4-11 shifts ended, and the party began. We would also ditch our cars after dropping off the booze so we didn't have to worry about drinking and driving, grateful we could walk most places in town, including our respective homes. One time, I even remember stuffing the alcohol into the trunk of the police cruiser when a cocky summer cop asked us to do just that. And somehow, he managed to get away with it.

I was ready for the seasonal work and seasonal fun. And living with a new family member in my house was sure to be interesting. It was good I was home; Samantha and my mom weren't doing so well. Samantha had spent a lot of time by herself downtown as a child, and the kids my mom saw as delinquents, (always fighting, always in trouble, always accused of new crimes) were more like

Samantha's street guardians. My mom didn't understand this and whenever Samantha was accompanied home by one or two of these troubled teens, my mom would get upset and punish her. My presence helped calm the tension, although I had no idea why.

When the Fourth of July arrived, I had the night off, but my friends were all working. I ventured down to our neighborhood beach with my mom and a grounded Samantha to watch the fireworks. There were plans for a party later, but until then I was hanging out with my mom and her young charge. The three of us sat on an old blanket and tried to keep the conversation light and patriotic. And it would have stayed that way if not for my glancing to the right of us and seeing, just a few yards away and already settled, Richard, Patty, baby Jesse and some of their friends. I felt sick to my stomach. Watching them felt like watching an intense, private moment unfold. I knew I shouldn't look, but I also knew I couldn't turn away.

If Patty saw me, she didn't seem to react. But Richard saw me at the same time I saw him. Both of our bodies going from relaxed to rigid. I didn't want him to see me with my mom. He didn't want me to see him with Patty. But there we were. Worse, since you had to claim your beach spots early, we had a frustratingly long wait for the fireworks to begin. Richard had once told me he had also grown up on this same beach, so why did it not occur to me they might be here? Of all the beaches and places in our little town to watch this light show, how did we wind up sitting so close to each other?

I thought of leaving, but the friction between Samantha and my mom seemed about ready to explode as many of Samantha's troubled friends were there too; running around us, almost taunting my mom, and leaving the poor kid clueless about how to handle it. My mom was too absorbed with that drama to notice Richard, and if not for the magnetic pull between us, it might have taken me a while to notice him, too. The beach was pretty packed.

But since we met, we had always seemed to sense each other's presence immediately, the draw between us too hard to resist.

The thing was, I wasn't sure that I could make myself leave, for this was the first time I was seeing Richard's son. When I first glimpsed their group, all I could spot of the baby was a very blonde head lying in his mom's lap. Waking up from the brief rest, it was not long before he was up and about, exploring the area. He must have been just under a year old, although I didn't know his actual birthday. He had his mother's complexion with fair skin and light hair, very different from the darker look he might have inherited from Richard. Yet, even at that age, he seemed to have his father's stance and from what I could tell, or maybe imagine at the slight distance, the same spark that was in his father's eyes.

As Jesse got his post-nap energy back, complete with a sippy cup sugar rush, he took off, alternating from awkward walking to super-fast crawling. It was Richard who got up and followed him; all the while seeming to do everything he could to divert his eyes from me. Richard looked like a natural father, showing Jesse the cool shells and hermit crabs they found, and instinctually grabbing him before he would toddle fully dressed into the water. And Jesse, this very little boy, seemed in awe of his dad.

I wanted Richard to be happy, and I wanted him to be a good father. It was just hard to watch, especially with the boy's mother so near. Patty was in this scene. This WAS her scene. I was the outsider looking in and it was breaking my heart. How could I keep getting hurt from this relationship when Richard had never actually done anything to hurt me? I'm sure my eyes following his every move didn't help the situation, but I just couldn't miss anything of this self-imposed pain.

After the sun set, Richard scooped up his son and Jesse nestled into his dad's neck. They went back to the blanket where Patty was. I watched as Richard pulled out a sparkler and lit it, carefully showing it to his son — enough to capture his attention but not allowing him to get close enough to touch it. Richard and I never made eye contact and yet never stopped being aware of each other-not really. I knew that even though I was the one watching him, he was equally attuned to my presence. Despite the crowd that had continued to gather and occupy every open spot of sand, I could feel him as if he were right beside me. The pleasant breeze didn't distract me. Neither did the brutal mosquitoes. I was with my mom, my young friend/foster sister, and hundreds of people. But all I could sense was Richard. I was completely alone.

Mercifully, the fireworks finally started. I could no longer see him or his group in the dark, amidst all the many other beach goers. When it was over, I jumped up and started for home, my mom and Samantha trailing after me. Richard and Patty weren't that far behind us, but I did my best to lose them in the crowd.

I was shaking with new knowledge. Seeing their child with my own eyes made the pain real. They were a family. As parents, they had a bond I could never broach. It was time to get these dreamy ideas out of my head and let memories of my first love die.

On Commercial Street, I said goodnight to my mom and Samantha and, while walking away from them, pulled out my fake ID. I walked to the little market and bought whatever that summer's drink of choice was, a pack of cigarettes and a cheap lighter. In college, I continued to bum a cigarette here and there, especially when drinking. While smoking was not an actual habit for me, it was slowly becoming more common. I grabbed both bad habits and returned to the beach. The idea was to both wallow and forget about the happy little boy and his beloved daddy.

Later that evening, partially intoxicated and thinking hard about not thinking about him, I realized another, more depressing reason things had changed between us. Tonight had been the first time since we met that Richard did not look at me with that special smile that was all his own and seemed all for me.

part II

living

chapter 16
visit

I had done what they asked. My parents had insisted that I graduate from college and *then* make decisions about my future, whatever those decisions would be. Their thought was that after I discovered all the amazing opportunities available to me in school, I would have little interest in returning to town and taking any old job. Well, I had graduated, magna cum laude no less, with a degree in English. And now, I just wanted to be home.

The most obvious plan was to move back with my mother while I made money over the summer. I still had no idea what I wanted to do, but staying in Provincetown was still my plan; my hope for a year-round town job was still the only future I could foresee. I had made a lot of friends in college, which meant they had a place to crash on Cape Cod, which was great. My mom liked having summer company, within reason. I still didn't care about the idea of college itself. So much so, I did not even attend graduation. U-Mass Boston was huge, and the ceremony would take hours and be filled with boring speeches by important people I did not know. As thrilled as they were with a college diploma, my parents were not terribly excited about sitting through a long, hot afternoon either. My mom threw me a small party at home, and I received my diploma in the mail. I was back at my gift shop job and loving summer more than I ever had. It was 1991, and this was the second summer that I was of legal age to drink. Made better by the fact that all of my local friends were, too. Bars and dance clubs were high on our agenda.

After she had lived with my mom for six months, Samantha was placed in a more permanent home. Now it was back to just my mom and me. But there was a new member of the family nearby, absorbing a lot of our attention. Laurie and Andy had a baby, Drew, and he was the highlight of my life. He was an eight-month-old adorable redhead, and I helped his parents by babysitting him whenever I wasn't working or partying. Technically, I was helping them with their childcare issues. In reality, I was having fun with a precious baby and reinforcing the idea that someday I wanted to be a mom.

Heather was back in town too, thankfully. She was still with Sean, and now they had three children, the youngest just a few months old. She was also still the one working the most in the relationship, waitressing to make ends meet. Because of this, we didn't get together as much as before but between her kids, my little sister and brother, Drew and the baby daughter of my friend Shannon, who had also become a mom, I had lots of little kids and babies to play with and enjoy.

When my single friends and I met up for drinks, we were arrogant. We were among the youngest of the local population's partying, straight females and cute and thought the world, the drinks and the guys, were ours. I never would have described myself as cute in college. But at 22 and back in my hometown, I felt cute and went with it.

Sometimes, I would see Richard when I was out. We would flirt, dance maybe, but we never seemed to take it further. I didn't think he was with Patty on a regular basis, but I did not know for sure. I had been in a relationship in my senior year of college but had broken it off. I just didn't love the guy. He claimed to love me, but I'm not sure that he really did. I think it was more like I seemed a good fit to him. I was from a nice, responsible, Portuguese family like his own but, unfortunately, I just did not want to be with him. So, Richard was no longer the only guy I had been with, but he was still the one that made my heart flutter whenever I saw him. Despite the confidence and happiness I felt, I did not feel I could ask about his relationship status. Was I frightened by the bond that must have existed between him and the mother of his child? Was he seeing someone other than Patty? Was he still doing coke as all the folks in the rumor mill loved to report? Was his flirting based on memories of our earlier pairing, or did he still have feelings for me? Was it possible that his heart fluttered a bit when he saw me, too?

The bars were getting to me, and one night, I opted to stay in. A quiet night at home with my choice of TV after my mom fell asleep seemed like a great idea. But Serena was disappointed. I was *always* the one who would go out with her. She had established a Piggy's routine for us upon arriving at the dance bar. We would be let in and then head straight to the bathroom like we needed to go. We didn't. It was an excuse to scan the bar and see who was where, so we could discuss it in the ladies' room and decide which area we should settle in when we came out. Later, I learned that some bar patrons always assumed we were into coke too — rushing into the bar to get a line in before hitting the dance floor. When I learned that, I quickly stopped that habit for both of us.

Around 11 on the night I decided to stay in, I had just gotten into bed when I heard something outside my open bedroom window, the window nearest my mom's own bedroom window. My mom had been asleep for hours, so the noise was not coming from her room but from somewhere outside. This was odd. The window looked out on our backyard, and no one should have been there. I was not frightened. Ptown was a safe place and neighbors would catch anyone trying to break in before they could do any real damage. It was a high window so I couldn't see out. I sat up to listen. It was quiet, but I heard the sound again.

"Psst, Yvonne?"

And then again, a bit louder, and not my imagination.

"Yvonne, wake up. Yvonne, can you hear me? Go to the living room window."

I got up and went into the living room. It was Serena who was calling me.

"What are you doing? If you wake my mother up, she'll freak. I'm not going out tonight," I whispered through the open picture window.

"I know, you said. I brought you something. Go to the front door."

What was wild Serena up to now???

I opened the door and there was Richard, looking at me like I was the best thing he had seen in a long time. I could not believe it, and yet I knew it was right. It felt like everything that had happened since I first met him had led to this very moment. Here he was, standing outside my door, reaching out to me when there was no longer anything or anyone keeping us from being together. I fell into his arms as I heard Serena drive away.

With me barefoot and just in my frilly summer nightgown, we walked the few steps from my front door to the patio. There he told me how he had been hoping to see me out, had asked Serena where I was and then, over shots of Southern Comfort, told her how much he missed me. Serena was a "get things done" kind of girl and craved adventure. She had offered to drive him to my house, mom or no mom, and wake me up if necessary. He had instantly taken her up on it. And so there we were, me sitting on his lap on the wooden Adirondack chair and resting my head on his shoulder. The awkward position of both of us in the chair should have been uncomfortable, but it wasn't. It felt like it was the place I was meant to be. We spent most of the night in that chair, talking and often kissing, until the early morning sky was just about to lighten.

And, like that, we were dating. For real this time. I did not make a formal announcement, but I did not hide it either. I'm sure Andy told Laurie who told my mother, but we just didn't discuss it. There was nothing to say. I had fulfilled my end of what was hardly a bargain. As the obedient daughter, I went off to school as directed, did well, turned legal age, and could now make my own choices.

Richard was not with Patty. He told me that for a very long time, their relationship was off and on. Both preferred the off status as they really did not get along. But they liked doing coke together, and he liked being around his son and thus the dysfunction that was their life. But now he was renting a room in the home of a friend and was working steadily. He wanted to stop using. And he wanted to be with me. I was out from the shadow of my protective parents. He was trying to live a better life, and I could not have been happier.

Our first date after that early July night was very romantic. We went to the bay beach at the bottom of my street, where he "borrowed" a rowboat lying on the sand. He knew the owner and knew he didn't lock the chain as he could never remember the combination to the lock. Richard also knew that the guy left his oars underneath the boat, so he wouldn't forget to bring them when it was time to go fishing. It was this little skiff Richard took to row us out to one of the nicest speed boats moored in the harbor, that owner unknown. We tied up to the same mooring and climbed aboard. There we made love under the stars and slept for a bit in each other's arms.

Trying to stay away from cocaine did nothing to diminish Richard's 'naughty little boy' playful side. On another date, we drove to an ocean beach in nearby Truro. It was after 1 a.m., and the beach was deserted. We carried a blanket, a bottle of wine, and two cups down to the shore. Before we knew it, alcohol, romance and desire took over and we were fooling around. Although we were alone, someone could show up at any time and clearly see what was going on. This was completely out of my comfort zone, but I wanted him so badly that I did not think about it too much. Clearly, I was not a timid little girl at that moment.

Getting dressed afterward, I had no sooner pulled my blouse over my head, when a police cruiser pulled into the lot and the officer shined his lights on us. I was mortified. Richard waved and then laughed hysterically.

"How can you laugh at this! Minutes earlier, he totally would have caught us!"

"I know, that's why it's so funny! Come on, don't you think that's funny?"

He was laughing so hard he was having trouble catching his breath. If he had wanted, the officer could have charged us with public drinking. But to do so, he would have had to hike down the steep dune, under a waning moon in the middle of the night. We were spared.

It was not my dad's police department, but as neighboring towns, they knew each other well. And the cops would have likely run the plates of my new to me, used car, the Firebird having died a tragic death two years before. If they could see it was Richard I was with, I do not know. If they told my dad I was on the beach with some guy innocently looking at the water, I don't know that either. But little by little, our relationship came to light and my parents knew they had to suck it up.

chapter 17
bob

While I was away at school, Richard had lost his construction job. I didn't know the details. Losing the job meant the loss of the company truck, but Richard was resilient. And in Provincetown, wheels were nice but not a necessity. Between walking and bumming rides, he got where he needed to go. And he had started fishing. As the granddaughter of fishermen, I knew fishing was noble, hard work. I was proud of him. But since the fishing industry now faced extreme regulations, it wasn't the lucrative career it had once been. After paying rent to Tanya, the friend he was renting a room from, Richard never seemed to have any money. Buried under student loans and payments for my car, I didn't have much either. But it was ok. We didn't need to go out to fancy dinners or on expensive dates. Between us, there was enough money for cheap beer at the Bradford and sandwiches here and there. We were together and happy, just as I always thought we would be.

By August, my family knew about the relationship. Richard even brought my mom lobsters from his trips every once in a while. I still did not like them or the disgusting smell they made when you boiled them, but that was ok too. He would drop them off just before one of our dates, and my mom would cook them while I was gone. She liked Richard, but she still did not approve. She chose not to say much about it.

The boat he fished on was a distinct steel western-rigged dragger with a high bow. It would often come in from a trip as I finished my day shift at work. As I walked home, I would catch glimpses of it making its way back to the pier when the pathways between shop buildings offered a precious harbor view. I knew soon he would get a ride to Tanya's, clean up, and then call me. I told my grandmother how romantic it was, seeing his boat round the point under the late afternoon sun. She became very upset. It was the only time she ever yelled at me.

"Romantic! It's not romantic at all! There's no romance when the boat is late, and no one can raise it on the radio or have seen it in days. Or when the boat is only catching bottom feeders and you're feeding your family trash fish for days on end. Or when there's no fish at all. How about when it's wartime and, on top of everything else, you have to worry about German submarines out there. Don't tell me seeing a boat rounding the point is romantic! That's just foolishness!"

I was humbled by her words and reminded of why, in the old photos in her albums, all the men are smiling on their boats while, on the shore, the women look forlorn and do not smile at all.

Richard had taken me to Tanya's. They were around the same age, and she was a single mother. I liked her a lot. If I had any worries about him being involved with her, they were quickly dispelled when I met her and saw how they interacted together. There clearly didn't seem to be anything but friendship between them, and I trusted him. He told me they had a brief fling in the past but in the end were not right for each other.

We spent time there, hanging with her and hanging by ourselves when she and her young daughter were not home. He talked about Jesse, who was now three and who he had only been able to see a few times since leaving Patty's house. It was not that Patty refused Richard's visits; it was just that they always fought when he was there.

I did not want to be the kind of girl who ditched her friends for a guy. And I didn't want to alienate my family, either. So Richard and I did not spend all of our free time together. We had a dating system that worked well. His boat would often come in from a trip in the early evening. He would go to Tanya's to shower and nap for a bit while I watched Drew or stayed home with my mom or hung out with friends. We would meet up later, at 10 or so, and spend hours together. Many were the nights when I would drop him off at the pier around 4 a.m. for his daily voyage. His strict Portuguese captain would politely nod to me, but it was clear he did not approve. More likely, he was grateful that I was not his daughter, running around at all hours with a fisherman over ten years older than she was. Richard and I would kiss goodbye, and I would tell him to be careful and then would go home to bed for a few hours until it was time for my shift at the gift shop.

Some nights, I would drop him off earlier and he would sleep on the boat before his trip. We made it work. There were nights when I would be at the bar with my friends, and he would join us later. If Richard was doing coke on those nights before he met me, I was not aware of it. Here and there I would see Patty out, with her own friends and sometimes with a guy or two. We never acknowledged each other. It was weird seeing her, especially if Richard and I were together. But luckily, that was also rare. We each did our own thing and out in public, Richard and Patty were always civil to each other.

On the third week of August that year, Provincetown was paying attention to Hurricane Bob. As far as we knew, Richard was the first to come up with a slogan that would be popular with the gay community.

"Just wait. By the end of the week you'll see all these guys wearing t-shirts that say, 'I was blown by Bob.'"

He was right. We should have made the shirts right away and made some money on it. Unfortunately, someone else thought of it too.

At first, the warnings were vague; Bob could blow out to sea. But as the day got closer and meteorologists could see its destructive potential, Provincetown began to prepare. Laurie was off from the gift shop that day and she and Drew would stay with my mother at my house. Andy, as a volunteer firefighter, would be at the station on duty, so it was best to have my sister and her baby with my mom. I was due at work and my boss planned on taking the storm one hour at a time. Richard intended to wait out Bob on the boat.

"The captain and the other guys have families and houses they'll need to be checking on. If someone has to stay on the boat to help prevent any damage, I'm the most likely guy."

I did not like that plan. We were a couple now and should be together when a hurricane was bearing down on us. I thought maybe I could stay on the boat with him, although I wasn't thrilled with that idea; less because of the dangerousness than the fact that the bathroom was not much more than a bucket in a corner of the hull. I was young, and still a bit uptight. It didn't matter. Richard said his cautious captain would never allow a non-crew member, especially a girlfriend, on board during a dangerous storm. The day before the hurricane, the harbormaster announced there would be extra staff on the pier and all the boats were tied down and prepped. Richard's captain did not want anyone on the boat at all. He didn't want to be responsible if one of his crewmen got hurt doing something stupid during the storm. He prepared as much as possible and would just take his chances.

That left me with another idea. There was no way anyone would be comfortable with Richard being with me at my house, but Laurie's rental house would be empty. It was an old house on a busy street with many ancient trees surrounding it and yards nearby with lots of junk piled in them. What if something happened to it during the storm? Richard and I could be there to keep watch on the place. My mom was not thrilled and tried to argue. I would not budge. The thing was, Andy and Laurie were worried about the property; it was very likely a branch could land in the yard or crash through a window. Having someone watch the place was not a bad idea. They could have just asked Richard to do it alone, but I was putting my foot down.

They projected the storm to reach the Cape in the late afternoon. As I went to work that morning, Laurie gathered Drew and all their immediate needs and took them to her childhood home where my mother was cooking up food for them and looking forward to cuddling and playing with her first grandchild. The quiet of the streets was eerie. It wasn't just that the town looked deserted already, unusual for an August morning, or that some of the businesses were boarded up and looked abandoned. It was that the air seemed charged with danger, as though Mother Nature herself was holding her breath. If it is true that there's always a calm before the storm, our usually peaceful bay was not aware of it. I could see churned-up ocean-like whitecaps crashing viciously outside the breakwater. The harbor was abandoned too. Owners of smaller vessels had removed their crafts, making the choppy, empty waterfront look like winter. Yet it was near 90 degrees and the winds had not started yet.

Before I unlocked the door to the gift shop, I glanced directly above me. The monument rose above, as high and strong as it ever had been. It wasn't worried about Bob. A little hurricane was nothing compared to the well-made granite tower, thankfully. My childish nightmares of it toppling over notwithstanding, the tower, like the town, was ready for a little rough weather.

Richard called me at work several times and told me he was at the Bradford, only three blocks down from the store.

"Has your boss said when he's going to let you go? I can't believe he's even open. Call me here and I'll come get you."

My boss was kind, and he was fond of me. He came into the store just before 11:30 in full panic mode. The radio reports stated the hurricane was advancing quicker than expected and he worried about having opened at all. In a rush, he helped me close down the shop and offered me a ride home. Since I was meeting Richard at the bar, that wasn't a good idea.

"I'll be fine, Kurt. It's out of your way and I'm a fast walker. It's still pretty calm out."

"Ok, but please tell your mother that I'm sorry for keeping you. You're going straight home, right?" he asked. I nodded and left.

With my boss's arrival, there had been no time to call Richard for an escort and no need as even though there was a weird feeling in the air, the weather was still quiet. The notion that this could be very serious was heightened by the fact that Donald Thomas wasn't in the square. He was the Provincetown policeman known as the 'Dancing Cop' to tourists. His means of directing traffic was an art form that exhibited both precision and safety, complete with dance steps to help keep things moving along. Townies, washashores, tourists, and entertainers from lowly street musicians to night club headliners all stopped at the busy intersection that led vehicles to the main parking lot and the pier, but only if Donald told them to. Even the Cher impersonator on a motor scooter known for taking over Commercial Street stopped at Donald's whistle. Without him, this part of town should be in chaos on a late August morning. But with the streets empty, he had nothing to direct and no way to keep us safe if the weather predictions remained accurate.

When I got to the Bradford, Richard ordered me a quick drink while he finished up his own and the bartender set to closing down. As we walked to Laurie's not far away, the wind was kicking up, and now it was raining.

At the house, we discovered some leaks already starting, and we pulled out pots and towels. Then Richard announced he was going out.

"What? Where are you going? The storm is starting, and we're supposed to be keeping an eye on the house."

"We will. I'm just going up the street. I'll be right back."

His friend Ronny lived just up the street, but this was ridiculous. We had all that we needed, and this was no time for a casual visit. Ronny couldn't need Richard's help; he had a whole family to help him. True to his word, Richard was back within 20 minutes, but told me he had to go out again and left as soon as he came in.

It was then I realized what he was doing. He was looking for cocaine to help weather the storm. Far be it for Richard to spend a hurricane without a little coke in his system. I was furious. And I felt like a fool. I could be at home, playing with my nephew and eating my mom's homemade cooking. The idea had been to spend the storm with Richard in a mature, responsible way, helping to protect my sister's house, not alone, bored and a little frightened. I thought about going home but knew that was a dangerous idea. And if I did, how would I know if Richard was ok? How would I explain to my mom why I walked through town in the middle of a hurricane?

When the power went out, I called home to check in before the phone lines went dead. Drew was napping, and my mom and Laurie were playing *Scrabble*.

"How's it going there? Are things ok so far?"

"They are," I told her. "There's water coming in a few places, but I'm on them."

"And Richard's with you, right?"

"Of course," I replied, feeling ashamed to admit the truth. It was the second time I had lied because of him in just two hours. My mom did not need to know where he was. In her mind, as inappropriate as our relationship was, she believed that Richard always had my best interests at heart.

While he was gone, I continued to mop up the multiple leaks that the wind blew in through the windowsills and the roof. I noticed debris landing in the yard but was too afraid to go out and grab it myself. The hurricane was raging at that point.

Finally, I saw Richard reappear outside. He was moving about the yard, securing what debris had landed in it, so it didn't cause any harm. I opened the door to help, and he yelled to me to stay inside. He would be right in. So, with him on the outside and me inside, we completed what we had promised; we helped protect the house from as much damage as possible. When Richard came in, he was soaked, windblown, and a little off. Not terribly off, but enough that I understood he had found at least a bit of what he was looking for.

"How's it been here? Everything ok?" he asked.

"Did you get your errands done?" I replied without responding to his question.

He flashed me the sheepish version of his grin. I did not grin back.

"It was just a little bit, no big deal. I haven't been doing any at all, but I just had to have a little."

"Jesus, Richard, why? And if you 'had to have' it, why not get it before the storm? Before I was with you?"

"I wasn't going anywhere until I knew you were safe and settled somewhere. It was totally ridiculous that you had to work at all today and I wanted to make sure you weren't out in this alone."

While hardly the point, he was right. I had made only one sale in the two hours the store was open: a few postcards to a customer who was upset that we didn't already have Bob souvenirs available. Tourists were an interesting breed.

"But it was ok for you to be out during the height of this, for something as stupid as a little bit of drugs?"

"I'm here now. You're fine. The house is fine. It's not a big deal," he said again.

We spent the next couple of hours holding each other and listening to the sounds of wind vs old, creaky house. At some point, Richard dozed off, and I lay next to him, thinking about his behavior. The afternoon had not gone at all as I had imagined. When I might have needed him the most, he bailed, for cocaine, no less. But, as he said, he had made sure I was safe before he set out on his quest. *That had to be worth something.* The thought did little to comfort the apprehension that was surrounding me, apprehension that had nothing to do with a hurricane.

For the first time, Richard's drug use was in my face enough so that I could not ignore or minimize it. Nor could I explain why this great plan I had for us to ride out this storm together was not enough for him. It was clear there were bigger storms for me to worry about.

chapter 18
apartment

By late afternoon, Bob had moved on. Richard had awoken from
his nap, and we sat in silence watching the winds abate. We made
ourselves' sandwiches from the supplies I had brought, opening
the refrigerator as quick as possible since the power was still out
and we wanted to keep the inside as cold as possible. It was a
useless exercise; the whole town was without power, and my sister's neighborhood would be one of the last to get it back, over
four days later. Richard said he wanted to check on the boat. We
locked up, and he walked me straight home. In front of my house,
he gave me a quick kiss goodbye and then headed off for the pier.

It was not until the next day that I saw the destruction the
storm had caused and learned that winds had reached over 100
miles per hour. I went to work, and my resourceful little town
made do without electricity as best it could. We wrote up our few
sales with pen and paper and shared hurricane stories. Mine were
pretty brief. And, like that, summer was over. Technically, there
were still two weeks left in the season. But with boats damaged or
already pulled from the water, campgrounds flooded and abandoned, and tourists evacuating before the direct hit, the season
was done.

Once the hurricane was over, Richard and I didn't talk about
his disappearing act. With no formal discussion of any kind, we
drifted away from each other. Being angry with Richard was for-
eign to me. I had *been* angry on his behalf; standing up for him

when people tried to tell me bad things about him, but I had never been mad *at* him. I loved him but was confused. As we spent more time apart, I understood that his "just have to have a little" had led him back into regular use. I told myself I did not care. I was 22, where I wanted to be, and had my whole life in front of me. I wanted the Richard who was at least trying to break free from addiction. And the Richard of late August was no longer trying.

The early end to summer meant I could start working on my future right away. My simple plan was to work at the gift shop as long as possible and then collect unemployment while I continued to apply for year-round jobs, preferably one with insurance. And I wanted my own apartment. There was no way I could afford a regular year-round rental. But I could manage the cheap off-season rents offered by property owners who wanted to keep their units occupied until the next lucrative tourist season. Most of these places came furnished. Though I would have to move out by Memorial Day the following year, I would have my own place until then. My mom agreed this was a good idea, hoping the long winter would help me figure out what I wanted to do with my life while giving me a taste of having to pay bills like rent and heat.

The apartment I found was small, but adorable. The first floor was a combination kitchen/living room with a tiny table, an uncomfortable pull-out couch, and a bathroom. In between the table and couch was a spiral staircase up to the bedroom, though it was more of a loft space than a separate room. My friends were convinced I would come home drunk one night and kill myself on those spiral stairs. I never did, but I also never admitted that many was the night I would come home late and buzzed and would just crash on the lumpy pull-out, being buzzed but sober enough to not even want to attempt the stairs.

Just after Labor Day, I moved in and was excited about being on my own. I missed Richard as I thought about my fantasy for us to move in together. But I hadn't even seen him around town, which was not a good sign. If he was not out and about, then I did not want to even think about what might be occupying his time. I knew from Andy that he wasn't back with Patty, at least not officially. He was still living at Tanya's, but I didn't know who he was doing lines with. The fact was he preferred cocaine over me, and that was not what I wanted our life to be about. I did not need him in order to be happy.

This point was proven shortly after I settled in. One afternoon, my older sisters brought Drew over. He was just a few weeks shy of his first birthday. While they sat on the sofa and I sat in a kitchen chair across from them, Drew took his first steps — towards me. He walked so naturally it seemed as if he had always known how, but never had anything he cared enough about to walk towards. But that day, he walked across the room to cuddle with me, and it further confirmed for me that I had done the right thing by coming home.

Things are good, I thought as I left for work one gorgeous fall morning. I approached my little blue Escort, parked on the side street of my new place. Something about my car was off, but I wasn't sure what. It just did not look normal. It took me several seconds to figure out what was wrong. My license plate was screwed on upside down. It had not been like that when I came home the night before. And I knew this was not a silly prank from local kids. It was Richard saying hello. He must have asked Andy where I had moved. While I slept, he was outside my apartment, goofing around to let me know he was thinking of me.

He asked Andy for my new number. Laurie asked if they should tell him to get lost.

"Of course not. I still care about him. He can always call me."

And he did, several days later. I told him about my new place and how much I loved it. "It even has hardwood floors," I rambled. "And a cool spiral staircase that everyone keeps saying I am going to kill myself on, but it's been two weeks and I haven't stumbled once!"

From the noise in the background, I could tell he was calling from his special phone, the pay phone at the Bradford. He asked if he could come see the place. I told him yes without even thinking about it.

He arrived within 15 minutes, covering the distance from the bar to my apartment easily with his fast long legs. He came in and looked around.

"I hate to tell you, darlin', but these aren't hardwood floors."

"They're not? Huh. That's what I thought you called this type of flooring. Then what are hardwood floors?" I asked.

Neither of us cared what kind of floors they were. This time, our conversation was a little awkward. Basic conversation between us had not been awkward since the night I had called to ask him to buy alcohol for my friends and me, over four years before.

"Did Laurie tell you that Drew took his first steps on these non-hardwood floors, right across the room to…"

Before I could finish the sentence, he was kissing me, a long, deep, loving kiss. The kind of kiss that takes your breath away. The kind of kiss that screams that everything is going to be ok. The kind of sweet, yet urgent, sexy kiss that you think can't possibly be real, but it is, and it's more than you could ever hope for. I kissed him back, surrendering eagerly. I wanted to be with him so badly and it felt so good to be wrapped up in his arms. It always had.

Reluctantly, we separated. He told me he missed me. I asked him about the coke. I didn't want to. But I knew if we were going to give this another shot, I had to.

"I know. I fucked up. I never should have gotten some; that was just stupid. Once I did a little bit, it was harder to give up."

"Who were you doing it with?"

"Friends. Whoever was holding, basically."

"And what about Patty? Where is she in all this?"

"Nowhere. Other than the mother of my son, Patty is in the past."

"Are you sure? Because I don't want to be a part of some twisted triangle with the two of you. I'm not willing to share you with anyone. And I don't want any part of the drug scene or the drama."

"You're not a part of it or sharing me."

I believed him.

While never completely giving up his room at Tanya's, he wound up staying with me. And before I knew it, we were living together, doing domestic things like shopping and cooking, with all the romance and excitement that I knew there would be.

It was exactly what I wanted.

chapter 19
message

Less than two weeks later, on another brilliant morning, I lost track of time before going to work. I didn't have much of an excuse. I had lingered over my morning tea and cigarette, smiling about the playful interaction that had occurred at 4:00 a.m. One comfort of dating a fisherman was that if he was in bed next to you, and the phone rang in the middle of the night, it probably wasn't an emergency. It was more likely a captain or a crew mate reporting that the winds were favorable, the boat was leaving in 20 minutes and if anyone wanted a ride to the pier, they needed to be at their street corner in ten. Richard had come back upstairs to get dressed after answering the phone and tried to wake me up, pawing at me mischievously as if we had time for more than a quick kiss. I kissed him and told him to have a safe trip. Then I gently pushed him away and pulled a pillow over my head. He yanked the blanket off me and laughed when I shrieked. Then he playfully put it back and kissed me again before going to meet his ride. I loved his teasing so much that I even enjoyed wasting time remembering it over and over.

And now I was rushing to open the store. I saw the answering machine flashing after I got out of the shower. I played the message while I gathered my lunch.

"Yvonne, this is Patty, Richard's girlfriend. Please call me back."

Richard's girlfriend! What the fuck? Patty was pretty ballsy to announce herself on my machine like that. And what could she possibly want? What the hell did Richard get me into? I did not have time to call her back just then. And I wanted to fume a bit longer before I did. I couldn't help but think that she left me such a message to intimidate me in some way. Yet, it had the opposite effect. Ironically, she was the one who sounded nervous on the machine.

Hours later, Laurie came into the gift shop to give me a lunch break. I told her about the call.

"What are you going to do?" she asked. "You're not going to call her back, are you?" Patty had come to town from a city outside of Boston and had a reputation for being tough. But Richard was too important for me to care.

"Of course I'm calling her back. I want to know what her problem is. I'm calling her right now, in fact. I just couldn't do it while I was here alone."

I called in front of Laurie. The store was pretty quiet, but if one of the elderly ladies on a day trip that we called blue hairs came in, it was Laurie's problem. Laurie looked nervous herself. Was she expecting her meek little sister to break into tears during a phone cat fight? That Yvonne was gone. Richard had helped me get rid of her.

"Patty, it's Yvonne. I got your message."

"Thank you for calling back. I wanted to talk to you as there are some things I think you should know. I don't know you, but I know Laurie, and you seem like a good person, so I thought we should talk."

"Fine, but first off, what's up with the 'Richard's girlfriend' thing? Last I knew, you guys had broken up, months ago. Am I wrong about that?"

"Well, no, we're not actually together right now, but we'd been together for a while and so it just seems like…."

I cut her off. "Patty, did you kick Richard out last spring, and have you guys been split up since then?"

"Well, yes."

"Ok, glad we got that cleared up. What did you want to tell me?"

"I'm just not sure you know, but Richard is really into drugs and some of the people he does coke with aren't so great."

"Ok, thank you for telling me. Anything else?" I wasn't being rude, but I certainly wasn't being polite either. Laurie stood in front of me with her mouth hanging open.

Patty seemed to stammer.

"Well, there's more I guess, but that's the main thing I wanted to tell you."

"Ok, thank you. Have a good one," and I hung up.

While I did not know her, I knew some of the people she hung out with and the games they played. I wasn't interested in their games. Maybe I should know all the details about the other side of Richard's life. But if I asked, he would tell me himself. I did not need to hear it from Patty.

When I played him the message that night, he looked amused, seeming to enjoy the idea of two women fighting over him.

"I don't think it's funny," I said. "I'm not interested in this crap. What's this about?"

"Well, for one thing, she's lying. We're not together, haven't been since the spring."

"I know. She admitted that when we talked."

"You called her back?" he asked, his amused look turning into something like pride, pleased that I had not cowered from her. "Good for you. But if she told you we weren't together, why are you mad?"

"Because I don't want to be a part of this stupidity. If she kicked you out, why is she bothering me?"

"Who knows? Maybe she's jealous. She probably didn't expect me to find someone else, especially someone who's not in the scene. You know, someone like you."

I did not need to ask him what he meant. I was not a part of the drug-fueled drama world that Patty and Richard had moved in. I wondered if her deepest fear was that he might really be able to get his life together. He had so many great plans for the future for when he could make real money. Not the least of which was being a better parent to his son.

"What did she want, anyway?"

"To piss me off and to get me pissed off at you. To tell me bad things about you," I said.

"Ha, you already know them."

"I don't know the details, though. Do I need to know the details?"

"You need to know that I don't want that life anymore. And that I'm trying."

And that was that. It was good enough for me.

* * *

I had never seen Richard drunk. His drink of choice was Southern Comfort, but since I had never seen him drunk, and he did not drink it at home, alcohol wasn't a problem. The only time he really drank beer was when we were hanging out with Laurie and Andy. And since he was a better driver, when we went out, he took the wheel. But in late October, we had planned a night at the bar, and I offered to be our designated driver. I was curious to see what he would be like with a good buzz going.

College degree or no college degree, Richard was smarter than I. The dynamic of our relationship was that I was the more responsible of the two of us, but he was by far smarter. That night proved it. He did get drunk. But he did not change much. His silliness got a little sillier and his dark complexion paled slightly. But, otherwise, he was still my Richard. Driving us home after last call, I could see he was going to be sick. All I could think about was getting him home as soon as possible and so I sped up. As he leaned his head out the passenger window and threw up, I drove faster. We made it home, and I parked and helped him into the house. It had started raining before we went out and while we were in the bar, the rain had picked up considerably and had added some vicious nor'easter winds.

In the morning, trying to curb his incredible hangover with coffee, he said, "You know, when someone gets sick like that, usually the driver pulls over to the side of the road and lets the sick person do what they need to do."

"Well, why didn't you say something?" I asked, completely clueless.

"Umm, I was kind of busy. I figured you were trying to punish me for getting sick."

"Of course not! I was just trying to get you home quickly."

He looked at me and shook his head in wonder, but his eyes still held his loving grin.

The storm raged all that day, and we stayed in. But the winds quieted that night and the next morning his captain picked him up for gear work. When I went out to my car later, it was covered in puke. With all the rain, we both thought the car would clean itself. But the wind had caused the opposite effect, sticking the disgustingness with an extra hardness on the whole passenger side of my car. Since he would not be home for hours, I cleaned it myself. Lesson learned, next time, pull over.

Soon after, we learned this storm was being called "The Perfect Storm," wreaking havoc throughout the state, and leading to the sinking of the fishing boat, *Andrea Gail,* out of Gloucester. The loss hit another fishing community, not ours. But it almost felt like our own. We did not talk about it much, each reflecting on the sadness and fear in our own emotions.

chapter 20
jesse

It was good that I hadn't pulled too much of an attitude when I returned Patty's call. It was not my nature. More importantly, there was another reason not to alienate her, Richard's son, Jesse. Richard didn't like the way Jesse was growing up, and he knew that, as his father, he was a big part of the problem. At three-and-a- half, and very smart, Richard said Jesse had little structure or rules and had witnessed way more than a child should. While people were in and out of the house constantly partying with his parents, Jesse watched it all from his perch on the sofa, where he chose to hang out until he fell asleep. Richard could not remember him ever sleeping in his actual bed. Just a kid, he was an innocent amid the adult craziness surrounding him. Richard wanted to be a better father and wanted to offer his son some stability but knew that would not happen as long as he continued to be a part of the drug scene. Richard had dreams that included starting his own small car repair business and getting at least partial custody of his son. He just needed to get clean and get some money.

We had been together long enough that it seemed time for me to meet Jesse. But I worried about how he might react to me. Dysfunctional home or not, the child loved his mom; how would he feel about another woman being such a good friend to his daddy? How much did his young, wise eyes understand about the adult relationships in his life? Concerns aside, I wanted to meet him. And I desperately wanted to help Richard get closer to him.

Richard called Patty and asked if we could take him out for the day. She seemed almost comforted that I would be a part of this visit. Maybe she was hoping Jesse would not like me, or maybe she wanted him to report back details of his dad's relationship. Or, possibly, the mom instincts she did have thought it best to have a second adult as part of the outing. She had seen Richard at his worst and maybe knowing he would not be alone with Jesse all day brought her some relief and assurance.

Richard drove up to the house late the morning of the visit. In the passenger seat, I was nervous about everything. First up, would I go in with him? How awkward would that be?

"Maybe it's better if you wait here," Richard said, seeming to read my mind.

I didn't argue. I sat and resumed analyzing how best to handle the day. I did not want to come on too strong, but I didn't want to seem cold or bored either. I wanted the child to like me. How did I make that happen without forcing it? I had a great relationship with all the other kids in my life, but I had known them all since birth. And the circumstances here were quite different.

Richard walked him out to the car and buckled him into the backseat. He was big for his age. And he looked like his mother with her complexion and her light blonde hair, which she let him wear long, just past his shoulders.

I looked back, smiled and said, "hi Jesse. My name's Yvonne." He did not return the smile or respond. He looked at me suspiciously and then turned his bright eyes towards the window.

Although it was November and cloudy, the day was actually pretty warm. We decided to start our day at the playground and then just see where our time together took us. When Richard opened the door for him to get out, Jesse immediately ran to the jungle gym. Only then did it occur to me that maybe we should have brought Drew. While Drew was only 1, he might have been a distraction for us. He would at least need my constant attention, giving father and son some space. Before picking him up, I had suggested that maybe Richard should take Jesse alone, at least for some of the day. Perhaps giving them some time alone would help ease into the part of the visit that was about a child meeting daddy's girlfriend. But Richard had been insistent that I join them right from the beginning.

At the jungle gym, Richard helped Jesse climb up. He was still silent and still glaring at me like he did not know what to make of me. *Richard was wrong,* I thought. *Jesse needs his dad to himself for a while.* I turned away, thinking I would try to find something, anything, separate from them to busy myself with. It was then that I heard his little voice call out, "Hey! Where are you going? Aren't you going to watch me go across the monkey bars?"

And, like that, we were good. We hung around the playground for a while and then brought a pizza back to my house. I already had coloring books, crayons and a deck of Go Fish cards for my little sister and brother, and so we played and colored. The time was going so well that Richard started thinking about keeping him overnight. There was one problem, though. Jesse was potty trained, but he had not used the bathroom since we had picked him up hours before. We asked if he needed to go and each time he had walked into the bathroom and then immediately walked out, saying he did not have to. After lots of juice, it was clear he was dancing around and would have an accident if something wasn't done. Richard tried to be the stern dad and insisted he go. Jesse cried and said, "I can't use the potty. There's poop on it!"

The germaphobe in me freaked, and I ran into the bathroom to see if he was right. Father and son followed. I inspected the toilet seat and there was nothing.

"Jesse, what do you mean? Show me where you see poop," I said.

He pointed to a speck on the seat itself. This speck had been there so long that Richard and I didn't even see it anymore. It was a small chip in the white paint of the toilet seat, exposing the dark wood beneath. The poor kid had been having fun but had been holding it in all day because of the speck. We told him what the "poop" was, but he didn't believe us. I grabbed a sponge and some cleaner and made a big production out of cleaning the toilet. Then I left them alone and Richard had to pull down his own pants and sit on the seat before Jesse would finally go.

While I boiled water for spaghetti and Jesse watched cartoons, Richard called Patty and told her we were keeping Jesse overnight. I was worried; he announced it instead of asking. That attitude might not help. But surprisingly, she said yes. When he hung up, I asked if we should all go to his house to get his things, or did he think it was ok if I stayed with Jesse and made dinner while he went?

"What? What things?" Richard asked, looking honestly perplexed.

"Uhhh, duhhh. Things he needs to stay over—a toothbrush, pajamas, his favorite toy or blanket. You know that kind of thing."

"Yvonne, he just falls asleep on the sofa in his clothes or just in his underwear when he gets tired. And I think he usually brushes his teeth in the morning. He'll be fine for one night. Patty didn't mention he needed anything."

"Seriously?" Drew was a baby, so I couldn't really compare. Still, I thought of my six-year-old sister and three-year-old brother, their bedtime routines and the many items used to put them to sleep.

"Jesse, buddy," Richard said to him, "you want to sleep here tonight, right? You don't need anything from home, do you?"

He seemed almost too excited to spend the night and shook his head no.

After dinner, Jesse got rambunctious as kids do before bed and dropped a glass. It shattered on the floor just below the spiral stairs.

"Whoa, hold up buddy, stand here on the stairs for me, ok?" I told him, so his bare feet wouldn't get cut.

He started to cry.

"Jesse, it's ok. These things happen. I just don't want you to get hurt," I tried to reassure him.

He didn't seem convinced. I sat next to him and pointed out funny things on the cartoons while Richard cleaned up the glass. After a while, he was happy again.

When it was getting late, I pulled out blankets and a pillow from the closet.

"I don't know, Yvonne. I know being close to the bathroom is a good idea, but I think he'll be scared down here by himself."

"I think so too. So, I'll sleep on the sofa."

"What? Why? That's dumb."

The bed in the loft/bedroom was king-sized.

"There's plenty of room for all of us upstairs," Richard continued. "You don't need to sleep down here."

"Richard, that'll be wicked confusing for him. And it's not necessary. You guys sleep upstairs. I'll crash here, no big deal."

"That's ridiculous. Jesse, do you want to go watch TV in a really big bed? Do you want Yvonne to come with us?"

Jesse nodded. I tried to whisper, "That's great, but don't you think his mother will flip out? It's not unlikely that it'll come up."

"I don't give a damn what she thinks. He's my kid and I say it's fine."

"You want him to stay again, right? She can keep that from happening."

"She won't. If he's happy with us, it's a party night for her. Trust me, she's not worried about what's going on here." He wasn't whispering, and Jesse seemed to take in every word. Against my better judgment, I agreed.

Richard slept in sweatpants, and I slept in my most matronly pajamas. We didn't even kiss goodnight, but Richard teased me about being such a prude. Jesse sat on the bed between the two of us. Richard fell asleep right away, leaving Jesse and me to search for something age appropriate to watch. We did not have much luck as the upstairs TV that came with the apartment didn't have cable and there wasn't much on the basic channels at night that would hold a three-year-old's attention. Eventually, Jesse grew bored and fell asleep, and at some point, I did too.

I woke up early and tiptoed down the stairs. I made tea and sat alone in the living room, thinking about the day that had just passed. We could do this. Jesse could come and stay with us sometimes. Richard could build a healthy relationship with his son, and he could be a large part of the future we were building together. This sweet kid was another part of Richard to love.

After a while, I heard moving around and whispering. Jesse was up and had woken up his dad. Richard tried to mollify him with television, but Jesse was excited to start his day.

"Ok buddy, guess we're getting up. Do you want to go see what Yvonne is doing?"

Richard helped him down the twisted stairs and sent him to the bathroom. We had English muffins and watched more cartoons, and Jesse jumped around being silly until it was time to go. Richard grabbed my car keys and called to his son, taking him home before going to work on a friend's truck. When I said goodbye, Jesse walked over and hugged me. His smile filled my heart with joy.

One hour later, the phone rang. It was Patty.

"I'm glad he had a good time with you guys, but he told me he slept with both of you. I don't think that's a good idea." She went on for a bit. I listened, torn between agreeing with her, which meant throwing Richard under the bus, or defending the love of my life by talking about all the fun things we did and how dare she question Richard's decision. But she was right. And she was being reasonable, stating her concerns calmly. I could freak out at Richard when he got home. Right then, I had to keep her on my side. I sucked it up.

"I can see your point, Patty. Nothing happened between us, but I can see how that would bother you. I promise it won't happen again."

And I wanted there to be an again.

chapter 21
cars

Laurie and Andy didn't have a car. Andy had been a mechanic by trade and so we worked out a deal. We would share my little blue escort and Andy would do all the upkeep on the vehicle. He was in charge of regular checkups, oil changes, and addressing any potential problems, hopefully before they showed up as an actual problem. He was working as a truck driver for a local produce company and so had access to their garage and their tools. Richard had as much vehicle knowledge as Andy, maybe even more, but no tools. Often, they worked on vehicles together, which I appreciated as I trusted Richard more than my brother-in-law, who was known for doing things a little half-assed. Because of this arrangement, I got used to driving my car around with Drew's car seat in the back. Since I was now seasonally unemployed, I had a lot of free time and Drew was often with me, anyway; if not just with me, then with me and his mother together.

Neither Laurie nor I had a washing machine or a dryer. By this time, she and Andy had moved from their rental house to the apartment above our childhood home, making my mother their landlord. But we were only allowed to use my mom's machine for washing emergencies, as the house had a septic problem that caused repeated use of the machine to require expensive pumping. Due to similar water issues, Provincetown did not have its own laundromat. Laurie and I spent a lot of time together that early November, making a fun day trip once a week to go do our laundry together. We liked a place in Dennis, about a 45-minute drive away, as it was big and clean, near a Burger King, and in the same town where Laurie's friend Michele lived. While Andy worked his regular job and Richard picked up work here and there, fishing, construction or doing minor repairs on a car for this one or that, we would buckle Drew into his seat, pile Laurie's laundry basket next to him in the backseat and mine in the trunk and go for a ride. We took turns playing with Drew at the nearby playground while the other one of us took over our washing and drying duties. Afterwards, we would pick up burgers for lunch and go over to Michele's, where Drew would play with her son, only a few months older than he was. Then we would meet the guys back at Laurie's and hang out until Richard and I went on our way. Making a fun day of it made the laundry chore much easier.

Richard and I had been together solidly for about six weeks at that point. We had not had Jesse over a second time as Patty started visiting her family more, often traveling to her home city, about two hours away. It seemed like they were not around very much.

One night Patty called and asked to talk to Richard. She told him to put the TV on channel 17; Jesse was going to be on the local news. Jesse on TV? We were excited and as she filled Richard in on the details, I searched for the remote and changed the channel. The news came on and the feature was about a new food co-op program. In exchange for limited community service, low-income eligible families could take part in a food share and receive free produce and other healthy groceries once a month. It was a good program and Patty played a big part in getting it off the ground, as the news told us. The feature interviewed her and showed all the work she had done to pull it together, as well as footage of her and her friends unloading a truck from J&E Fruit and Produce, the company Andy worked for. As they talked about the community service part, they aired women gardening and sorting through items at the local church thrift store. We scanned the entire screen, and Jesse wasn't even in the background. The feature seemed to be the Patty show and while she deserved the credit, we would have rather seen her son.

She called back and asked Richard if he watched and said that they must have cut Jesse out. He had been in the thrift shop, and they were supposed to show him to convey that even young kids were excited about the program. Then she told Richard that she was having trouble with her brakes and he would need to fix them before the weekend. He hung up and told me they must have cut Jesse out of the segment.

"Why would they cut out a little kid helping with the food share? Seems like that would be great PR for the program," I commented.

"I don't know, that's what Patty said. And I need to work on her car before her next road trip," he told me.

"Seems kind of manipulative," I replied. "She calls and makes a big deal, so we'll watch and see how great she is and then she needs a favor?"

"She's the mother of my child and you're just going to have to get used to that!" He snapped at me.

I was shocked. Richard had never snapped at me. Was I being petty? I didn't think so. Any way I looked at it, I stood by my comment. And I was not normally a bitchy person, so I didn't think I deserved the attitude. In the seconds it took for me to realize that I got mad and snapped back.

"What the hell are you talking about? I've never, ever forgotten that she is the mother of your son and thus will be in our lives. You know me better than that, so don't pull that crap with me. Plus, you're the one who always tells me how manipulative she is, and that, to me, was manipulative. 'Get used to her being the mother of your son?' Give me a fucking break."

This was our first fight that wasn't about drugs, if you could even call it a fight. And, as I assumed people who are in a healthy relationship do, we made up just as quickly, and talked about it.

"You're right, I'm sorry. You're not like that, and she probably was showing off. They might have cut Jesse out, though."

"Maybe," I admitted. *Unlikely* I was thinking…

"I'm not thrilled about having to go over there and get her car and then deal with her. But if it's unsafe…."

"If it's unsafe, then you need to fix it. She can't be driving Jesse around in an unsafe vehicle. And you definitely don't want her breaking down outside of Boston."

"I guess *I* get bitchy just thinking about it," Richard laughed.

He fixed her brakes before her next long drive. But then there were other long drives, drives where her new boyfriend would take her car to New Bedford to get coke for them and their friends. And, as these trips had nothing to do with the safety of Richard's son, she sometimes paid him for working on the old car with some cocaine of his own. Just a little bit, which he would do at some other friend's house or alone in the room he still rented from Tanya. We had a real fight about that; he was supposed to be staying off drugs. And making up after a drug fight was not so easy.

While responsible and much less timid, I had been naïve. I had not understood that the cocaine Richard was doing was no longer lines but being smoked in a make-shift pipe made from plastic soda bottles. I had heard the term crack, but that was a term reserved for actual junkies, those who were mostly homeless and lived in cities in abandoned buildings and did nothing but smoke all day. I knew of Richard's addiction but had no idea how his need had changed and grew before I had returned to town.

This knowledge lead to us breaking up, and thus it was that he spent Thanksgiving by himself at Tanya's; she and her daughter having left to spend it with her family out of town and his son spending the holiday with his mother and grandparents, also out of town. Richard watched TV until the bar opened and he could hang out there, using Southern Comfort as a holiday sedative now that the coke he received for car repairs was gone. I, of course, spent the holiday with my family, playing with Drew. I was sad and frustrated by how easily he fell into the habit again but was not sorry he was alone on Thanksgiving. He had made his choices.

* * *

For several days, Laurie and I noticed the car making an obnoxious noise. Unfortunately, it was one of those noises that would come and go, and when Andy drove it, he wouldn't hear it. Still, he swore he did an overall inspection, and nothing was wrong; we silly women were just hearing things. One sunny but cold day in December, Laurie and I set out on our weekly trip with plans to do some shopping in addition to our laundry. She had some Christmas gifts on layaway at Kmart she wanted to pick up. We headed to Hyannis first, about an hour from home, and the closest place with a real shopping center. Laurie was driving, and she dropped me off at the mall. I had to return some things for my mom and wanted to look at a couple of stores there. We made a plan that she would swing back by the Sears entrance in 45 minutes to pick me up and then we would head out to lunch, stopping to do our laundry on the way back to town. A busy, four-lane roadway separated the mall and K-Mart. I was at our meeting place at the right time, but Laurie, Drew and my car were not. I waited another half hour, getting more annoyed as each minute passed. Of course, neither of us had cell phones. They existed then, but only wealthy or very important people had them. Small town girls on unemployment did not.

About 40 minutes after our meeting time, I saw a woman holding a baby as she tried to cross the dangerous intersection. What was that crazy woman doing? I breathed a sigh of relief when she made it across unhurt. When they got closer, I recognized them as my sister and my nephew. I ran to them.

"What the hell?" I shouted through chilly puffs of air.

Drew's nose was running, and his cheeks were pink. Laurie looked cold and panicked.

"I can't get the car to start. I've been trying to start it over and over and giving it a little time, but it's dead. K-mart called Sears and asked them to page you, but you must not have heard it. I didn't know how else to get you."

I hadn't heard the page because I was waiting for them in the vestibule of the store.

Terrified of the swift traffic, the three of us made our way across the treacherous intersection once again. I was carrying Drew this time to give Laurie a break and I could see why she appeared so upset. The crossing was even scarier than it looked.

We got to my car, and I buckled Drew into his seat while Laurie opened the hood. I tried to start it but as she had described, the car was dead. Laurie stood in front of the engine, trying to look like she knew what she was looking at. I had lights and the radio, so the battery didn't seem to be the problem. My sister took a screwdriver from the mini toolkit Andy kept in the trunk and started banging away at various parts of the engine. I yelled at her to stop. She yelled back.

"Shut up! I don't know what else to do and I don't care about your precious car right now!"

"It has nothing to do with the fucking car! You have no idea what you're doing, and you could get hurt! You could have something break and start a fire or explode or something. Stop it right now!"

From his car seat, Drew wailed. We argued for a few minutes until a guy in a pickup truck came over. He tried starting the car, confirmed the battery wasn't the problem, got his own toolbox out of his vehicle and spent about 20 minutes fiddling with the engine. Laurie went back into K-mart and bought Drew some animal crackers, an exciting new treat for him at 14 months, but they didn't appease his sobs. Eventually, our good citizen got the car started but told us we should get right home because it likely wouldn't start again without some major maintenance. He also told us to keep the speed under 50 and to be careful.

"I would drive very gently until you get this to a garage," he said.

I didn't have a garage. I had Andy. Andy, whose son had just been forced to cross a very dangerous roadway twice. Andy, who was responsible for my car. Andy, who had just given my car a clean bill of health. I grew furious as we thanked the guy and tried to give him some money. He just said Merry Christmas and wished us luck.

Laurie took the wheel. It was her choice and though I loved her, and we got along great, she could be bossy. Since this was a hazardous situation, she felt as the oldest that she would be the better driver. I didn't care. I was too enraged about the situation. Drew continued crying and nothing I offered him seemed to help. Laurie decided he needed to be picked up, but we were afraid to pull over, not knowing what was wrong with the vehicle. So, in between the front seats with Laurie driving slowly so as not to upset the precarious engine, I reached over and did my best to unbuckle Drew and bring him to the front with me. As close as we were, my holding him did not help. He wanted his mother. Laurie instructed me to put him on her lap as she drove. With every risky step we took on this journey, my fury grew. Once on his mother's lap, Drew's tears subsided, and I took him back. He fell asleep in my arms in the front seat; on top of worrying about making it home safely, I worried about Drew being unharnessed in the front seat. If we had an accident, even a minor one, could I protect him? I was also worried about getting pulled over. Not only because of a pricey ticket, but because of not getting the car started again after a traffic stop.

We made it home, laundry undone, exhausted, hungry and me on some sort of red-hot auto pilot. Once Laurie stopped the car, I bounded out of it, not stopping to help her grab Drew or the dirty laundry. I opened the door to the stairway that led up to her apartment and was surprised by the presence of a friend from my childhood.

I calmed down enough to say, "Hey Alan, how are you? What are you doing here?"

He was an electrician and told me my mother had called him to fix some minor wiring issues in the hallway. We chatted a little and then, when I could not contain my fury any longer, I said goodbye and threw open the door at the top of the stairs. To my angry glee, I found both Andy and Richard sitting in the living room, casually hanging out while downing cans of Budweiser. I yelled at them both like I had never yelled in my life. The whole town must have heard me. Alan, who knew me as a quiet, shy girl, certainly heard me. Laurie, carrying the now quiet Drew, certainly did as well. I did not care. I screamed at both the guys. And it *was* at both of them. My car's maintenance was not Richard's responsibility, but that didn't matter. In my torrent, I got out the details of what happened, accused Andy of both lying about looking at the car and being an incompetent, stupid asshole who was not able to see what was clearly a major problem. My tirade lasted a good ten minutes and included a lot of swears and a ton of sarcasm.

"How's the J& E truck, Andy? Did it make to the market ok? I would hate to think of the town's vegetables being stranded on the side of the road!"

"How about Patty's car, Richard? How's that doing? Did it get to New Bedford safely? Wouldn't want the local drug supply to be diminished by any engine problems! What would we do then?"

Richard was braver, or more foolish, than Andy, and he dared to respond.

"Patty's car has nothing to do with…."

I cut him off with another, even louder outburst than before. He grew sheepish, his gorgeous dark skin turning pale. Laurie brought Drew into the living room and tried to calm me down while defending her husband. "It's nobody's fault, Yvonne."

I was not having any of it.

"Are you freaking kidding me? Don't even try. Remember dodging speeding cars coming from four different directions while carrying Drew across Route 132? Remember having to do it twice? Remember driving with Drew on your lap? Don't you dare say another word!"

I ended by telling Andy that he was going to take my car himself to the garage and not leave for any reason until it was fixed, 100%, and that he better make sure it was perfect because after he was done with it, I was going to take the car to a professional garage to check his work.

"And don't either one of you," I finished, by declaring both to Andy and Richard, "dare to even look at me until my car is the safest vehicle ever made and you have groveled at my feet and Laurie's feet and Drew's feet in apology!"

At that, I kissed the top of my nephew's head and slammed the door as I left, not caring that my mom had just pulled into the driveway, and she would not be happy about slamming doors. I stopped in the hallway.

"Sorry you had to hear all that, Alan. It needed to be said."

"Hey no, no problem. I'm just glad you're not mad at me!"

Yes, Richard had taught me to speak up and defend myself. And at that moment, it sure felt good.

chapter 22
christmas

After I smoked a cigarette and calmed down from my outburst, I
borrowed my mother's car to get myself and my still-dirty clothes
home. I had to return it before she left for work the next morning.
Opening my door at 7:00 a.m., I discovered slightly frozen flowers
on my front step. They were cheap convenience store flowers, but
they were still a token. I had been up late the night before, drinking wine and smoking many cigarettes while analyzing the day's
events. When I had gone to bed, I mostly just tossed and turned. I
would have heard Richard if he knocked, whatever time he had
dropped these off. I knew Richard well, and he knew me even better. If he wanted to come back, he knew I would welcome him. I
missed him and could not help thinking there had to be some way
to make this work. I smiled to myself as I pictured him walking
through town in the middle of the frigid night, carrying a bouquet
of flowers. But he had chosen not to knock and so the flowers at
my door meant only that he was genuinely sorry, which was intri-
guing considering that the car problem was not really his fault.
But he felt bad about it and wanted me to know that, but he wasn't
ready to get back together. Which also meant he was not ready to
give up the drugs. My smile soured as I wondered where else he
had walked and what other errands he might have been up to.

Later in the day, Andy called me. He had inspected the engine
and discovered the problem. My car needed a new, expensive part,
but he had ordered it, and would have it installed the very next

morning as soon as he got it. Right now, my car was not drivable, but did I need anything? He could pick up whatever I needed or wanted and would figure out a way to get it to me. He was sucking up as he should have been, but I needed nothing and if I did, I would turn to my friends or my mom; they were far more reliable. Our conversation was short. He brought the car to me the next day, and he swore it was as good as new. He had checked it before the shopping disaster. He really did, he claimed. But the reason he did not see the problem was because of a bit of an oddity with my particular engine that made this problem impossible for anyone to notice in advance, blah, blah, blah.... more of Andy's typical bullshit. His greatest skill was in his storytelling abilities, stories created to make him look better when he screwed up. If professional bullshit artist was a career path, Andy would have had it made. But the reality was that I could not afford to have another mechanic check his work, so I just had to hope for the best.

Several nights later, I went out with Serena. With most of the usual businesses closed for the winter, the Bradford had become a regular part of our night outs. Considered a "straight" bar, it often featured live bands and dancing in the summer. But this time of year, it was dark and dingy with music playing from an outdated jukebox. Still, it was a great place to play pool and people watch from the large windows overlooking the town's main street. The Bradford was in the center of town and was the center of what little social life the off- season offered to young, heterosexuals in town.

Richard was sitting at the corner of the bar when we entered. From the first time he smiled at me when I was 17, until even after we were practically living together, when I would see him unexpectedly, my heart would do an excited little flip. Our issues of late had not changed my feelings for him, but my reaction to seeing him was now different. It was less excited, maybe a little cautious, but also hopeful. I wanted him back, needed him back. But there did not seem to be an answer to the drug problem. When we had started dating the previous summer, I once asked to do some lines with him. I thought maybe if it was something we did together, he would have better control with me than when he did it with Patty. Coke was everywhere, and even Serena had dabbled in it a bit. Perhaps I was also curious about the fascination. Richard would not hear of it.

"No way. Don't even try it. You have no idea how quickly it can mess you up. Please, please stay away from it. I don't want you to have anything to do with it, ever."

And so, if he was still using, we were at an impasse. An impasse he felt was best and, probably, rightfully so. But it was agonizing just the same.

He bought Serena and me drinks, and I thanked him for the flowers.

"Is your car running better?" he asked.

"Yes, definitely, but what's the story? Did Andy just blow me off when he said he checked it? He gave me some sob story about how the problem was obscure and impossible to find and even the manufacturer would have missed it and some other crap like that."

Richard rolled his eyes. "Well, you know my buddy Andy."

"What's the real story?" I asked again.

"He did check it when you said something didn't sound right. The problem was, he assumed he knew what was causing the sound and only checked that."

"So when he claimed he checked it, he was completely half-assed about it?"

"Basically. But I could've looked at it too. And I didn't."

We left it at that. Serena was back and forth between chatting with us and flirting with the few guys in the place. As hard as it was, Richard and I went our own ways at the bar with him leaving before I did, saying something about a fishing trip the next day. Not kissing him goodbye, not walking out together, not joking and flirting like we usually did — it all tore me up. But it was the way it had to be.

* * *

There are some people in the world, religious or not, who choose not to make a big deal out of Christmas. My mother was not one of them. We had grown up with all the fun of the holiday. Not necessarily with expensive gifts, but with fun. And I had inherited her traditions. Though I had little money to spend, I was still excited. Before the latest break up, I thought less about what to get Richard for Christmas — as he was one of those people who did not need much — and more about how we would spend it with Jesse. I had been thinking about the holiday since the night he stayed over and had lots of ideas to make the time with us special. I knew we would not be able to be with him on the exact day, but figured maybe we could do something nice at my place with him right before. Hiding presents and giving him clues to find them. Cheap presents likely, but still. Then we could drink hot cocoa and watch Rudolph and other holiday tv specials. Maybe take a ride to see all the lights and then come home to a fancy dinner. I would do some of these things with Drew, and my dad's kids, but I was eager to think that we could do them with Jesse, too. How would Richard and I give him presents—from both of us? No, I decided, it would be better for the really cool gifts to be from his dad only and I could give him smaller gifts just from me. Or, better yet, from Santa.

But as the holiday week approached, and Richard and I were not back together, there were no gifts for Jesse at my apartment. I did not know what to get him or when I would see him, or if it would even be appropriate to give him a gift now. With such a lean budget, I did nothing.

One afternoon, three days before Christmas Eve, I was wrapping presents while carols blasted from my stereo. That was one of my traditions. No wrapping presents unless Christmas music was playing. Somehow, through Elvis' fun version of "Here Comes Santa Claus," I heard someone knocking at my door. I opened it and let Richard in. It was grey outside and looked like it might snow. It didn't, but snowflakes would have only made the scene too sappy to be believed. I fell into his arms, and we stayed like that for a long time. Just hugging tightly and me projecting all the warmth I had onto his cold body.

He told me he had been almost completely straight for two-and-a-half weeks. He'd had one minor slip, sharing just a bit with a buddy, and regretting it deeply.

"I needed to try to do it on my own for a while. I wanted it out of my system before I came back. But I miss you too much. The night I left the flowers, it was all I could do to walk away from your door. And now Christmas is coming, and I don't care about it so much, but I know you do, and I didn't want you to think I came back just for that but...."

I kissed him before he finished. The details did not matter. He was back. And he was straight, or at least trying very hard to be. How long did it take for someone to be rid of the addiction? I didn't know, but I was thrilled to be with him, regardless. We spent the winter afternoon cuddled under a blanket, just enjoying being together. We left to go to the grocery store at some point so that he could make me dinner. On our way back, I asked him to pull into the liquor store. I came out with a big bottle of Southern Comfort.

"Did you get that for me? That's pretty expensive and I don't really need it."

"It's kind of for you, but it's also for me too...." I told him.

"Since when do you drink this?"

"Since I learned that it's delicious in eggnog."

He told me he had given Patty some money from his last two fishing trips for her to buy presents for Jesse.

"But what did you get him?" I asked.

"I just gave Patty the money—she's better at that kind of thing than I am. She knows what he wants."

Patty had already left to spend the holiday with her family, and it broke my heart to think Jesse's dad would not be a part of it at all. Richard saw the disappointment on my face.

"It's ok. I don't really get along with Patty's family and they don't have much use for me. But they love Jesse; he'll have a great Christmas with them."

Of course, I was glad that Richard's son would have a nice day. But it did not seem enough. Jesse was prime Santa Claus age. Richard had no clue the fun he was missing, the joy on a kid's face when he sees Santa has been by.

"Well, that's good, I guess. But I wish he had something special to open just from you. Maybe when they get back you could take him shopping, just the two of you?" I suggested.

"Ya, that would be fun."

Holiday joy with his son would not be what I had hoped, but at least Richard was back, and we had a whole future to spend with each other and with Jesse. We spent that night drinking eggnog and playfully fighting over TV—me arguing for Christmas specials and him pretending to hate them.

He would not go with me to my mom or dad's house on Christmas Eve. He saw my mom at the unemployment office and had brought her lobsters several times. And he regularly saw my dad around town. But we had never spent time together with either of them and, combined with our recent breakup and the holiday atmosphere, he thought it would be more than he could handle. Instead, while I visited my family, he visited several of his friends, stopping by their homes for a little merriment. I worried about what else he would get into but had to trust him. And when we met up later, he was still drug free. A little bleary from the festive shots shared at the various places he stopped, but not high. Definitely, thankfully, not high. And since he seemed to have missed me in those short hours while hanging with some couples celebrating together, I hoped he would consider spending at least some of the next day at my mom's. He did. Since he was slightly hungover when I woke him up early Christmas morning, we came up with a plan. He would stay at my place sleeping off the night before while I went to my mom's for presents. Then I would come get him at noon, so he could join us for dinner.

When I got back to my apartment, he was clear-headed, showered and shaved.

"Are you ready?" I smiled as I took his hand to go.

"Right now? Are you sure you don't want to hang here for just a bit? Maybe celebrate with a bang our own way?" He was grinning his mischievous grin.

"We did that this morning, remember? I've never started Christmas like that before. It was awesome."

"What, that? That doesn't count. I was barely awake."

"You seemed pretty awake to me! Come on. It'll be fine. And then we'll come back here and spend the evening doing all those things your brain is conjuring up."

"It's not my brain that's doing the conjuring," he laughed.

My mom would not allow help in the kitchen, and she made this very clear. Not in the "it's ok — I've got this — you sit down" way, but in the "get the hell out of my kitchen — you're in my space and it's ticking me off" way. Because of this, while Laurie was getting dressed, and Audrey was watching Drew, I set about to cleaning up the living room from all the piles of ripped wrapping paper. Richard joined my brothers-in-law, Andy and Billy, on the sofa for a guy chat. Billy was a likeable guy, but he was not very quick-witted. Andy, knowing how much my mother was not a fan of his, gave her lots of space when they were in the same place together. So when my mom yelled from the kitchen that she needed a big strong man to help her drain the heavy boiling pot of potatoes, it was Richard who jumped up. And my mom appreciated it. And she did not kick him out of the kitchen. My sisters and I would have been kicked out the second we appeared in the room, but I did not see my boyfriend for over 20 minutes as he helped my mom finish dinner. He seemed relaxed and part of the family, even taking a turn filming Drew's toddler antics with the video camera my mother had borrowed from a friend. He turned the camera on me at one point and left it there until I protested and he chuckled; a special moment between us caught on film.

It was dark when we left and, in the car, Richard said he had one more stop to make before we called it a night. *Oh, Richard, please no,* I thought. *It's been so good. Please don't.*

"Where?" I asked, an edge to my voice.

"I can't tell you. It's too hard to say. It'll be quick. I'll direct you."

"Are we visiting somebody?"

"I just need to pay my respects."

I had no idea what that meant. He was being evasive, and I did not know what to do. Ignore his directions and just drive us home and fight about it there? I did not want to fight. It had been such a great day. Maybe I was wrong. Maybe he was directing me to his sister's house to say a quick Merry Christmas or to another friend's house, hopefully a friend who did not celebrate every holiday with cocaine?

His directions lead me to the side of the road that bordered the cemetery. Was he meeting someone? I hadn't seen him make a call.

He told me where to park and then got out without another word. I watched as he went to what must have been his father's headstone, the parent Richard had lost when he was still a teenager. He bowed his head and stood there for several minutes while I waited. It was hard to look away but I wanted to give him privacy. I scooched down in the driver's seat and adjusted the rearview mirror to see the monument behind us, lit up during the holiday season. Gigantic strings of white bulbs were draped from the very top of the tower to the lawn over two hundred feet below, shining dazzling light above us and adding a wonderous feel to the day.

When Richard came back to the car, he kissed me. We did not talk about the pit stop. We didn't need to.

chapter 23
clothes

In the days after Christmas, we settled ourselves in for the long, cold winter as a happy, normal couple. Well, *normal,* as in what I assumed life for a normal couple in the deserted off-season of a small seaside town was. While the holiday magic lingered, Richard thought we should go see his mother. I had never met her, but this visit had less to do with a formal introduction than it did with him needing some of his foul weather gear he had stored in her basement. He was hoping for a winter fishing trip or two and wanted to be prepared.

We left after our morning caffeine. He drove the 40 minutes to her home in Brewster while I sat in the passenger seat and looked at the chilly scenery of the neighborhoods. When we pulled up to the house, Richard commented on a car in the driveway. He had that mischievous look about him. He whispered to me to be quiet and to close the car door gently. What was going on? Could his mother still be asleep? He had not told her we were coming, but it was almost 10.

I followed him to the back of the house, very confused, as there was a perfectly appropriate door directly in front of us. Richard knelt on the ground and lifted a basement window. What were we doing? He leaned in and yelled, *"Thomas!"* From inside, I heard a deep voice loudly grumble, "Crap! Who the hell is that?" Richard burst into giggles as he yelled back, "wake up bro, you've got company!"

Apparently, the car in the driveway meant that Richard's younger brother was home and was sleeping in the apartment he created out of half of his mother's basement. Richard got up, and we walked to the kitchen door. By that point, his mom was waiting for us, having heard the commotion but not recognizing the car. She greeted Richard, and he introduced me. She nodded but did not say much. We didn't sit down. Was it my imagination, or did she seem suspicious? Richard asked about her holiday and she told him about spending it with his sister and how Richard's nieces and nephew were doing. She did not ask about his holiday or about Jesse. Thomas came in then and poured himself some coffee. We were properly introduced. He asked if we wanted anything. Richard said no thanks, we couldn't stay. We couldn't? I didn't think we had much else scheduled on our December calendar.

"You mean you woke my ass up by shrieking in my window and I come up here to visit and you're not even going to stay? Not going to let me properly get to know this young lady with you?"

Richard grinned his grin. "Well, it was either yelling in your window or jumping on your bed. I need some of my stuff down there, so you were waking up regardless."

He left me then, heading to the basement to get what he needed, with Thomas following him. I was alone with their mother and it was uncomfortable. My mom and Richard's mom knew each other. Her son-in-law was my old gym and science teacher. We were both natives of a beautiful small town. How come we had nothing to talk about? Did she know who I was? Was she apprehensive about why Richard was there? Or wary about why he was there with me, a woman 11 years younger than he, but who was smiling and trying to be friendly? Had she already been through so much with this son and the women in his life? I wanted her to ask about Richard's Christmas or mine, so I could tell her how much fun we had and how he had helped my mom and that my mom liked him very much. I wanted to tell her we were the real deal. But she did not ask. She busied herself with washing her coffee cup as we both stood awkwardly in her kitchen.

Thomas came back, and we made small talk for a bit. Just a few minutes later, Richard came up the basement stairs. He had his neoprene waders and a heavy parka slung over his shoulder and was carrying a worn knapsack, so he used his free hand to slap his baby brother on the back instead of saying goodbye. He kissed his mother's cheek, and I muttered something about it being nice to meet them and we left. I thought that in the car he would say something about why we did not stay longer, but he didn't. His manner seemed to suggest mission accomplished—he had gotten what he needed and said a quick hi to his mother and brother. I was glad to put the awkward visit behind us. Maybe his family just needed time to acknowledge this new, healthy Richard.

* * *

For the first time in years, Richard was going to spend New Year's Eve chemical and somewhat alcohol free. Since drinking was not that big a deal for him, he had decided to be our designated driver. Getting dressed upstairs, I put on a new blouse I had bought with Christmas money, just for this night. It was pink with flowers, hung below the waist and had ruffles at the bottom. I thought the print was beautiful and that it made me look fantastic. But as I walked down the spiral staircase, Richard's face scrunched up.

"What are you wearing?"

"My new blouse. Why, what's wrong? Don't you like it?" I asked.

"It's not my favorite shirt of yours. You're so pretty and have so many pretty things, but that doesn't do much for you," he said.

I was annoyed. He was just a guy. What did he know? I felt insulted but loved my top and was going to wear it. As we gathered our coats, I hesitated. "What, exactly, don't you like about it?" I questioned.

"The flower pattern is old ladylike, and the ruffles are childish and ridiculous. The color isn't the best I've seen you in either. It also doesn't flatter your figure, and it makes you look like a grandma on top and like a little girl on the bottom."

My honest Richard.

"Well, I don't have a ton of clothes, you know," I told him. "There's not much to choose from."

"I bet you that in one minute I can find you something that looks gorgeous and will be way, way better than that."

I took him up on his challenge and before I knew it, I was wearing something totally different from what I had planned. Walking into Laurie's apartment to wish her, Andy and Drew a Happy New Year, my sister complemented me on my outfit. Instead of smirking, Richard said, "yes, doesn't she look great?"

"Richard made me change," I sulked.

"I did not!" he replied. "I just told her I thought I could find her something better than what she was wearing."

"Well, what were you wearing before?" Laurie asked.

"The flowery shirt I bought at Bradlees last week, the day we went to do laundry."

"Seriously, you were going to wear that out? That ugly old lady thing? I thought you bought that to wear around the house, as a nightgown, even."

Now Richard smirked. Apparently, besides many other wonderful things, he also had good fashion sense. It pissed me off a bit. I turned to my nephew for support.

"Drew honey, you don't care what auntie wears, do you?" I asked, scooping him up. He answered me in baby talk and then he made the face he made when he had a messy diaper. I put him down on his father's lap so the diaper was his problem.

"Don't smirk too much, Richard," I said. "You actually owe me a nightgown. You ripped the buttons off the one I was wearing last night."

"That's only because I couldn't wait to get it off you. That was old lady like too. You are much, much prettier with nothing...."

"STOP!" Laurie shouted. "This is a conversation I don't want or need to hear!"

We laughed and then said goodbye. We stopped briefly at the Bradford but wound-up spending most of the night at Piggy's. Patty was there with some of her friends and with her new boyfriend, a townie named Jason, who had a violent reputation. We nodded to them and I briefly wondered who was watching Jesse; maybe we could have had him stay over with us instead of going out? I had thought Patty was still away.

We spent the night dancing together; the way New Year's should be. I had too much to drink though and just remembered glimpses of what happened after midnight: Patty and Jason getting into a fight at the bar, my passionately attacking Richard on the sofa as soon as we got home, him helping me up the tricky stairs, and then insisting I drink some water and swallow two aspirins before I passed out. As I fell asleep, I thought how nice it was to welcome in 1992 being taken care of by someone I loved.

chapter 24
towel

January could be pretty bleak for townies. I was not concerned. It felt like the first time I was spending the winter in Provincetown. Sure, I had grown up here. But I lived with my mom and my sisters and I went to school. Now I was in my own place, living with Richard and appreciating every minute of it. While he picked up odd jobs here and there, I scoured the want-ads for a full-time job. I was relaxed, having the security of unemployment checks until May, when I would again start my seasonal job. When I was not with Richard, I was with my friends or my family. The dull, cold days, desolate streets, and boarded up businesses didn't depress me. Instead, they felt welcoming and encouraging. They felt promising.

We were home one bitter, dark night when the phone rang. Richard answered it and I heard a loud voice on the other end.

"Hey Richard, it's Dante. Does your old lady want some clothes?"

I feigned a 'what the hell' expression, and Richard shrugged his shoulders. He asked Dante what was going on.

"My old lady threw me out, the bitch. For no reason! I had like 10 minutes to get all my stuff and so I took some of her clothes to piss her off. I don't wanna take them to the thrift shop 'cause she'll just go get them again. What's the point of that?"

Richard had been there—at least in the getting thrown out part. He had sympathy for his buddy, who just happened to be in the neighborhood. Dante came over and we met for the first time. While he handed me a large, dirty trash bag, Richard handed him one of the three beers we had in the back of the refrigerator. I went through the bag and pretended to be appreciative while he told us the story of the fight that led to him walking around town with a garbage bag of women's clothing. I oohed and ahhed over several of the items while I tried to fold them carefully. Even if I had felt comfortable wearing stolen apparel, Dante's 'old lady' was a size zero. On a super thin day, I might have been able to squeeze into an 8, but I was basically a 10. Yet, I was new to this relationship stuff and did not want to seem ungrateful to Richard's friend, who thought he was killing two birds with one stone: pissing off his ex while gifting Richard's 'old lady' with a new wardrobe. I compromised by selecting and gushing over two ratty but common t-shirts that I could not imagine the ex would miss and, even if she did, would not recognize. I would never fit into them but made a mental note to drop them off at the thrift store. Maybe the ex would get some of her clothes back after all....

Not long after, Richard and I had a different sort of visit/clothes issue, except this one was about a lack of clothes. Richard had come home frozen and filthy after doing gear work on a friend's boat. As he was getting into the shower, I told him I was going to pick up Serena and bring her back to the apartment so they could talk about her car, which he had agreed to work on. When Serena and I came in, Richard was out of the shower and innocently watching TV, wearing nothing but a pink towel. Serena doubled over with laughter and could not get over the fact that he was just in a PINK towel. "Pink, that's what so funny! He's wearing a pink towel! I've used your towels and I know you have colors besides pink!"

Personally, I was furious and embarrassed. What was he thinking? Richard was hot and had a great body. Was he just trying to show off? Did he think we would be so enamored of his abs that we would both throw ourselves at him? I didn't think so. Richard loved me even though he knew I was pretty uptight. While Serena was far from uptight, it would still never happen. Mostly, he was just being his impish self, trying to shake the winter up a bit and have fun watching me turn bright red. I yelled at him to go get dressed like a normal person and he did. But not before making a production out of pretending to "almost" drop the towel on the staircase, which caused Serena to crack up even more.

Back downstairs and dressed, they talked about her car problems. Richard had looked at the engine the day before and knew what she needed done. He estimated what the parts would cost and said he would call them into the shop the next day. Once Serena had the money to pick them up, he could fix her car, no problem.

Serena was known for many things: a great sense of humor, being kind, being a flirt, being adventurous, and her incredibly big boobs. Dolly Parton had nothing on my dear friend, and she didn't mind if people talked about her chest. I was not lacking in the boob department that much myself, but Serena's were definitely bigger. She would not have been offended when Richard called the shop the next morning and spoke to a guy he knew that worked there. When he was done ordering the parts she needed, he told them that a very large-breasted woman would be in to pick them up.

"Why would you tell him that?" I asked.

"So they'll recognize her. And hey, you never know, maybe they'll give her a break on the price."

"You men are dogs," I told him.

A few days passed and Serena had the cash, but not the opportunity to get to the shop several towns away. On another one of my laundry trips with Laurie, I volunteered to go to the auto store for her. I told the clerk I was there to pick up parts Richard had called in. He leered at me and said, "I thought so." *Oh buddy, you have no idea what you missed had the original woman come in,* I thought. But I had to admit, I felt a little flattered.

Unfortunately, however, *my* boobs did not get her any discounts.

chapter 25
movie

We spent many evenings with Andy and Laurie. Laurie and I genuinely liked hanging out with each other, and Andy and Richard's friendship went back to their teen years. Plus, I could not get enough of my adorable first nephew. The baby, who took his first steps walking towards me in my very first apartment, had me totally captivated. Richard and I would go to Laurie's after dinner and play with Drew until his bedtime. Then we would have a few beers with his parents. I was in love with the new child in my family and I was in love with Richard. Spending the quiet, cold winter with them was even better than I had imagined.

One Saturday, my mom planned to keep Drew with her overnight, which left Laurie and Andy child free. We decided we would all go to the Whaler Lounge for a movie. Our town's movie theater was not open in the off season. One of the major hotels was open, but business was sporadic. For years, they supplemented their income in these lean months by offering a movie and free popcorn with the hope and expectation that they would make their money back by selling alcohol. And they did, as townies desperate for something to do attended regularly. The movies were post-theater release, but for drinks and socializing, it wasn't a bad deal. Especially since Laurie, never really a fan, had long grown tired of the regular bar scene.

Andy had a problem with alcohol. From the time they started dating, he and my sister fought over his drinking. Many was the night he would not come home and would have a story about how he was so tired after work that he lay down in his truck and didn't wake up until morning. Richard could verify Andy's claims and confirmed for my sister that her husband was not with other women those nights he didn't come home. Andy, as well as many other blue-collar workers in our town, would end the workday at the Governor Bradford. Too often though, he would let the alcohol and time get away from him and, being too ashamed to go home, would pass out in his work-issued truck, often at his job site so that he would not miss work in the morning. Then, he and Laurie would fight. He would dry out for a bit and then several months later, the same thing would happen again. But Andy was her husband and my sister loved him. One day, she hoped, the alcohol craziness would stop.

The trouble seemed to come from hard alcohol, so beer with us every once in a while was not usually a problem. But the night of our movie plan, Richard and I arrived at their apartment to discover that Andy was not home and had not called. Laurie was furious. We waited for a while. Richard even called the bar, looking for him. If Laurie called, they knew to tell her that Andy was not there; he was too good of a customer for the bartender to sell him out to his angry wife. But they denied knowing where Andy was, even when Richard called. Richard zipped up his jacket, deciding to just go to the bar and check for himself. But as he was heading out the door, he saw Andy walking up the sidewalk, almost an hour late, but only buzzed, not completely trashed. My sister and brother-in-law fought for a bit, but then we decided that they needed a night out, so we stuck to our plan.

The hotel lounge put out a schedule of movies, but it didn't matter what they were showing. The idea was to get out of the house. Any distraction would do. The film that evening was *New Jack City,* and I knew it was a guy's type of action movie and had something to do with gangs. Richard and the bleary Andy were eager to see it. Laurie was just eager to be out. And I was eager to be out with them; not as the tagalong baby sister I had been most of my life, but as part of a couple. Since our sister Audrey lived several towns away, and Billy and she did not drink, I was her social sister. I was eager to be there as Richard's girlfriend and as Laurie's buddy. And we looked the couple friends' part too. Andy and Richard talking guy stuff while Laurie and I talked girl stuff. We bought our drinks, ordered appetizers, chatted with other bored, eager to be out locals and munched away on free, stale popcorn. The earlier argument about Andy being late was forgotten.

The movie started. It turned out that *New Jack City* was a deeper look at the rise of crack cocaine in the slums of New York. Wesley Snipes played a drug dealer at the heart of the crack epidemic. If I knew the subject before the movie started, I did not appreciate its significance. To me, this was a movie about gangs, ghettos and junkies. A world I felt so far removed from the world I was in, that the drama of it was to be embedded only in plot twists meant to entertain. I assumed I could not possibly relate. But the very first scene pierced me like a dagger.

It opened in broad daylight on a high bridge with a young woman in hysterical sobs. Next to her, a guy was holding her boyfriend by the ankles, suspended several stories over the water. A car pulls up and the dealer Snipes gets out. The guy hanging begs for more time to pay back his drug debts. Snipes says his time is up as the other dealer lets the guy go. His terrified screams echo his girlfriend's as he drops to his death right in front of her.

The couple did not look like homeless junkies from the streets of a hardened, ugly city. They were normal looking. I was stunned.

I felt like my heart had stopped, and I was sure I was going to faint. I looked at my companions, and none of them seemed affected. It was just a movie. Even Richard seemed indifferent, just waiting for the next scene.

Didn't it scare him? How many times had I heard rumors about him shorting people for drugs because he just couldn't control himself? Sure, I wasn't worried about the locals he bought his drugs from. The locals were his friends. But they had to get the drugs from somewhere, didn't they? This frightening world was a world Richard knew. Earlier that night, I had a sense of superiority that it was my boyfriend rescuing the evening, ready to drag Laurie's husband away from the bottle so he could join us for what was supposed to be a fun double date. Richard was where he was supposed to be, out with me, having a drink or two, perfectly innocent. Meanwhile, my poor sister's undependable husband had to be tracked down for something as simple as a night out. But getting alcohol did not come with the kind of danger that buying crack did. Here, in my face, was an example of the not at all innocent lifestyle Richard often lived in. A place I did not like to think about too much.

They sat unmoved. Andy whispered something that made them all chuckle, the sound of Richard's distinct laugh ringing in my ears. I excused myself and went to the bathroom. At the sink, I noticed I was shaking and covered in sweat. It was obvious I was terrified about the world my boyfriend, my first love, my Richard, moved in. But he was done with that world and we were moving forward. This was just a movie, and Richard was trying to get clean, be a good dad, and have a future. He was in a relationship with me and together we did not live in that world. I told myself that I was too sensitive, a total wimp about a movie, for crying out loud. I was letting myself get worked up over nothing. If Richard did not recognize himself in the guy dangling over the bridge, then there was no need to for me to recognize myself in the screaming girl next to him. This relationship was what I wanted, and things were good.

I splashed water on my face and told myself to stop being silly and paranoid. Back at the table, I took a sip of my cold beer and lit a cigarette. I leaned against my boyfriend's strong shoulder as I sat back to watch the movie, pretending it had nothing to do with me.

chapter 26
deals

Though things felt great to me, towards the end of January, Richard started to get restless. He had been coke-free for almost a month. And in the previous six weeks, he had only one slip up. But he was bringing up drugs again; how he didn't want to go back to his old way of life, but how this cold turkey thing was hard. I tried to be encouraging. *Hang in there, I'm here for you, you can do this* were all frequent comments I was reciting at the time.

"I think if I could just do a little bit, a line or two, I think it would help me through this bad patch," Richard said.

It seemed like a bad idea to me, so I did everything I could to distract him and the moment would pass, for a little while anyway.

He fixed Serena's car for her and while there had been no talk of payment, Serena was generous, and I knew that when she could, she would pay him for saving her so much money at the garage. Serena was seeing Greg again, a local she had spent time with the summer before. I didn't like him. He was just too full of himself, which was ridiculous, as he did not seem to me to have anything to be full of himself about. Also, I worried as he had toyed with my friend in those brief months when they were together. As if those weren't reasons enough for me not to be fond of him, he was also one of the town's small-time drug dealers. He liked to boast as if he was a total bad ass. Yet people who got drugs from him were more frightened of his odd dealing partner, a large brute of a woman named Shelly. At least, we thought she was a woman. She liked to act as if she was Greg's bodyguard, but the whole thing just seemed pathetic to me.

One night Richard and I were at Piggy's, trying to shake away the winter blues with dancing and booze. Serena and Greg were there and before long, we were all talking, shouting over the music as we had grown accustomed to doing. Serena apologized for not yet having paid Richard for the work on her car. Richard said not to worry; the off-season was tight for everyone. Greg commented that he would be happy to pay Richard on her behalf if Richard would take the thank you in the form of a little blow. Richard looked at me. I pulled him away from them, towards the bathrooms where it was only slightly quieter.

"Don't do it Richard. It's a horrible idea. Plus, you need the money. Serena will give you some cash, probably from her next unemployment check," I told him.

"I know, I know. It would be totally stupid. But I've really been struggling lately, and it won't be a lot. I'm thinking maybe this is what I need, just a little bit to take the edge off. Maybe giving it up completely is too much."

I had no clue how anyone got off drugs. If Richard was so obsessed with cocaine now, maybe a little bit would help him get past this bad patch, with each coke-free period getting longer each time. He was a grown man and didn't need anyone's permission to do anything. But he was asking me about this issue, seeking my approval. Was it the two White Russians in my system? Was it my intense desire to make him happy? Maybe I wanted this to be all it took, a line or two here and there to carry him over until he could stop for good. Whatever it was, I looked at him and said, "Only if you really, really think this will help." I knew the instant I said those words that it wouldn't.

At least he brought his "payment" back to my apartment, so there was a finite amount and no chance of socializing with his regular coked-out crowd. And he insisted it was only a little and that was all he would need. That night, we foolishly told ourselves that would be the end of it. The problem was that now Serena and Greg wanted to hang out with us. Serena sometimes felt uncomfortable around Greg's idiotic cohorts. Shelly in particular, would act like Serena's best friend when Greg said he was crazy about her and then would be obnoxious when it seemed like he wasn't. Being with Richard and me instead seemed like a good solution to her. Just a few days after Greg "thanked" Richard for working on his girlfriend's car, they invited us to join them at Serena's place, temporarily all her own, since her grandparents were out of town.

I loved Serena, and I loved Richard, but I did not want to go; especially when I noticed how much Richard wanted to go. I didn't relish being the downer, the goody-two-shoes in the group. But, since we didn't have any other plans, there was not a valid excuse to refuse. So we went, one couple visiting another.

Serena must have told Greg about the pink towel story. Not to be outdone, he said he was tired and was going to bed, which was weird as it was very early, and we had only been there a few minutes. He excused himself and before we had even gotten comfortable, he came running out of Serena's bedroom in only his briefs. I had to admit, it was pretty funny. He did not have a good body and looked a lot like Homer Simpson in his underwear. We couldn't help ourselves and cracked up.

The night was not as bad as I worried it would be. They all did lines, though, and there was not even a question about whether or not Richard would join them. *What happened to "just a little bit?"* I wondered. It did not seem like the best time to ask. At least I didn't witness it, the three of them sharing who knows how many lines together away from me. They gathered in the bedroom for several minutes while I sat on Serena's grandmother's sofa, smoking, drinking and staring blankly at the TV. Assuming I would not be getting high, Greg preferred they do their coke thing in private, just in case I, the cop's daughter, turned narc on him. It was fine with me; I had no interest in watching them get high. It was not long after they came out of the bedroom that we got mellow pretty quickly. The night wasn't fun anymore. I had thought cocaine was supposed to make you energized, but that was not the case here. Maybe it was like a drunken stupor; you are silly and fun for a short time and then you get depressed, quiet and boring. Richard and I left not long after and I was glad to end the evening, feeling relieved that at least it was somewhat controlled with just the four of us, not the whole Greg/Shelly posse.

Before I knew it, we were spending a lot of time with Serena and Greg. Now, they stopped keeping the coke away from me. That was how I realized they weren't doing lines anymore; they always just smoked it. One night Greg asked me why I never did any. I was not quick enough for an honest, polite answer. And there were so many honest, polite answers—because it's dangerous, because it's addictive, because it's illegal, because it's expensive, because it could ruin Richard's life. But as I sat there, I did not know what to say. I still couldn't imagine what all the fuss was about. Was the high that great? When I didn't answer him right away, Greg asked if I wanted to try it, just a small taste among friends. I waited for Richard to say something, but he didn't. He was looking at me, but I couldn't tell what his expression meant. I looked at Greg and nodded. I don't even know why. Serena smiled, and Richard showed me how to hold the bottle/pipe and how to inhale. Greg and Serena seemed pleased that I had joined their club. It was not until the next morning that I remembered Richard's words from August "please, please stay away from it."

Apparently, he did not remember them either.

I didn't even enjoy it. I may have done it with them on one or two other nights, but I never got the high, if there was any. *This* is what people were destroying their lives over? I was happier with a bottle of cheap wine. Even though they now saw me as part of their cocaine world, I stayed straight enough to protest Greg's next suggestion. He was too well known, he said. So was Shelly. He needed to change things up a bit to stay under the radar. Why didn't Richard start delivering for him?

"*No!*" I shouted. "That will never work. Richard. Don't do it. We both know that with that much around, you won't be able to control yourself."

I was being the wet blanket, the pessimist, the wicked straight arrow. This was perfect for Greg and, in his high mind, it worked out perfectly for Richard, too. He would get paid either with cash or coke, whichever he preferred. We all knew what his preference would be. He wanted to want the cash, but his body would go with the drugs. Since Serena wanted to please her boyfriend, no one listened when I said, "This is a huge, huge mistake."

Everything happened so fast. It had only been two weeks earlier that Richard had been clean, and I got freaked out by a scene in an action movie. Now he was helping a dealer, and I had actually used myself. Richard's new employment opportunity was the final straw for me and my brief involvement with cocaine. While we continued to hang out with them, I refrained when the drugs came out. I just did not see the point and one of us had to keep a clear head. Since Greg knew I loved Richard, and Richard was now embroiled in the drug scene right in front of my eyes, he no longer feared I would turn them in. And I wouldn't have, no matter what. Being a narc went completely against the whole small-town spirit I had grown up in. No, I wouldn't report anyone, but would just try to deal with the consequences of Richard's "job" myself. And with the drugs around us now, there was no point in talking about taking Jesse for the night. Things felt no more stable at my apartment than they were at the house he was growing up in.

It didn't take long for the first repercussion to arise. Richard was late getting home one night. Neither of us had a set schedule, but it was still later than I expected him to be and he had not called. When the phone did ring, it was Serena.

"Hey, listen, where's Richard?" She asked.

"I don't know. I was wondering that myself."

"Are you sure he's not there? Put him on. You need to get him on the phone." I did not like her tone. I answered in a tone of my own.

"I can't put him on as he isn't home. What's wrong?"

"He may have ripped Greg off. This is very bad, very, very bad. He's in big trouble if he doesn't come up with cash or coke, like, right now."

"Well, that sucks, but I'm not surprised. I told you guys this was a mistake and he wouldn't be able to handle it. What did you expect?"

"You're not getting it," she responded loudly. "I'm trying to keep things under control here but if he can't pay Greg back immediately, then someone is going to get hurt. You've got to get him to give the drugs back or pay Greg for them before it's too late. Can you come up with it for him?"

In an instant, I was beyond furious. Short of feeling threatened, I was angry. I was angry at my friend from forever who was being so manipulated by a total scumbag that she thought scaring me was actually helpful. I was even angrier at the scumbag himself who put his girlfriend up to this type of call. He was probably right by the phone, directing her as to what to say. I was angriest at Richard, who had fallen back into this drama and had allowed me to get pulled into it too. Yes, I had let myself get involved, but fuck, this was his crappy world, and he was supposed to keep me out of it. The same townie vibe that kept me from being a narc also kept me, perhaps naïvely, from being afraid of Greg "Big G" Collins, of all people, let alone being afraid of one of my dearest friends.

"Serena, is Greg trying to get you to threaten me?"

Her voice changed and got calmer.

"I'm really just trying to keep things under control...." she repeated.

"Well, keep me out of it! I told all three of you this was a mistake, so don't put this on me! This is not my problem and I won't be paying Greg anything. If you have a problem with Richard, take it up with Richard. Or, even better, tell Greg to grow a pair and do his own dirty work! What, Shelly's too busy pushing people around so he's got to get his girlfriend to do it? Fucking unbelievable!"

I slammed the phone down, knowing that Greg might have heard every word and wondering if I was being a little too cavalier about the seriousness of all of this. But in my frustration, I refused to care.

When Richard got home, he was high. I was not surprised, but I was still furious. I told him about the call. In a clipped, pissed-off voice, I told him to fix this problem and not to bother coming back until it was. "And best friend or not, our couple outings with these two are fucking over!"

He went out again and was gone for a long time. He hadn't dared ask me for my car keys so I knew whatever he was doing, he was walking the deserted, icy streets to get it done. I stayed home worrying about what came next. He came back after midnight and said things were all set. I did not ask for the details. He promised me that there was no reason to worry, and he had made it up to Greg and would no longer be running for him. Probably, Richard borrowed from someone else to pay Greg back, and I hoped that would not be a problem later. By the next morning, Serena, Greg and Richard acted as if the whole incident had never happened. Serena called like we had not even talked the night before. It occurred to me she was probably high herself when she made the call, and our friendship went back too far to let it come between us. So, I pretended the other call had never happened either. She did not ask, however, when the four of us could get together next, and I certainly did not mention it. If I never saw Greg or cocaine again, it would be more than fine with me.

chapter 27
bees

Life quieted down and seemed drug-free for several days. Thus, it was a surprise when I received another threatening phone call. This time it was from Patty.

"Yvonne, listen. You should know that Jason is looking for Richard. I don't know if you know him or not, but he's a wicked violent guy, kind of crazy, too. He was trying to make me give him your address, but I wouldn't. But, you know, it's not going to take him long to figure out where you live and then I'm afraid of what he'll do."

Emotions collided within me as I processed what she was saying. I only knew Jason as the short, muscular guy Patty was dating who had quite a reputation, a reputation I suspected because of the story of the bees. On one of the nights that Richard and I had hung out with Serena and Greg, before the first threatening phone call, Greg had shared the bee story. He said he liked telling it because he hated the local VFW. Seems Greg was banned from ever entering the VFW and so the story made him feel better. I couldn't help feeling like the story was a slight jab at me too, as in Greg's version, my dad did not come out so well.

While technically a private club for veterans, the VFW in our town featured a bar open to the public as long as you signed a guest book. Since everyone knew everyone, everyone was considered a guest of one veteran or another. Dark and smoky, the bar was in the basement below the regular VFW Hall. The steps were in the back of the building and once you entered, it was like entering an American cave filled with medals, flags, memorabilia and memories of our town's heroes. The guest book was right at the entrance and after your eyes adjusted to the haze, it was hard not to find a familiar face sitting at the bar. Especially since you had most likely surveyed the parking lot before heading down the steps. It was a great place to play pool and get strong, cheap drinks.

Jason had also been banned and was pretty furious about it. According to Greg, Jason had shown up one-night years before, drunk and belligerent, and was ordered to leave by Pick, the bartender. Jason not only refused, but supposedly opened a box full of trained bees he had with him, unleashing them into the club. The mostly drunk townies freaked out as the bees magically zeroed in on people to sting. The police were called, and my dad, alone in the cruiser, went into the bar and also freaked out at all the bees. Not knowing what else to do, my dad and Pick begged Jason to gather the bees, and promised if he saved everyone from the swarm, they would lift his ban. Only then, did Jason snap his fingers and calmly walk out, the bees following close behind.

While listening to the story, I indulged Greg, but did not believe it for a second. My dad was known as a fair, cool cop who would give people a break if he thought they were being honest with him, mostly because he hated writing tickets and arrest reports. But if you would not pay attention to reason, then he would take you in and was not afraid to do so. I couldn't imagine my dad losing it over some obnoxious insects, and the whole incident was too crazy to be believed, even in my quirky town. On the way home that night, I had asked Richard if he knew the actual story.

"Well, I wasn't there," he said. "But the way I heard it was more like Jason showed up drunk, Pick kicked him out and he stood in the doorway yelling and swearing. There must have been a nest over the door because, while he stood there, a couple of bees came in. The police were called and when your dad showed up, he told Jason to calm the hell down. When he wouldn't, your dad took him into protective custody. Less paperwork than an arrest, I guess. I think I heard Pick complaining about the bees Jason had let in and your father said something like, 'well, get a fly swatter for Christ's sake. I have handcuffs for people, not bees!'"

Richard's version of the story made more sense and again reminded me that my dad was tough and cool and most of the reason was because he did not have to tell people he was tough and cool. If Greg and Jason had to brag about how badass they were, didn't that mean they really were not tough at all? And using bees as a weapon? It just made both of them seem incredibly lame.

Still, I could not help but react to Patty's call. It was one thing for my friend to call and try to scare me, but Patty calling to threaten me? I thought of the movie Richard and I had seen with Laurie and Andy. Wesley Snipes was the main dealer, maybe unknown to the guy hanging from the bridge, the big shot in the operation. The drugs were coming from somewhere and what about the people who were providing them? I knew nothing about them. Could Jason be working for them? Still, I knew the drama they lived in and wanted to back away from it as soon as possible. I thanked Patty for calling and letting me know. She did not want to let it rest.

"Well, what are you going to do? I can't keep your address from him forever. If he doesn't find it on his own, he will get it from somebody or ask me again. Even I'm a little afraid of him when he's been drinking," she told me.

"Thank you for warning me and I appreciate it. Don't worry about keeping my address from him, it's pretty well known, and my car is always on the street. You don't need to piss him off on my account."

"Yvonne, what are you going to do if he shows up there?"

I didn't know, but I refused to let any of this crew know that or think I was afraid.

"It's fine Patty, I'm not worried. Gotta go."

As I hung up the phone, I realized my hand was shaking. The sound of someone opening the door made me jump until I saw it was Richard himself.

"What's the matter? You don't look so good," he asked.

"I'm not surprised," I said. I told him about the phone call.

"What an asshole!" he responded. "I don't owe him that much and I just talked to him yesterday. He said I could pay him back on Friday. They're playing games, either him or Patty. It's just bullshit."

"Why are they playing them with me?" I cringed at the whininess I heard in my voice. "I told you I wanted no part of this crap. Threats, games, whatever the fuck it is, I don't want to be a part of it!" I realized I was tearing up. Dammit — I didn't want that either.

Richard hugged me then and said he had no idea what this was about. He called Patty to clarify. She insisted Jason *had* asked for my address, and he had been livid when he did. Richard and Patty were still on the phone when Jason showed up at her place. She handed him the phone. Richard beckoned me to the receiver so I could hear the conversation. Jason confirmed the agreement Richard had told me about.

"I was just curious where you were living," I heard Jason say through the phone, not sounding so tough at all.

When they hung up, everybody was fine. Except me. Later, I told Richard why I was so concerned. I told him I thought the locals were full of it, but I worried about the people supplying them. Richard told me not to worry, that he was barely involved anymore and everything he did was small time. He agreed with my instinct that Greg and Jason and even Shelly just liked to act big time, like they were in some kind of movie of their own and that it was all just stupid crap they made up to get through the boring winter. Again, Richard apologized for how it was coming down on me.

Richard paid Jason on Friday and on Saturday Serena called to tell me that Jason's son was throwing a huge party that night and it was going to be a blast. Richard and I should come, and we could all drive there together. Since the house was in Truro, the next town over and near where Greg lived, she was going to meet him at the party and did not want to walk in alone.

"You're kidding me, right? I don't even know the kid, or Jason, for that matter. I know that Jason's dating Patty, and I don't really want to socialize with her. Plus, I wasn't invited. No, don't think I'm going to make it."

"Invited?? Seriously? It's a party—you don't get invited to a party; you just show up. That's a dumb reason not to go. Come on, don't be so uptight. It'll be fun. You're going," she said decisively.

"No, I'm not." I replied. I did not want to tell her about Patty's phone call.

That evening Serena came over anyway, trying to get me to change my mind. She reminded me again that I was being silly as I didn't need a special invite. I told her I did not care; I wasn't going. But Richard wanted to go. Of course, he wanted to go. With Serena present, we got into a bit of a standoff about it.

"Well, if you won't go, then what if I went without you?" he asked, his voice containing a slight note of disdain.

"I'm not your mother, Richard. Do whatever the fuck you want."

And he did go, getting a ride with Serena. *Some lovely people they were going to hang out with*, I thought, *threatening me one day and then wanting to party like it never happened the next*. It wasn't just that I wanted no part of the drama of this crew. I also wasn't sure I totally believed Richard about the dealings being small time. The scene from *New Jack City* stayed in my mind, and

I couldn't shake it. What if this gathering was a set up? What if there were people we did not know sent there to beat the crap out of Richard, or worse? I would not be able to handle that. I sat alone in my apartment, smoking Marlboro Lights and devouring mint chocolate chip ice cream as my emotions went from being hurt, to being angry, to being scared, and then to beating myself up, feeling that if something was going to happen to him, I should love him enough to be there to try to prevent it.

Evidently, the party was not all they had hoped. They called me once, taking turns getting on the phone and saying it was no fun without me and that I should come meet them. They would give me directions. As if not knowing the party address was the reason I wasn't there. I refused and to prevent my mind from being changed, I got into my pajamas and took off my makeup. Richard called me again at 11. He said that the party was really boring, (translation no drugs to be had,) and that it was mostly teenagers. Jason's son was 18—what did they expect? At 18, he was closer to my age than Richard was, but somehow, I felt way more mature than this kid, being of legal age and all. Richard told me that Serena was spending most of the night driving kids around and buying beer for them at Greg's insistence.

They were leaving and moving the party to Piggy's, Richard told me. When Serena got back from the latest alcohol run, they were going to drive into town. Would I meet them at the dance bar in 20 minutes?

I felt as if I had won somehow. He missed me and wanted me to be with him, more than he wanted to be with this group. Yet, I felt like I could not completely cave.

"I don't want to meet you there," I said. "If it's so important to you that I go, then have Serena drop you off here and we'll go together."

I was just finishing my makeup for the second time that day when he came in. He kissed me long and hard and apologized for going to the party, for the drug business, and for all the crap of the past couple of weeks. Outside the bar, he took my hand, and we walked in together, past Greg, past Jason, and past Patty. We danced and kissed on the dance floor, oblivious to the dancers around us. Richard and I were not about any more drama that night. We were just about enjoying being together.

chapter 28
valentine

Clearly, Richard was not completely ready to commit to being drug free. But he agreed to keep it away from me and to use sparingly, just once in a while, and always in small doses. With us away from the cocaine lifestyle, I believed he would slowly get over it. We'd had an awesome Christmas, an even better New Year's, and managed to come through our dalliance with Greg's drug-filled world with our relationship intact. I had tried cocaine myself and found it lacking. With other things to keep him happy and busy, I believed Richard would eventually find coke lacking, too. I desperately clung to this belief.

With unemployment benefits still being our main source of income that February, we did not have much money with which to go out and have fun. But I held to the cliche that our feelings for each other would be enough. Valentine's Day was approaching, and I hoped for an evening built on the stuff of the sappy romantic novels I could not stand. I didn't expect much, only magic. I assumed that at the very least, we could recreate the excitement of our very first date, the one where Richard made me dinner and kissed me like I had never been kissed, and I was both thrilled and terrified. I did not need expensive things, but I loved holidays and I had high expectations for this one. This was a chance to redo our first Valentine's Day; the one that started with the emotion of our first date but ended badly. My parents had flipped about our relationship and I had been forced to walk away from the sweet evening Richard had planned.

I wasn't going anywhere now. I did not outright tell him all of these wishes, but I figured he would come up with them on his own. Between the coke and the threats of the last month, there was a part of me that felt Richard owed me a bit of extra tenderness, and I was eager to be spoiled with sentiment and passion. Of course, it did not turn out that way.

On the morning of February 14th, Richard kept flashing me his grin as if he had a big surprise. He told me he would cook us dinner that evening and I figured the night would just get better from there. I pictured him scoring some scallops, the gems of the sea, to recreate our first dinner and walking in that evening with a bottle of wine and maybe even flowers. He left early to go get some things at Tanya's. He had some minor engine repairs for a buddy lined up — under the table work that would not jeopardize his unemployment check. I did some errands and then spent a big part of the day at Laurie's. Laurie left Drew with me while she went shopping for her and Andy's Valentine's Day. I tried not to feel smug as I thought about how if they had a fun night, it would be because Laurie was doing all the work to make it so while Richard would be doing all the work for our night. I went home in the late afternoon to wait for him. We usually saw each other or talked by phone around five. Our phone calls occurred with Richard tracking me down at home or Laurie's by using the pay phone at the Bradford. He used that pay phone so much that his fellow barflies considered that section of the bar his personal office. That he often wrote notes or carved important numbers on the scarred wood surrounding the mounted wall phone further solidified the image.

Five came and passed and then six did, too. I considered going to look for him but decided no, that he should be the one coming to me, not the other way around. In reality, I did not want to leave the apartment in case I missed his call. I had thought I would be drinking wine by this point and was annoyed that I didn't have any to keep me company. I had smokes, though, plenty of them; my own and two packs of his brand. The cigarettes, a new lighter and a bottle of Southern Comfort were my lame Valentine gifts to him. I knew of better presents, but alcohol and smokes were the only things I could afford that he would appreciate.

It was almost quarter of eight when he walked in, sans flowers, food, or wine. He apologized for not calling and said that he had worked on his friend's car before going to Tanya's and then had fallen asleep. I believed him; Richard didn't lie to me. But I guessed that wasn't the whole story. He had probably left Tanya's and then stopped at the Bradford to call me on his way here. Once there, he likely found a friend with some coke and since Richard had a few bucks in his pocket from the car job, instead of surprises and dinner for me, he had done some to pass the early holiday evening. He did not deny it when I told him my theory.

"Come on, don't be mad. I know that was a screwup, but it's early and I still have plans for us for the evening. We just need to go to the store."

I so badly wanted to salvage the night. He was home and so what if it was later than I had hoped, and he was almost out of money? It was his plans and special attention that I wanted. And we were both hungry. I did my best to cast aside my initial disappointment and decided to just see what he had in mind. Once at the grocery store, he had enough cash left to buy the makings of a basic spaghetti dinner. It didn't matter that he called it a romantic Italian dish; I could have made pasta myself. Though the fishing had been sparse that winter, Richard had a lot of friends and it probably would not have taken much to find some scallops if he had put his mind to it. I used the little cash I had to pick up a bottle of cheap wine, my Valentine gift to myself.

Out in the frigid and near empty parking lot, we found a stray cart blown against my car. There was a grocery bag still in it. Richard opened it and pulled out two T-Bone steaks, baby potatoes, asparagus, a loaf of French bread and a pint of Haagen-Dazs chocolate ice cream. For a second, I thought he might have staged the left-behind bag as a surprise, but just as quickly realized that was not likely. I thought we should take the bag to the courtesy desk inside the store. Richard argued against it.

"Seriously, this is a gift, fate, even. Here's our fancy Valentine dinner and you want to put it back?"

"It's somebody else's Valentine dinner, Richard. They're going to come back for it and it must have cost them a lot. We can't keep it."

"Do you really think the store is going to save it for them? Stevie's on the courtesy desk. You know how cheap he is. We take it back in and he's just going to put everything back on the shelf, and these folks will still have to buy the stuff all over again. Come on, let me show you how sorry I am with a fancy, romantic dinner."

He talked me into it. It didn't feel right, but I knew the store manager and Richard's argument about him putting everything back on the shelves won me over. Back at home, he did the cooking and cleaned up while I chased a light buzz. Though the found groceries were delicious, the Valentine magic I hoped for had disappeared somewhere between 6 and 7:30 when I had not heard from him. As we ate the Haagen-Dazs, he apologized again.

"I really did have plans," he said. "The works—candles, music, the whole bit. I was thinking I would run a scented bath, put you in it and then give you an incredibly sexy massage. We could still do it now, you know."

By that point, it seemed silly. I told him I would take a rain check. I realized that I had to let those perfect moments come unexpectedly, like they had on our first date. Magic wasn't really magic to the one who planned the magic.

* * *

A week later, I was at Laurie's when Richard called from his "office" phone. He asked me if I wanted to go out to dinner. Of course I did! We had never done that before. We had done cheap take out but never had a meal at an actual restaurant. Richard had money when we first started dating, but we had to be careful about being seen in public together. Now we didn't have to worry about that, but neither of us had money. Richard must have gotten paid for some other job and was making plans to spend that money on me before he did something stupid with it.

I raced to the Bradford to meet him. He took my hand, and we walked down Commercial Street, passing the boarded-up businesses. There weren't many restaurants open this time of year and as we walked away from the bar, I tried to guess which one we were headed towards. But the restaurant was not quite what I expected. It was actually our Town Hall where the annual Year Rounder's Festival was taking place, complete with free food for all in attendance. Richard had heard about it as he went about town earlier in the day. The Year Rounder's festival was not something my friends and I had ever paid much attention to. It was a fairly new event and seemed to be created by folks who had come to town previous summers to work hard and play harder and then stayed. We townies called these folks 'washashores.' The festival gave them some fun in the off-season. Not surprisingly, we did not know many people there. Many of the locals we knew were hibernating in the cold or warming up with shots at the bar. But it was ok. We were both friendly. The people were a pleasant mix of young and old, gay and straight, artists and intellectuals, and the food was good. And it was free. I might have been disappointed at first, but the invite had been classic Richard. I pictured his teasing expression as he called to "invite me out to dinner." That playfulness was one of the things that attracted me to him. That date wasn't quite the romance I had hoped for the previous Friday, but it was fun and made a great story. And for a long, dreary winter, that was pretty good.

chapter 29
search

Sometime after Valentine's Day, Richard came up with a new plan. If he could keep the coke on hand, doing a little at a time, he could wean himself off it. He gave me his supply and asked me to keep it for him. His instructions were that in order for his plan to work, I needed to hide it well and only let him have a small amount each night. I had my doubts. But what did I know? I wanted to help him, but I was so far out of my element, I was willing to try anything. It had been a long time since Richard had a woman in his life who knew about his drug use but wasn't interested in doing any herself. Maybe, just maybe, this plan might be the answer.

The first night was great and I remember feeling like this way might work. Maybe we had finally figured out how to limit the role of this insidious powder in our lives. The next night was different. I gave him the little he asked for. The evening was mundane. For a while, we just played Scrabble and Rummy. Then he got anxious. He wanted a little more. I said no, reminding him of his own instructions. He let it go. An hour later, he asked again. Again, I said no. We argued. I refused to give him any more than he had allotted himself for the evening, any more than what he had already used. He grew angry. This didn't surprise me. I knew I was helping him to get off the stuff eventually so that we could move on with our lives. It would not be easy, but that was ok. It was what we needed to do, and we would do it together. Thirty minutes later, he asked me again, this time with an edge in his voice that I did not recognize.

"Richard, forget it—I'm not telling you where it is. I know it's not easy, but you just have to let it go."

"I just want a little bit; a little bit will help."

"If I get it out to give you a little, you'll know where it is and won't be able to stop. You were fine last night, and each night will get easier. Just chill for a bit, okay? Come on, watch TV with me. Or do you want to go out? Take a ride or go have a drink somewhere?"

"That sounds great, after you give some of my stash."

"If you want it, you find it. I'm done with this."

I sat on the couch and flipped through channels on the TV. Richard began the search.

The cocaine he had me hide for him the day before was wrapped in a plastic bag and was smaller than the palm of my hand. I pretended to be busy looking for something good to watch, but I was really just observing him, hoping he would give up when he couldn't find it.

Before my eyes, he changed into someone I had never met before. Even the few times I had watched him actually do coke looked nothing like the person he became as he hunted for his drugs. He seemed to develop this creepy, intense air about him, that of someone not totally with it, and yet in complete control at the same time. He started in a corner of the living room. Soundlessly, this stranger meticulously took apart the entertainment center, sliding VCR tapes out of their boxes and inspecting them. The frightening thing was that he would put each back into place when he was done checking it. There was no rush to his search, no violent pulling apart of this world we had created. That he was so focused and in control scared me more because it was this same control that was seeking what could be our downfall. He moved through the few books and magazines we had on the shelves around the TV, on hands and knees when necessary, lifting the carpet, sliding the TV over, whatever needed to be moved to make sure he didn't miss one inch of a possible hiding place.

He moved into the bathroom with the same painstakingly dark manner. I was afraid, but I was not sure of what. I did not feel threatened. I wasn't in danger. Yet, I didn't know who or what I was dealing with. In the bathroom, he lifted the top of the toilet tank and inspected every item in the medicine cabinet. In the cabinet under the sink he did the same, pulling out each bottle and looking it over, then putting it back. He came to my box of tampons. He sat on the floor and pulled out each one, ripping the paper each came in to make sure I had not opened one, put his coke in it and then tried to disguise the hiding place by folding the paper to look like it had never been opened. After being convinced there was nothing in each tampon, he folded the paper and put it back in the box. How long would this go on? When would he give up or forget about it, or decide to just wait the urge out?

I tried to make a joke to relieve the tension. "It doesn't melt if it gets near heat, does it?"

It's impossible to find a word to describe the look in his eyes when he spoke—not violent, not threatening, not angry, not amused, not annoyed, but severe; obsessively severe and dark.

"Of course it melts."

He left the bathroom and glanced at the wall heater lining the baseboard in the living room. He stepped away and went into the coat closet. From the top shelf, he removed the small tool kit that came with the apartment. He was going to take the heating unit apart as carefully as he had inspected each tampon. I had enough.

"Stop it," I whispered.

I had hidden the drugs in a dingy, scratched pan that was stored in the bottom of a cabinet filled with other pans and cooking utensils. Ironic, since it was Richard who did most of the cooking. But this particular pan was buried under several others in much better shape and so it seemed unlikely that he would come across it making one of our small meals. I knelt down in front of the cabinet and broke the uncomfortable silence as I purposely clanged pans around in the small space. Then I handed him the baggie and climbed the spiral stairs without saying a word. I wanted to get away from this person I no longer knew but felt it would be a bad idea to leave. If I left, he might leave too, and where would we be then?

I got into bed and stayed there all night without ever falling asleep. Within minutes of crawling under the covers, I heard him click his lighter; the pink lighter I had bought him for Valentine's Day as a gag gift—none of his bar buddies would steal his lighter if it was pink. I smelled the sickening burnt plastic smell of his makeshift soda bottle pipe and buried my head under the pillow.

I think Richard stayed awake all night, too. He never went out, and I did not hear him move around at all. He got high and sat on the sofa. Again I asked myself, what was the point? What could he possibly get from an insane search for coke, only to sit for hours in a spaced-out zone? I did not understand the obsession. On different floors of the tiny apartment, we were both aware of each other nearby, and wide awake.

When it started to get light out, I heard him get up, use the bathroom, and start up the stairs. I turned on my side and pretended to be asleep. He knew I wasn't. I waited to see what he would do. He lay down on the bed and tentatively came towards me. When I did not move away, he curled against my back and put his arm around me. Out of habit, I raised my head slightly, allowing him to put his left arm under and around me as well. We stayed like that for a long time, neither talking. In my head, I analyzed the night, over and over, as I had been doing for hours. Who was this person who had been in my apartment? It felt like it was Richard lying next to me now, my gentle Richard. The man I had loved since I was 17. The man I wanted to build a happy life with, even start a family with; first with Jesse and then with kids of our own. I could see it so clearly. But the events of the night before did not fit. I didn't know this creature who so deliberately tore apart our little piece of the world, looking for poison that could destroy us. That possessed person did not belong in the picture.

Richard did not move. He only held me. I had to be sure who it was lying next to me. I turned to him and kissed his neck. He held me tighter. I kissed his mouth, and he stroked my back. I kissed him harder, in a desperate search for him; trying to prove that I knew who he was—that this was no stranger holding me. I needed to get his body as close as possible to mine to make sure he was still my Richard. Less tentative, he kissed me back and soon we were moving together and it was all I wanted. It was Richard loving me, making love to me. The person I had seen the night before was gone, and I was with the man I loved so completely.

Afterwards, we lay together for a long time; not talking, often kissing, briefly sleeping. Eventually, we got up and went downstairs. Over our late morning caffeine ritual, I found my voice, the voice that he had given me to use to stand up for myself.

"I can't see you like that again."

"Ya, I know. Clearly, keeping it around and just doing it in small bits isn't the answer. And it's not fair to you. It's also not really a good idea to keep it in the house."

I did not bother to ask if he had any left. I knew he didn't.

"So what do we do?"

"Well, I went without it for a few weeks in December. Maybe I have to go back to giving it up altogether."

"Do you mean it?"

"Please, come here."

He wrapped me in his arms and smiled down at me. Not his playful, twinkly eyed, ear-to-ear grin, but a sincere, full-on smile.

"I love you," he whispered as he held me. "It will be ok."

Maybe that was it, the bad part. The rock bottom everyone talks about. It had to be. We could make it. We would make it. He had great plans, things he wanted to do with his life when he was done with the crap and it was out of his system. We both wanted it and we loved each other. That was all we needed....

chapter 30
betty

The last few days of February were quiet, which, in my world, meant things were great. My head filled with plans. We would see Jesse more. Spring would arrive soon and that would mean steady work and regular paychecks for both of us. I wasn't happy that with summer we would have to leave the adorable little apartment, but I had a plan to make that ok too. Richard still had his room at Tanya's and that would work for a couple of months. I would move back to my childhood bedroom, but just for the summer. We would not be able to live together for a short time, but we would date and save and, in the fall, we could get a more stable year-round apartment. My dreams were coming true.

And then the murderer Betty Broderick came into our lives, bringing with her the end of those dreams.

On a quiet night in early March, Richard and I were home, hanging out, and looking for something good on television. Part 1 of the Betty Broderick story was on. We cuddled under a blanket and watched it, both of us enjoying the movie. I found the story fascinating and was drawn to the details of the Broderick's life, the family drama within that life, and the crime. I wondered how seemingly normal people could suddenly become violent and so quickly spin out of control. What Richard seemed to appreciate was that the younger woman Dan Broderick leaves his wife for was named Linda Kolkena. He kept remarking how much the name sounded like cocaine and he giggled about it several times.

Part 1 ended with the enraged Betty driving her car into the new home of Dan and Linda, shattering the large bay window and half the living room wall. We were looking forward to watching Part 2 the next night.

The following morning, Richard left to help a friend with a small construction job. I was home. Serena called, hysterical. Greg had broken up with her. She didn't know what to do and could not sit still. She was thinking about taking off—just getting in her car and vanishing for good. We talked, and I thought I calmed her down; she sounded much better and encouraged. The phone rang a second time. It was my mom whispering from her job at the unemployment office.

"I can get in a lot of trouble for telling you this, but there's something you should know. Remember when Richard brought in that tax statement from the fishing job last year—the one he didn't file unemployment on because he thought he was getting paid under the table?"

"Yes."

"Well, we filed a claim just to see what would happen, and it turned out his salary was on the books. He won. He doesn't know it yet, but when he picks up his check in the mail today, it will be way more than he expected."

"How much more, Mom?"

"I can't tell you that."

"Hundreds?"

"Yes."

I thanked her and hung up. Receiving an unexpected windfall in his check would be a challenge for him. But he had been doing better these last couple of weeks and his commitment this time was strong. I tried not to worry. There was no way he could possibly blow that much money. Richard had a post office box and would check it when he finished helping his friend. I thought about trying to find him, but I had no idea where that friend lived. And I was not supposed to know this information. I could only stay home and wait for him to call when he was done with the job. I had to trust that he would call when he discovered the extra cash, before temptation overcame him.

The phone rang again. This time, it was Serena's grandmother. She told me that Serena was very upset, and she was really worried about her. They had just had a big fight. Could I do something? Could I come get her and try to talk to her?

It was still early in the day. Mail didn't get placed in boxes for at least another hour. I had time to see what was going on with my friend. I picked Serena up and brought her back to my place. Her grandmother was right. She was out of control, chomping at the bit and eager to do something dramatic to grab Greg's attention. She insisted on going for a ride. The walls were closing in on her, she said. She claimed she was going crazy and needed air. I felt what she was really getting at was that if we went for a ride, she might find Greg and beg him to change his mind.

"Serena, I can't. I'm waiting for Richard to call, and it's really important that I'm here when he does. Let's just chill and talk this out."

"If I don't get the fuck out of here, I will lose my mind. I swear I will."

Maybe it was better to get out and about. Perhaps I could find Richard even before he went to the post office and way before he considered anything crazy. Maybe I could even be with him when he went to check his mail. So we left my apartment and went on a long ride. I periodically made the post office and the Bradford part of our drive. Eventually, Serena calmed down. She seemed to be doing much better when I took her home less than two hours later.

Snow was predicted for the evening and cars couldn't be parked on my little street in case plows were needed. I left my car in the parking lot of a closed for the season restaurant a block away and walked home, hoping to find Richard already there.

There were two messages from him on the machine. One, his standard, silly, "HEL-lo." The other more serious, "alright, just trying to reach you. I'll try again in a bit."

I sat by the phone for hours, smoking cigarette after cigarette, waiting for him. When it got dark, I called Patty's house. She said she hadn't seen Richard.

I waited. Betty Broderick Part 2 came on. They replayed the driving through the front window scene. I smoked.

At 11, I called Patty's again. This time, I did not give up so easily.

"He and some guys took my car to New Bedford. They left a while ago," she eventually admitted.

New Bedford was where the drugs came from. My heart broke. I sat up all night, willing the phone to ring or to hear his key in the door. Neither came.

When it got light, I drank tea and smoked even more relentlessly than I had the night before. Then I dressed and went outside. It had snowed about four inches. The plows had not been by yet, but I could no longer just sit and wait. I walked to my car and drove the slippery roads to Patty's, skidding here and there along the way.

As I parked, I noticed for the first time that Patty's rental house also had a bay window. A rather shabby one compared to the wealth and elegance of the movie window, but a bay window just the same; this one dripping sharp icicles onto the yard below. Like Betty Broderick, I envisioned driving right through her house. I pictured the noise and the glass of that fucking window shattering all around the stoned losers inside. Why not? Why did I always have to be the "always in control, responsible" one? Fuck them! That would get their attention for sure.

But I would not drive my car through her house, remembering what Richard had said about Jesse falling asleep on the sofa, just inside the door.

It was barely seven. I got out and trudged through the snow up the walkway. I calmly knocked like the sane person I was. Jesse, in only his underwear, answered.

"Oh, it's you. Are we going to your house? Are we?"

He tried to step outside towards my car. Though not even four, he was a big kid, and he moved fast. His speed surprised me, and I could not lift him that quickly. I managed to grasp his naked shoulder before his right foot was completely covered in snow.

"Let's go inside, buddy. It's freezing out and you don't have your shoes and jacket."

He stepped back and let me in.

"Jesse, are your mom and dad here?"

"Mommy's here," he said, as Patty walked into the living room looking as haggard as I had ever seen her. She sat down and clung to her son. He squirmed and wriggled away, walking back to the sofa and cartoons on the TV.

"I'm sure you have a lot of questions, Yvonne. I want you to know that you can ask me anything and I'll be totally honest with you."

"All I need to know is where Richard is."

"Are you sure? I think you would have a lot to say to me, a lot to ask." There was no way I would trust anything she said to me. Richard had the answers I wanted, not her. It was between me and him.

"Where is he, Patty?"

"He said he was going to Tanya's."

Tanya's: neutral territory.

"Thank you for telling me."

I turned to say goodbye to Jesse but, used to being disappointed by the adults in his life, he would not look at me. My already broken heart cracked a little more.

Tanya answered the door in her bathrobe, with a cup of coffee in one hand. She nodded to me and cocked her head to the left.

"He's in the spare room."

I walked in without knocking and found Richard sitting on the edge of the bed. He was not surprised to see me and didn't ask how I knew where he was. He kept his head down as he stared at the floor.

"What happened?" I asked.

"I got some extra money and I couldn't handle it."

"Is there any left?"

"I owed the guy and couldn't get any more until I paid him back."

"Fucking hell, Richard."

"I know."

We both were quiet. Me, thinking of all the things I wanted to scream. Him, knowing there was nothing to say, nothing at all.

Finally, when I couldn't take the agonizing stillness any longer, I asked, "So, do you want to go back to being with Patty?"

He raised his head and finally looked at me.

"You know that's not what this is about."

I did.

"What happens now?" I asked.

"I don't know. I've been sitting here trying to figure that out."

Come on, Richard, I pleaded silently, *give me something, anything. Tell me you regret it. Tell me you would take it back if you could. Tell me it was a mistake and if you could go back, you wouldn't do it. Blame me even; tell me if I'd been home to get your call, I would have been able to talk you out of it. Give me something to let me know that there is still hope, a way around this.*

He said nothing.

He looked like hell and was clearly miserable. The past evening hadn't been about fun, or pleasure, or desire. Yet, he could not tell me he would do it any differently.

I waited.

"You can't expect me to hang around while you figure it out."

"No, I guess not."

More quiet, more nothing. The realization broke like a gut-wrenching strike, so debilitating, I actually shuddered with its force. This was my Richard. And this was how he would always be. He might have loved me and wanted to be with me, but the addiction would always come first. He would never be able to save money, never be able to walk away from the high. Even as he hated it, he would always run to it.

"Then I guess I need my key back."

He stood and pulled his sparse key ring from his pocket. There were few things in his life that warranted keys. Slowly he detached my apartment key from the ring, the key that could lead to a happy life, a future, and handed it to me. Then he held me. I hugged him back until I cried. Then I walked out.

And my already fragile heart completely shattered.

chapter 31
restroom

Sobbing, I drove home through the snowy streets. The plows had been out by then, and the sun was breaking through the cloudy sky. What had been a raw path of white less than an hour before was now turning into a dirty brown slush covered roadway. The ugliness of which matched my mood.

I wallowed in the depth of my sorrow for three days, not leaving my apartment and barely talking to anyone. My mind shifted constantly from the futility of it; why couldn't he let the drugs go? To blaming myself—if I had just been home to get his call? To guilt—maybe I walked away too easily? And back to the finality of despair. Whether these thoughts were relevant did not matter. The bottom line was this: I loved Richard, and he loved me. But the drugs completely controlled him, making him incapable of living a drug-free life. And no matter how much I tried, I couldn't make a life with cocaine work. We had no other choice but to go our separate ways.

I was not able to wallow for much longer than three days. Off-season or not, I had things to do. Lynn was getting married in less than two months, and as a bridesmaid, I had responsibilities. Serena kept calling to try to cheer me up and to talk about brides-maid stuff. What are you making for the shower? Did we confirm the stripper for the bachelorette party? Serena always recovered quicker than I did and after her initial freak-out over Greg, she was back to her normal self. I tried to keep up but was not doing so well.

When I finally left my apartment, the first thing I did was go visit Drew. I knew my adorable nephew would boost my spirits. My sister, however, was another story. She had heard about the break-up from Andy and was hardly sympathetic.

"Come on, you didn't really think this would work in the long run, did you? He's probably doing lines at Patty's as we speak. He just likes his drugs too much."

She might have been relieved and eager for me to date somebody different, but belittling the pain made it hurt even more than I thought possible. I had no energy to fight, and I did not want to scare Drew. I did my best to ignore her while I played with my nephew and then left as soon as I put him down for his afternoon nap. I had spoken to my mother on the phone during my exile and she was sympathetic. Funny how she had been so furious about Richard and me dating in high school, but now that she had gotten to know the side of Richard that I knew, she was sad for me.

The next thing I needed to do was to mail in my RSVP card for the wedding. I just hadn't gotten around to it yet and it was hardly necessary. I talked to Lynn all the time and could let her know if I was bringing a date or not. But it was a formal wedding and Lynn's mother was formal and so mailing in the RSVP was important. Writing the number one on the silly card brought another round of tears. Richard was supposed to be going with me. Of course, he wouldn't walk down the aisle with me; he only knew Lynn as my friend, and she paired me up with one of her brothers for the march into the church. But it was Richard who was supposed to drop me off at Lynn's home for the ride in the limo with the bride and the other bridesmaids. I had thought it would be Richard who would meet me at the church and then drive me to the reception when the 'just married' couple took over the limo. And it was Richard I wanted to be dancing and toasting with during the reception. Just another set of hopeful plans gone and there wasn't anything I could do about it. It would have been so much easier if I could be mad at him. But I could not work up any anger, at least not enough that would help me heal. The only emotion I seemed to feel was of overwhelming misery.

Serena encouraged me to go out again. It was not a bad idea. I had been hitting the local bars with and without Richard for a while at that point and always had a good time. I knew lots of people in my small town and being social might be good for me. So I agreed to go out with Serena one Friday night.

We walked into the Bradford and as much as I tried not to, my eyes scanned the bar for Richard. What would I have done if he were there? Tell him I wanted to try again? There had to be a way. But since there wasn't another way, it was probably good that he laid low for a while himself. Perhaps he did not know how he would react if he saw me.

We weren't in the bar long when Serena had to use the restroom and asked me to come with her so that she could fill me in on the guy who seemed to be checking her out. The bathroom in the Bradford was tiny, smelly and gross. There were two stalls when there was barely room for one. It was not an ideal place to hang out and have a conversation. While she went into a stall, I fiddled with my unruly hair in the mirror. The door opened, and Shelly came in, followed by Patty. When she saw me, Shelly gave me a vicious smirk. She was clearly looking for trouble, yet as far as I knew, I had done nothing to piss her off. But with the drama of the drug crowd, there didn't need to be a reason to screw with people. Shelly looked right at me and said, "Ha, it's you. What are you going to do now? There's two of us here who can kick your ass."

She had at least 50 pounds on me and I had only been in one physical fight my entire life. A fight that I was asking for when I was an obnoxious 11-year-old and a fight I had promptly run away from as soon as it began. But that was when I was a kid. And it was before Richard had taught me to stand up for myself.

Suddenly, the rage from all that had happened in the last few months overwhelmed me; the drug crap and the threats that came with it, not being with Richard because of it, not being home to get Richard's call before he ruined our lives, my sister being unsympathetic, all of it tore through me and before I knew it, I wanted to fight too. With Serena doing her best to finish up in the stall so she could back me up, Patty gasping at Shelly's threat, and Shelly trying to intimidate me with a "you're dead," expression, I stepped toward her. I got so close that her ugly face was only an inch from mine. With fury and a seriousness that surprised even me, I said, "Let's go."

Her cocky look vanished as she tried to step back, bumping into the sink behind her.

"Come on. Take your best shot, Shelly. Let's do this. Do you want to kick my ass here, or should we go outside?"

She seemed to stammer. Serena came out of the stall as Patty stepped in. "Nobody wants to fight you, Yvonne."

That was not enough for me. Now I wanted to kick some ass myself.

"Weren't you listening, Patty? Shelly just said she wants to kick my ass. So let's go. What's the matter, Shelly? You don't look so tough anymore. Are we gonna do this or not?"

Serena grabbed my arm and said, "Yvonne, enough," as there was banging on the door. Our friend Paul was the bouncer at the Bradford and knew the behind-the-scenes details of the bar patrons. He had seen Shelly and Patty follow us in and was prepared to burst into the ladies' room if he needed to.

"So that's it, we're not gonna do this?" I demanded.

Shelly said nothing, just looked at me, dumbfounded.

"You're pathetic," I said as I squeezed past her.

"You're alright kid," she called out.

With the door open to Paul's worried face, I looked back. "Just stay the fuck away from me, Shelly. You and I have nothing to do with each other."

It felt good. It felt 'down a couple of shots' good, which I did. They stayed in the bar and left me alone. I wondered if Patty and Richard were back together. Was Richard home with Jesse, waiting and hoping that Patty would come back with some coke from her night out? I wondered too if she would tell him about the scene in the restroom and if she did, would she tell him the truth about it? If she didn't, I decided, then I would definitely kick HER ass.

By the end of the night, Paul, who lived over the bar, announced that he was throwing an after-hours party. There would probably be coke there, but Paul knew I wouldn't do it. He didn't care and invited me, anyway. He trusted me. Shelly and Patty wanted to go to the party. They were not included. Shelly came up to me like we were best friends and asked to go with us. Serena was too into the new guy to be distracted by them, so it was my attention they sought. "You've got to be kidding me, right? It's not my party—get your own invite." Still, when Serena, her new love interest and I walked up the back stairs to Paul's apartment, they followed us like we were all best friends. At the door, Paul told them to get lost. Drugs or no drugs, I was their contact that night and it felt good to tell them to fuck off.

The natural high from my almost-fight in the bar bathroom stayed with me and I started going out more. Lynn's future husband, Michael, was a pretty good pool player and Wednesdays were tournament nights at the Bradford. It was on one of those nights that I met my own new guy, a washashore named Kevin, who had been in town for a couple of years. The good thing about being from a small town like Ptown is that it's somewhat safe to pick up somebody in the local dive bar. Kevin and I started talking and soon we were flirting. He bought me a drink and shortly after, I excused myself. On the way to the restroom, I stopped several times to get the scoop about Kevin from about five different people, including my always reliable bouncer friend Paul. Was he with anyone? Where did he come from? Was he violent? An a-hole? The final positive report came from Paul, who was like a wild, kind uncle to us and who gave Kevin a thumbs up. He was ok to date.

By the end of the night, Kevin had my phone number. He called me a couple of days later when I wasn't home and left his own number for me to call him back. I waited a day or two and then called from Laurie's one afternoon when I was babysitting Drew and he was napping. A woman answered the phone, and it was all I could do not to hang up. It was good that I didn't, as the woman turned out to be Kevin's sister-in-law. He did not have his own phone and had given me his brother's number. Eventually, we connected and scheduled a real date.

After about five dates or so, Kevin and I were at the VFW playing pool with some of his friends. His group of friends consisted of people I kind of knew, but not that well. After I scratched in one game, I headed to the restroom. One of his friends followed me in. Like Shelly, she was older, a lot bigger than me, and also had a reputation for being tough. But she did not follow me in to threaten me; she followed me in to sing Kevin's praises. I liked him and already knew he was a good guy. But if his friend wanted to fill me in some more, I was ok with that.

"I'm so happy to see you with him, and I can tell how much he likes you."

"Thank you, I like him too. I'm glad we met."

Then she took it too far. "I know you were seeing Richard. Kevin is so much better for you. Richard is a complete loser who…" I cut her off as my fury came back.

"Wait, are you freaking kidding me??? If you want to tell me how great your friend is, then fine. But you don't need to bash somebody I care about to do it. I don't need you to tell me what Richard is or isn't. If I'm with Kevin, then I'm not with Richard, and that's the only thing you need to know."

"I just thought you should know what Richard's like. A nice kid like you doesn't belong with a guy who's into all the things…."

"How the fuck do you know if I am a nice kid or not? Jesus, I don't even know you. It wouldn't be any of your business, anyway. And do you really think you're the only one who has warned me away from Richard? People way more important to me than you have also tried that, and it didn't work with them and it's sure as hell isn't going to work coming from you. Richard and I are not together and that is our business, but it doesn't mean that I want to listen to people talk shit about him. Now, if you don't mind, I came in here for a reason."

She left then, and I splashed water on my face and calmed down, realizing that this was the second fight I'd had in a bar restroom that had something to do with Richard. Thankfully, and thanks to him, I had held my own in both.

And at least this one was bigger and cleaner.

chapter 32
kevin

Despite the anguish of March, it turned out to be a pretty good spring. I continued to date Kevin, whom I really liked, even though he was very different from Richard. Where Richard had a Portuguese appearance, dark in skin, hair and eyes, Kevin was much lighter, with a paler complexion and light-brown hair. Where Richard was usually clean-shaven, Kevin had a mustache and a close-cropped beard. Another distinction between them was that while Richard was built, Kevin was not. In fact, he was almost scrawny, just my height and thinner than I was. I joked with Serena that both of his thighs put together would still be smaller than one of mine. It was a little unnerving for me to be larger than the guy I was dating. But, like Richard, Kevin had a good heart and a fun personality. And while he liked a joint or two, and a drink here and there, he wasn't into the hard drug scene.

He became my date for Lynn's wedding, sort of. They held the reception in the dining room next to a popular bar in the next town over from ours. Because you had to drive to Goody Halletts, I had not been there much. While only a few miles away from the places I usually frequented, it could seem a lot further when you were drinking. If you had too much, you couldn't just walk home, and it wasn't as easy to bum a ride from there as it was from the Ptown bars.

Originally, the side room had been a restaurant, but it did not do well. The new owners ran the bar and rented out the kitchen/dining part for private parties. Kevin was friendly with the owners, and with him, I hung out there a bit before Lynn got married. For the wedding itself, Kevin volunteered to be the bar-back, carting ice and cases of beer back and forth and washing glasses. That meant he could spend some of the evening with me, dancing and flirting here and there between his bar duties. And it was a fun wedding. It was good that he was my pseudo-date, as I allowed myself to get pretty drunk. My friends and I were into Grape Crushes at the time and I had quite a few. Kevin wound up driving me back to his place where I kind of remember jumping up and down on his bed in my blue satiny, puffy bridesmaid dress. I think I was lucky, or maybe Lynn was lucky, as I don't think the alcohol really hit me until the reception was ending. No one told me I did anything embarrassing, at least not until Kevin brought me to his place. And then he only told me about my behavior so he could enjoy teasing me about it.

The other huge thing that happened that spring was that I finally found my town job. The job that I was hoping for and had been a big part of my future plans with Richard, came to fruition, complete with a decent salary, benefits and even an employee union. It was working as a library assistant. It was only part time, which meant that I would still work at the gift shop in the summer, but the job was pretty perfect for me. I had always been a bookworm and so it fit nicely. The library was in an old sea captain's home that had been remodeled. There were three floors and while there was an elevator to fulfill the disability regulations, it was so slow that the staff hardly used it. Running up and down three flights constantly helped keep me somewhat in shape, as did walking to work. By the end of May, I was back in my childhood bedroom, which was only a few blocks from the library.

It was a great summer as well and it was interesting getting used to dating someone else, someone who was not Richard. I had dated one guy in college, but since it was in the city, it felt different from dating in my hometown. And since the only person I had ever seriously dated at home was Richard, this all seemed new, especially since Kevin and I could afford to go on real dates; out to dinner, to movies, even to a John Cougar Mellencamp concert once. Kevin's best friend, Beck, met us at the concert, making the evening even more entertaining. I had met Beck soon after meeting Kevin and every so often he would come to Ptown to hang-out. Beck was the epitome of the biker stereotype; super tall with long, thick, dark wavy hair held in place by a leather cap, lots of tattoos, boots, a leather vest and a wallet hanging by a chain from his belt. He was as tough as he looked. But he was also a sweetheart. As we were leaving the concert, enveloped by a mob, Beck stayed alongside us, guarding every step his short friend and his friend's short girlfriend took, jostling anyone who got too close to us. Beck was a trip. I wished I had someone I could fix him up with, but at that point, all of my townie friends were seeing other people.

The concert itself had been a blast, but the next morning found me in a particularly disconcerting situation. The venue was an hour-and-a-half away and since we met Beck there, I knew it must be somewhat close to Kevin's hometown. Since Kevin hadn't mentioned staying overnight, I just assumed we would come back afterwards and did not bother to pack a bag. But claiming fatigue and a slight buzz, Kevin found a cheap motel to crash in. I had no change of clothes, a hairbrush or a toothbrush. When you are 23, you worry less about that stuff and I was fine with roughing it. Driving back to the Cape the next morning, however, I was surprised when Kevin took an exit soon after we got on the highway. I thought maybe he needed coffee or a bathroom break. But instead of pulling into a gas station or a McDonald's, he drove us to a pleasant, modest home, where he pulled into the little driveway like he lived there. Apparently, he had. We were at his parents' house.

This was the morning he decided to introduce me to his parents? I was floored but had no time to protest. His mother saw the car through the front window and was already walking toward us while I was slightly freaking out. Responding to my gaped expression, Kevin said that it was not right to drive by his hometown without stopping. Maybe so, but a little warning might have helped.

His father was out, but meeting his mother was awkward enough. After introductions, she mentioned that there was something wrong with her bicycle, which caused Kevin to take it for a ride to check it out. A long ride it felt like to me. That left me sitting alone with her, trying to make small talk in wrinkled concert clothes and day-old, smudged make up. I was not having luck with boyfriends' moms, it seemed.

Or maybe it was the circumstances in which I was meeting these moms, as a very different experience of meeting a date's mom happened several weeks later. One sunny August afternoon, Travis came into the gift shop. He bought one of our most popular offerings, a small stuffed lobster that was bright red and right near the counter at the front of the store. (I never quite understood why tourists liked these red lobsters so much. If they were supposed to represent the real thing, or a toy version of a pet, they would be dark brown. Didn't people understand they were buying fake, already dead, cooked, and prepared lobsters?) But Travis was not a tourist. He had grown up in Provincetown just like I did, though he was a few years older and in my sister Audrey's class. As underclassmen did with the upperclassmen, I remembered him from the stories of awe I heard or witnessed. In Travis' case, it was his singing and acting talent that made him the star of the high school musicals when I would go to watch them but before I could participate. I knew him to be one of those who stuck around town after college, had a good job and wasn't much in the bar scene. Turns out, the purchase of the touristy lobster was a ruse. He had really come in to ask me out. I didn't know what to do. Travis was cute, and by all I knew, a nice guy. But I was seeing Kevin. Were we exclusive?

I gave Travis my number, but that night asked Kevin if we were seeing other people. To my surprise, he said of course we were, he already had been. I tried to hide my disappointment. When Travis called, I accepted his offer of a date. He immediately mentioned taking me to an expensive restaurant in Truro. I felt bad about this, as I was not sure how I felt about us going out at all and asked if we could go somewhere more casual.

On the assigned day of the date, Kevin stopped into the store to make our usual getting together after work plans, but I told him I was busy. Now it was his turn to be surprised, and I was pleased with myself. Travis picked me up and took me to a local fast-food restaurant, similar to the Dairy Queen. In fact, this restaurant had been the Dairy Queen when I was growing up. I didn't care. I knew the food was good, and I had asked for somewhere casual. What I didn't know was that Travis' mom and aunt both worked there, were on the clock and after meeting me and taking our order, smiled at us and waved whenever their shifts gave them a free minute. This mom seemed delighted I was out with her son. I'm sure she knew my family and roots, and I was much more together than I had been with Kevin's mother, but it was unlikely she knew my dating history. After my date with Travis, Kevin tried to find out where I had been and who I had been with. "So my boss said he saw you at Piggy's with a red head from out of town."

"That's weird, because I didn't go to Piggy's. And the only red head I go out with is Drew." There was no way I was telling Kevin where I had really gone.

In the end, my secret date made Kevin realize he did not want us to see other people, which I didn't really want either. And there were no sparks between Travis and me. I worried I had led him on by agreeing to the date in the first place, but Travis was fine when I explained the situation. His mother, though, she was the one who might have been disappointed.

When summer was over, I found a new winter rental. It was tiny and not as cute as the previous one, but it was cheap and wasn't at my mom's. It was on the bottom floor of a two-story building with a kitchen so small that the stove, refrigerator and sink were less than three feet from the wall facing them. Had I gained too much weight, I might not have been able to use them. Though they claimed it was a two-bedroom, the second room was more like a closet. It would be unlikely to fit even the smallest of beds. The main bedroom and living room were small, too. The biggest problem was in the bathroom where the toilet overflowed constantly. I had to keep calling the landlord to pump the septic system and he could not figure out what the problem was. It was months before he discovered that the elderly Portuguese couple who lived on the second floor were taking in laundry for extra income. This quickly filled the septic tank, and since I was below them, my plumbing was affected first. Despite these issues, the apartment was mine, and it was great to have my own place again, complete with a steady, year-round income.

Sometime that fall, Kevin had to leave his cottage as his landlords were selling the property. It just fit for him to move in with me. And I was glad. I loved being part of a couple, even if the apartment was not adequate for two people. It became even more crowded when two turned into three. On one of Beck's visits, he wound up getting some construction work alongside Kevin with the contractor Kevin worked for. Soon, Beck was offered a regular job, and he took it. He moved in with us. As tall as he was, he had to sleep on the floor with his head and torso laying through the doorway of the spare room and the bottom part of his body in the living room. During the night, his arm would dislodge the door stop and he would wake up banging his body against the bedroom door. Despite the ungainliness of the arrangement, I thought it was a lark being in a reverse set-up of the old TV sitcom "Three's Company."

One Friday night, we all went out and had too much to drink. I had a short shift at the library the next morning, 10-12 only, but, completely hungover, I was not eager to go. I went though, leaving

Kevin asleep in bed and climbing over Beck's comatose body as I got ready for work. They slept through the morning and were only just getting up when I got home. Minutes after I came in, a friend of theirs stopped by and asked why they hadn't answered the door when he had come by earlier.

"Man, I like knocked and even banged on the door a lot. I could see Beck's legs. Thought he might have croaked. How come you assholes didn't answer?" their friend asked.

"Ya Beck, what's up with that? I heard somebody banging on the door. Why the hell didn't you answer it?" Kevin asked groggily.

"Ya right, Kev," Beck replied. "Someone's banging at the door first thing in the morning and I'm going to get up with my bloodshot eyes and my whiskey breath and see Yvonne's daddy, the cop, standing there with his service revolver drawn. I don't think so, man. You want to live dangerously, you can. But me, I'm playing it safe."

Beck was not that far off. My parents were not thrilled with the living arrangement, but what could they do? I received the most pressure from another family member. Laurie and Drew were giving my grandmother a ride to the grocery store. They passed a construction site where Beck was stacking shingles. Laurie and Beck waved to each other. Beck definitely did not look like the boy next door. He looked like the boy who knifed the boy next door. My grandmother asked who the scary guy was.

"Oh, that's Beck. He lives with Yvonne," Laurie told her.

My poor grandmother gasped in shock. Laurie realized her mistake. She tried to correct it.

"Oh, no, it's not like that. Yvonne's boyfriend, Kevin, lives there too."

It was a miracle my proper grandmother didn't faint on the spot, only to be given mouth-to-mouth by scary Beck. I usually tried to visit her regularly, but after learning about that conversation, I purposely waited several weeks before I stopped by. And as soon as I walked in, she started, "Now, Yvonne, I know I'm old-fashioned, but girls get a reputation for a reason...."

Ironically, I spent part of that Christmas not with Kevin and Beck but with Richard, though it was a much different holiday from the one we shared the previous year. Kevin drove home with Beck to spend the holiday with their families and it didn't even occur to us to consider spending it together. I did not want to be away from Drew or my dad's kids and was so into the season that I didn't even think I might miss Kevin the short time he was gone.

The festivities were mostly still at my mom's, but this year Laurie wanted to make the dinner. My mom and I stayed downstairs playing with Drew and his new toys until it was time to head upstairs. We found Laurie and Andy having a heated discussion. Andy had invited Richard for dinner, as he had nowhere else to go. Laurie worried that would be tense for me or that I would do something stupid like leave Kevin for him or make a fool out of myself. I resented her worries. She still did not trust me and Richard together. Hadn't we proven that we were capable adults and had never actually been the caricature she thought of us as; the innocent, virginal teenager, and the seductive older man wanting to take advantage of her? I told her to relax. I had nothing but good feelings for Richard and if he had nowhere else to be, then he should be with friends. That was what Christmas was all about.

I had no sooner said that when we heard him open the outside door. My mom was still fond of Richard, still fonder of him than she was of Andy, and she welcomed him into Laurie's kitchen. I think we hugged and then I went to stay by Drew's side under the guise of keeping him busy while Laurie finished prepping the meal. I asked about Jesse, of course, how could I not ask about Jesse? From however Richard answered the question, it was clear that Patty and Jesse were with her family. What was unclear was whether Patty and Richard were a couple again. I should not have cared, but I did. I never would have admitted this to Laurie and Andy but having him there was tough. He looked great with a stylish new haircut that further emphasized his handsome face. Richard was attractive all the time, but I was so used to seeing his hair long, the short cut threw me a bit. He was also wearing a nice sweater that showed off his dark coloring.

What was hardest that afternoon was remembering that the holiday before he had been with us at my invitation, not Andy's. That was the day he won my mom over and we woke up that morning together and fell asleep Christmas night in each other's arms. On such a special day, my emotions were in overdrive. Apparently his must have been too as outside of pleasantries, we barely talked. Buried in our memories, and too weak to look at each other for too long, we did our best to act like all of this was normal, like we both did not still care desperately for each other. I would never have cheated on Kevin; I was not that kind of person. And Richard and I had split for a reason; a reason I had not forgotten. But going back to my cramped apartment alone on a day designed specifically for being with those you love was difficult, especially since I knew no matter what was going on with him relationship wise, Richard was going home alone somewhere too.

He left soon after dinner and we shared a quick goodbye hug. Back at my tiny apartment later that night, I grew melancholy about the day and felt lonely. It occurred to me I had not talked to Kevin. I called him, and we wished each other a Merry Christmas, but it was not the conversation you would expect of a couple in love, separated for the holiday. Were we in love? I had never really thought about it before.

When he and Beck returned, we went back to our casual, happy lives, partying a bit, working, and just being young and carefree.

One gray Sunday afternoon, we all went to play pool against my wishes. I had made lasagna for dinner and thought we would spend the chilly day at home, watching TV or playing games with or without Beck, who often took off for hours to give us some privacy. But when they insisted on pool, I went along with it. I put the unbaked pan in the fridge and made them promise we would only be out for a couple of hours. But at the VFW, we bumped into a lot of people we knew, and we all drank way too much. At 5, I was clearly smashed but remembered the lasagna. Serena was at the bar and I nagged her into giving me a ride home so I could finish it. Before I left, I told Kevin and Beck to be home within the hour for dinner. Against Serena's better judgement, I put the lasagna in the oven and then sat down, promising her I was fine. She went back to the VFW but, worried, returned an hour later where she found me completely passed out in bed and the cheese blackening in the oven, the whole thing smoking. She took it out and turned the oven off. I woke up hours later to the sounds of the guys stumbling in. They had dived into the cold, burnt dish, with the pan on the coffee table between them and each holding a fork. I went back to bed. But despite the next morning's nausea as I headed to work swallowing aspirins, it had been a lovely Sunday.

They liked to tease me about being a librarian and often called me a goody-two-shoes and other terms that were basically affectionate ways to call me a sweet geek. I surprised them one night when we saw the movie trailer for *An Indecent Proposal*.

"You wouldn't do that, would you, Yvonne? If you were the one in Demi Moore's shoes, sleep with a rich dude for money?" Beck asked.

In front of Kevin, I said. "Are you kidding me? Of course I would."

"What??" Beck seemed surprised.

"Beck, it's one night. It's Robert Redford, for god sakes, and it's a million bucks. That's a no brainer! I can't believe they even had to make a movie about it!"

Kevin leaned over and kissed me. "A million bucks, that's my girl...." he said.

Kevin could get jealous, but it always manifested itself in a silly, harmless way; mocking me lighting a guy's cigarette in the bar, back when we could smoke in bars, or noting me greeting an old friend at a party.

In a high-pitched, girly voice, he mimicked me, "Hi Kenny, how are you?"

"What else was I supposed to say to a guy I haven't seen since high school?" I asked, smiling to myself. I'm sure it didn't help that Kenny was very cute and had rushed over to give me a platonic hug, but I found Kevin's jealousy amusing and adorable.

He embarrassed himself with it one morning, however. As the new guy, Beck often got fewer hours than the rest of the construction crew. Kevin was due in at 8 and Beck was told to hang out until he was called to go in. I was due at the library at 9. When Kevin left, Beck and I were drinking coffee and tea respectively while watching the morning news. About 20 minutes after he left, Kevin was suddenly in the living room with us. As quietly as he could, he had slipped back into the tiny apartment, as if wanting to surprise us. He did. He surprised us as we were watching TV, neither of us having moved much since he had left.

"What's going on?" I asked him. "Is everything ok?"

I didn't immediately understand what he was doing back from work until that moment when his face turned red and he claimed he had forgotten something. He grabbed a lighter off the coffee table and put it in his pocket with his other lighters and hurried out the door. Beck looked at me and shook his head. Clearly, Kevin was concerned that he might find something else going on when he came home suddenly. He did not need to worry. Beck and I liked each other a lot, but in a big brother/little sister kind of way. That Kevin felt the need to check on us gave me a false sense of appreciation. He must really care about me if he needed to make sure that his friend and I were not fooling around behind his back. But this was a lesson that I needed to learn—jealousy and affection had little to do with each other, as it turned out.

Eventually Beck found his own place and soon after, Kevin broke up with me and started dating someone else. I was never sure why and was pretty miserable and confused. How could he be worried about me being with other men and then dump me for another woman? At least Richard and I had a reason why we couldn't make our relationship work. This breakup was outright rejection, and it hurt in a whole new way. Plus, it shook my confidence. The girl Kevin dumped me for was not that attractive, but she was very thin. Was that the reason he stopped wanting to be with me?

I got over it, though. And once I did, what I really missed was my friendship with Beck. I wished I could keep that, but he had moved back to their hometown and it would have been strange to stay in touch. I saw him a few years later in the Bradford. He was down for a visit and had come to the bar without Kevin. We talked a lot that night and met some people who commented on what a great couple we must have made. I was quick to correct them.

"Oh no, Beck and I didn't date. We just lived together."

Beck put his arm around me. "And we did a hell of a good job with it, didn't we, Yvonne?"

Yes, we had.

chapter 33
wild

The summer after Kevin broke up with me began a wild two years.
I was at my mom's house again for the tourist season and was
working both my library job and my seasonal gift shop job. I was
24, single and sleep mattered little. I enjoyed myself during the
brief times when I was not working. I was still responsible enough
to not allow my partying to get out of line and thus emerged from
this time period with my reputation intact but with many fun
memories. The insecure girl I used to be took the most pride in
two events I could never have imagined when I was a teenager.
The highlights of that time were the summer night a guy with a
Mercedes and a guy with a Harley fought over me, and the day
the following summer when one handsome fisherman brought me
haddock and another handsome fisherman brought me scallops.

Adding to the happiness of that season was the fact that
Heather and her children were finally free of Sean. She was dating
a new guy she was excited about and was trying hard to make this
relationship work. One night when her new beau was out of town
and her kids were spending the night with her grandparents, I convinced her to come out with me. Though she was tired from her
own two jobs and relished the quiet of a night home alone, she
also hadn't had a night out in years. It took a bit of cajoling on
my part, but after her waitressing shift, she met me at the Bradford. There we started talking to a bunch of bikers wearing leather
jackets that said they were from Sin City Cycles in Lynn, MA. I

had heard the phrase *Lynn, Lynn, City of Sin*. There were about 15 of them, a few with wives or girlfriends, but most of them were alone. Later, I mentioned Sin City Cycles to Smitty, a family friend from the Boston area who was a biker himself.

"They aren't really a gang," I told him.

"Darlin', anytime you got more than four guys with Harleys together, it's a gang!" he replied.

One biker was a guy about my age named Lance, who I danced with and who bought me drinks. I wasn't flirting as much as I was enjoying myself and enjoying talking to someone new. Also at the bar that night was a local guy, slightly younger, who had bought me drinks on previous occasions. He was handsome but in a too obvious, so obvious he was full of himself, kind of way. He drove a silver Mercedes and I guess that was kind of a big deal, but it did not mean that much to me. I should have favored him as he was a local, but he was so conceited that I had little interest. He reminded my friends and me of the Gerardo song, *Rico Suave*, and so that's what we took to calling him. We were not being mean exactly; we would call him that to his face. He did not seem to mind. He thought he *was* Rico Suave and took it as a compliment. That was why he was confused and annoyed when I was accepting drinks from Lance, the biker, instead of him. At one point, he even tried to interrupt us, and Lance may or may not have told him off. The drinks that night contributed to spotty memories, but I knew they were vying for my attention and I was beyond delighted.

Heather was enjoying herself too, mostly with karaoke and making sure I did nothing dumb. She was friendly with the biker crew, but cautiously so. She did not want to do anything that would jeopardize her new relationship. When the bikers asked us back to their motel for an after-hours party, I was ready to extend the evening. After much persuasion, she agreed to go with me and be my chaperone.

Their motel was a crappy, poorly maintained building that I liked to call the ugly stepsister of the Holiday Inn next door. Both businesses had the same owner, but one was kept up and the other was not. My new friends were in the latter. What was great about the place was that while it was cheap, it shared the same gorgeous view that its sister business did and that was one of the best views in town.

As Heather and I drove into the parking lot, we could see the crew outside their rooms playing music, eating, drinking, and smoking. But as Heather pulled closer to their area, every one of them ran into their rooms, slammed their doors, and shut out the lights. We couldn't believe it. Earlier, they had been friendly and had really seemed to want us to come. What was the instant scattering about? We probably should have just left, but instead we sat in her car wondering what to do next. As we tried to figure out what we did to make them flee, little by little lights came on and one by one they slowly came outside. It turned out the problem was one we hadn't even remotely considered. Heather's car was a dark blue Crown Victoria that she had bought dirt cheap at a police auction. The group recognized it immediately as a cop car and wanted no part of a police visit. As they peeked from behind the dirty curtains, they realized it wasn't the cops but the two girls they had invited and started to relax.

Gang or not, they were nice people, and it was a fun party. One biker told me he was their leader and had the best bike. He wanted a picture of me on his vintage Harley, which I happily agreed to. Smitty told me that there were now probably nude bike pictures of me hanging up in every bike shop in New England.

"That's ridiculous, Smitty. I was completely dressed!"

"Don't matter, darlin', they probably altered the picture to put your head onto some naked girl's body."

Rico Suave showed up as somehow, he had gotten an invitation, too. He did not stay long though, as this was not his crowd, and it was obvious that I was really into Lance. Rico jumped into his Mercedes and left in a bit of a huff. After a while Heather needed to go and I told her I would be ok. Lance promised her he would make sure I got home safely and there was a safe feeling coming from this crew. I wound up hooking up with Lance that night. Any guilt I may have felt over my one-night stand was erased by the way he took me home. An hour before dawn. I rode on the back of his bike as he sped and did wheelies down the deserted streets of my hometown. As dangerous as it was, I loved it.

I did not get to say goodbye to them before they left late the next morning, but Heather did, sort of. As they were riding out of town, they saw Heather's car at a stop sign where she was safely waiting for them to pass. Her boyfriend had just gotten home, and they were off to grab breakfast before picking up her kids. When the Sin City Cycles crew realized it was her, they laid on their horns, yelling and waving. A whole biker gang greeted her while she sat in her car next to the new beau and pretended that she had no idea why they were being so friendly.

Lance said they would be back later in the summer. They did come back, but this time when I saw him, he admitted he was having problems with an ex and there seemed to be a lot of drama in his life. The fun of the night we met was no longer there, but I was still thrilled with the memories.

Meanwhile, Richard and I circled each other in the dive bar scene. The latest gossip suggested that he was back with Patty, but that they were anything but happy. Once or twice, they would both be out, but often one would be stationed at the bar while the other worked the room, looking for whatever narcotics might be available. More often than not, being female and blonde, Patty would be out without him, having more luck finding cheap coke. After the scene in the bathroom the previous year, Patty and I politely nodded to each other, and we did not have any issues. I wondered about Jesse and though she was his mother, I refused to ask her. It just seemed like a weird sort of betrayal, although I was not sure who I would be betraying. Richard? Jesse? Myself? With or without Patty, when I saw Richard, we would always hug and say hello. Often while he was hugging me, he would look over my

shoulder just slightly, not for someone who might see us and report back to Patty, but to make sure he did not miss the arrival of
any possible drug connections. Despite all that we had been
through, every time I saw him my heart still fluttered, just as it
had done when I was 17 and was a shy, awkward girl with a
wicked crush. What I did not realize was that I had already started
a precedent. In the years that followed, whenever I went out, whoever I may have been dating or hoping to date, I always looked
around for Richard. It was not so much to be with him or to try
again, but to check in, to see how he was and to appreciate that
little rush that filled my heart whenever I was near him.

* * *

That fall I found an adorable cottage to rent that was near a beach,
affordable and actually year-round! No more moving home to my
childhood bedroom every May. It was a tiny, furnished, free-
standing one-bedroom unit that was filled with natural light. It
was not directly on the beach, but I could see the bay from the
sliding glass doors that were the entrance. The cottage was next
to a building that housed three separate apartments side by side.
The unit furthest away from mine housed a single mother with
kids ages 10 and 4. Next to her was a man I never got to know
but who I was told was very nice but kept to himself as he was
dying of AIDS and not up to making friends, a devastating scenario that continued to be far too common in Provincetown in
1993. The apartment closest to me shared my driveway and stayed
empty until about November, when two good-looking young guys
moved in. They were not locals. My first thought was that they
must be gay, but quickly I changed my mind about that. They just
didn't have the gay vibe. But no one in their twenties moved to
town just before the winter, to go fishing, no less. It made no

sense. That led me to believe that they must be narcs. What else could explain their sudden arrival in the off-season?

When the gift shop job ended for the winter, I picked up a new part-time town job as an assistant to the town's recreation director. That just meant that I worked in the library in the morning and in the late afternoon opened up the rec center for the various community clubs who used it and the teens who had nowhere else to hang out. When I went out on weekends or on the occasional pool tournament night during the week, I did not see these two guys much. If they were narcs, how come they were not out trying to bust people like Richard? I considered warning him about them and I think I did, but I must have also told him I had no idea what was up with these two good-looking guys. One of them was clean cut and so I, of course, thought the other one was cuter. With longish, wavy brown hair and a pleasant smile, it was hard not to notice when he came and went. When the weather warmed up in the spring, my neighbors and I had more of a chance to introduce ourselves. Their names were Colin and Tony, (Colin was the cute, slightly wilder one) and they had visited town with their families for years and decided that they wanted to move here and try their hand at fishing. Since several months had gone by with no major arrests made, I decided they must not be narcs after all. If they were, they were the worst narcs ever. I was interested. But I was clueless about what to do about it.

One night, I went out with friends and saw Richard. By then I had heard that he was no longer with Patty and was either still keeping a room at Tanya's or was bouncing from one friend's sofa to another's. He bought me a drink and then another and then a shot and we sat and talked and slowly got drunker and drunker. I was too drunk to drive and, always trusting him, my friends left knowing that he would make sure I got home ok. Richard was always the better driver, even with alcohol in his system, and he had a much higher tolerance than I did. He took my car keys and drove me home. My little cottage was not within walking distance of any of his friend's and even if it was, it was terribly late for him to knock on one of their doors. He spent the night.

I was a mix of emotions. This was my Richard and everything we did, every move we made, felt so familiar. Yet, none of the bad had changed, and was not going to change, which made this hook up kind of sleazy. But how could it be seedy when I was with my Richard? The feelings weren't anymore settled the next morning as both of us were happy to wake up together, but also aware that this was not likely to mean anything in our lives. It had been a brief visit to the old, not another start to the new.

I had to work, and he had to see a captain about a site on a boat leaving that afternoon for a three-day scalloping trip. As I was driving us into town at 8 that morning, I had to stop for a construction detail. To my horror, I could see that my dad was the officer directing the traffic around the work zone. My dad almost always worked nights, so I did not expect this and there was no way around it; we were already in the line of cars waiting to pass. What could I do? When he signaled for the traffic to move, I waved. My dad nodded in response, but it was clear from his face that he realized that Richard and I coming from the direction of my rental, that early in the morning, could only mean that he had spent the night. Is it a one-night stand if you hook up with some-one you have loved for years and who you used to live with?

Richard thought seeing my dad was a riot and could not stop laughing once we passed him.

"It's not funny," I shouted.

"Yes, it is. It definitely is!"

My mischievous Richard. He left me a message later that af-ternoon that he had gotten the job and would be at sea for a couple of days. I noted the fact that meant he could not get coke while he was on the trip. He could bring some with him, I supposed, but since he could not parse it out, if he had any to bring, he would likely have done it before the boat left the pier. Could that be a decent start to a new future?

* * *

Several days later, I came home from the library to find a bag of fresh scallops packed with ice on my doorstep. No note was needed. They were my favorite, and I knew they came from Richard. He was back from his trip and was reaching out. This was not an easy gift for him to leave. My cottage was pretty far out of town, even for the Richard who did not have his act together enough to own a car and so was used to walking everywhere. Maybe he borrowed a car or got a lift from a friend. I was pondering that when there was a knock on my door. I looked up and there was my cute neighbor, Colin, holding a bag of freshly caught haddock. Apparently, he wanted to be friends, maybe more than friends. I was delighted, but oblivious. I thanked him profusely and took the gift. Then I called my mom and Laurie and invited them over for a seafood feast. I had to tell Drew, who was now 4, that the fish wasn't fish but "special chicken" to get him to eat it, but he still refused.

My friends wanted to know why I hadn't immediately invited Colin over for dinner. Isn't that what you're supposed to do when someone you're interested in brings you an edible gift? But I just froze and did not think of that. Why did I not go looking for Richard and invite him for dinner, maybe a dinner just like the one he had made me on our first date? When it came to Colin, I think the reason I did not share the fish with him was because, even though I was interested, it did not seem likely that I would be lucky enough for him to like me back. It seemed safer to assume that he was just being sociable. As for Richard, I just did not know what to do. How wonderful it would be if we could try again. But how unlikely was the success of that scenario? In his case, it just seemed safer for my heart to share his gift with my family rather than with him.

Perhaps I could have done something more romantic with those gifts than feed my family, who I saw all the time. Still, I was pretty ecstatic. Two handsome fishermen had shown up at my door bearing fresh gifts from the sea on the same day — a scenario only a Cape Cod girl could truly appreciate.

chapter 34
neighbors

Colin and I wound up dating, although it took a couple of attempts on his part, and some embarrassing moments on mine, to get there. In Provincetown, the last Sunday in June was always dedicated to the Blessing of the Fishing Fleet. The local bishop would come to town, and after Mass he would bless each vibrantly decorated boat from a staging area at the end of the pier as they sailed past him in a glorious procession. After the working boats were blessed, smaller boats came next and then all settled in the harbor for a long afternoon party. Each boat held a mix of captains, crews, family, friends, and even strangers. Everyone was always welcome.

That year, the day fell on a gorgeous blue Sunday, just perfect for the event. Lynn's husband, Michael, took his speedboat out and Serena, our friend Bob and I, hopped aboard. Though I had been in their wedding, I didn't know Michael that well. He seemed like a great guy, but reserved. He was usually quiet and did not say much around us. After watching the procession from the water, Michael steered his speedboat around to the fishing vessels so we could say hello to the many people we knew on the many boats we were familiar with. I kept an eye out for Richard among the people celebrating on the water but did not see him.

Mostly, I spent the ride yammering on to my girlfriends about my cute neighbors and how the cutest one had brought me fish and how he was so awesome, but I was too wimpy to talk to him.

In the distance, I saw the boat Colin fished on and I told my friends about it. Michael steered towards it leading me to believe he must know the captain. I wanted to hide. I did not want Colin to know I knew which boat he was on, and I certainly did not want him to see me in a bathing suit. I guess Michael had been listening to me whine about Colin. As he got closer to the boat, he shouted out, "Hey, Cute Neighbors!" I was horrified! All the time I hung out with him he hardly said a word and now he shouted this?

"Lynn, what is he doing??? Make him stop!"

But she didn't. Instead, goaded on by Serena who had also yelled "Hey, Cute Neighbors" too, she and Bob joined them. There were four people in a little boat, motoring around a larger one shouting "Hey, Cute Neighbors!" while the fifth person on the boat did her best to crouch down under the wheel and cover herself by pulling the beer cooler in front of her. Ideally, I wanted to jump off the boat and swim away. But that would mean standing up and showing my full bathing suited body for the two seconds it took me to get into the water. It would not be a bad swim. The bay was so calm we had already seen a local fisherman swim from one boat over 100 yards to another, all while holding his open beer in his left hand, back stroking with his right and slowing to sip here and there along the way. We locals had talent for sure. But I knew that if the currents did not allow me to swim back to the pier, it would be an even scarier sight watching Michael and Bob trying to haul me back aboard. So I did my best to disappear until Michael got bored and headed toward our final destination, Long Point, the place for most of the smaller boat parties that day.

Back at home, I hid due to complete humiliation, doing everything in my power not to run into Colin in our mutual driveway. When the Fourth of July approached, I had a party. During the parade that morning, I told everyone I could find, and to my surprise, many showed up right after the parade. A lot of the friends I had told were in the volunteer fire department and after they had parked their fire trucks, they were ready to hang out. Problem was, though it was fun, they drank all the beer I had bought for the party I meant to actually have after the fireworks. They promised to come back and restock my supply, but once they met up with their families, they didn't. After the fireworks, my close friends came over and we blasted music, but the only alcohol we had was a bag of wine I bought because it was the new thing and I thought the funky concept was amusing. When that ran out, we found ourselves stuck with a sticky sweet cranberry liqueur my friend Shannon had made for the past Christmas. At some point, Colin and Tony came home, heard the music, and drifted over. They had a few beers in their fridge, which was a slight relief to our party predicament. Eventually, filled with bagged wine and a disgusting liqueur buzz, I drifted outside to set off sparklers. Colin followed me, and I thought he was just being nice and helpful, providing a lighter and taking the sparklers out of my hand.

After the party wound down but before she left, Serena said, "Of course he likes you, dumbass! He was the only one who went outside with you to make sure you didn't light yourself on fire."

I was still not convinced. So I was surprised when Colin and Tony showed up at the gift shop a couple of nights later and asked if I wanted to meet them for a drink at Euro. Euro wasn't a bar my friends and I normally went to as it was seasonal and usually filled with more visitors than townies. And I had plans to meet Serena and Lynn at the Bradford after work. But how could I resist a direct invitation? Was it possible Serena was right? I rushed to the Euro and had a drink with my neighbors, planning to go find my friends afterwards. But it was not long before Tony made himself scarce and it was just Colin and me drinking, dancing, and talking. I blew off my friends and knew that when I explained the next day, they would understand. But it didn't take that long to fill them in.

As last call passed, and all the town bars - gay, straight, local beer and shot regulars and tourists (frozen drinks galore) - emptied onto Commercial Street, Serena and Lynn found me on the meet rack with Colin. They had Bob, and another friend named Jeff with them. I tried to explain why I had not met them, and they pretended to be angry. Lynn said Michael was home, hadn't wanted to come out but was up for an after-hour's party. Did Colin and I want to go? I didn't. I wanted to keep being alone with him and so I was vague in my response. They understood, but only slightly. They had to exact revenge for my disappearing act before they would forgive me completely.

Colin and I made our way home, and he came into my cottage with me. We were making out on my sofa when my phone rang. It was my friends asking where I was. They could tell by the way I answered I was not alone, and they wondered among themselves why I had even answered the phone at 2 in the morning. They called again to ask me that very question. And again, I answered. They could not believe it. *What the hell was wrong with me? Why did I pick up a second time?*

Bob wanted a turn and so he called me next. When I answered, I heard them cracking up in the background. I told them to fuck off. Colin mentioned they were messing with me and I should stop answering, but, feeling guilty for ditching them earlier, I felt I should just keep picking up the phone. Michael called next and then it was Jeff's turn and each time they called, I answered. Colin shook his head and my friends cracked up.

Eventually they grew bored, and Colin and I grew tired and I fell asleep. He stayed until morning, even though nothing hap-pened between us besides kissing. When I later asked him why he didn't leave, he said he couldn't because he did not have a key to lock my door behind him and rationalized that it was a bad idea to leave me alone with the door unlocked. I thought that was sweet and finally, finally accepted that he was interested. We dated throughout that summer and late into autumn. He broke up with me at some point, another breakup I struggled with for a long time, and eventually, my cute neighbors returned to their own hometown.

While I was developing a complex about being dumped yet again, I also had a distraction. The local women's shelter was offering a three-day seminar to train new volunteers. Although I was working three jobs, the season was winding down and I would soon be down to just the library and the recreation department. I would have time on my hands, and I thought this type of volunteer work might be interesting. I signed up and when I arrived at the fire station multipurpose room where the seminar was held, I was surprised to see my dad and his fellow police officers there too. They were not happy. Their chief had mandated the training, and they were a little resentful. It was quite the dynamic-grouchy officers on one side of the room with eager, potential volunteers like me on the other. The interaction between my dad and me caused some comic relief for the group, welcome during an emotional training on the tense subject of domestic violence. In one exercise designed to show us how an abusive person can strip away their partner's identity, we were asked to discuss our names and what they meant to us. I was called on first and talked about how my name was always weird to me, as it was a French name, but my family was Portuguese. While I was explaining this, my dad sat back in his chair, crossed his arms and interrupted, "I didn't know this was such a problem for you, Yvonne. Perhaps we should go down to town hall right now and get it changed?"

The group broke into giggles; even the super serious instructor smiled, and the seminar continued. On the second day, they brought in a woman to discuss her position as the director of advocacy for crime victims at the local courthouse. Everything she said mesmerized me. It felt to me like she was describing the perfect job. As a police officer, my dad knew her well and introduced us. She agreed to meet with me to discuss her work more. I remembered wanting to study criminal justice in college and perhaps become a probation officer, and how Andy had told me that was not a good choice for me. He was right. But this, this field, it seemed like it was exactly what I was meant to do.

We met and later, when a position opened in her office, my dad's friend invited me to interview for it. I did not get the job. I was disappointed, but called to thank her and asked her advice for another interview I had just been able to schedule. In the months since attending the seminar and volunteering at the shelter, I discovered another agency with an opening. This position was just outside Boston and I surprised myself by how badly I wanted it. The girl who never wanted to leave Provincetown and who now had a great life there was looking for work back in the city, over a hundred miles away. But being a crime victim's advocate felt like a calling, a necessary career I had to try. If I could not get hired near my hometown, then so be it. I would have to keep looking. My dad's friend said I had interviewed well, but she had given the position to someone who had volunteered at her office previously. Unbeknownst to me, she knew the director of the program I was about to interview for and called him to put in a good word on my behalf. Only a week after that interview, I received a rejection letter.

About ten days later, the phone rang. It was the director of the program near Boston. The woman they hired instead of me had not liked the job and quit after only a few days. I was their second choice. Could I start immediately?

Samantha had moved from Provincetown by then and was living just north of the city. She said her couch was always available. So, with little thought, I gave my two weeks' notice to the town's HR department, said some sad goodbyes, packed up some of the nicest clothes I owned and left town for a new job, a new life and a new home. The goals I had fought so hard to achieve were swiftly dismissed. This move was sudden and exciting and even a little wild. But, amazingly, it was not as terrifying as it had been the last time I left town.

part III

leaving

chapter 35
gun

I was not wrong. Being an advocate in the criminal justice system was a good fit for me. The training I had received on the Cape helped me to ease into the role of being a liaison between crime victims and the overwhelming court process. There were many newbie mistakes and lots of jitters during the first several weeks. But mostly, I felt comfortable and knew I wanted to stay. I felt this career could be a permanent one. I quickly became friends with my coworkers and felt like I was part of a well-functioning team. I enjoyed spending time with them within the seriousness of the office and the courthouse during the workday, and on those evenings when we would socialize outside of work, complete with drinks, apps and a lot of venting. We were assisting people in crisis and a lot of what we did could cause serious repercussions in both positive and negative ways. Relying on each other was how we dealt with our stress. I knew that having the determination and strength needed to do this work was only possible for me because of Richard's advice long before, "you are as smart and as pretty as anyone and you have just as much right to be there as they do."

It was also good to spend time with Samantha. We had stayed in touch after she spent those six months living with my mom and we had become close friends. She was doing great, having completed her education and now living in a Boston suburb with an impressive job of her own. Her apartment was tiny and her sofa lumpy, but I could handle that in exchange for room, board and a Ptown connection to help steer away any homesickness, however small. The real problem was that though her apartment was technically a 45-minute drive to my office, with traffic, the ride quickly became 90 minutes each way. The commuter rail lines weren't much better. So, after one week, I packed my bags and moved into my aunt and uncle's house, much closer to work. It was a lucky coincidence that I had family in the area, my dad's brother having settled in Cambridge for factory work as opposed to the fishing opportunities Provincetown offered my grandfather.

My aunt and uncle were wonderful and kind-hearted, and since they only had boys, they enjoyed having a girl in the house. At least they seemed to. My youngest cousin was in his twenties and lived in a bachelor pad he designed for himself in the basement. I put my work outfits and briefcase into the closet in his old bedroom, a room I was now borrowing; a room decorated with posters of topless models hanging over one sports car or another. The arrangement worked, at least until I got more settled and found an apartment of my own. It was the Spring of 1995 and I was 26 years old. The transition from regular townie to professional was complete.

I could even hold my own at work, sometimes needing to argue with prosecutors when I thought they were wrong or needing to stand up for myself as well as for the downtrodden. Yet, I still struggled with confidence issues, especially with dating. I was interacting with lawyers, social workers and police officers and I could work with them and drink with them. But if one of them ever became flirty, I would immediately turn back into the timid girl who lived inside me. Once, a good-looking and intelligent attorney I was working with on a particularly gut-wrenching case thanked me for my hard work and then winked at me. I immediately ran from the hallway into the safety of the courtroom, where he'd be too busy to see me blush. For the rest of the case, I couldn't look him in the eye even as I argued that all three witnesses should be allowed to speak during sentencing, not just the victim's mother.

I dated a bit. But after two blind fixups that went nowhere, I unintentionally started dating only guys with a connection to my hometown. The closest I ever came to dating someone outside of my self-imposed safety net was a guy I met who was neither from, nor lived in Provincetown. But I had met him through townie contacts. I did not know why my dating tastes ran towards local guys or guys acquainted with local guys. Was that little bit of insecurity always with me? Was it because having a Ptown link was a starting point, a basis of conversation, a reference both my date and I could easily relate to? I could converse with a police officer about a case, but then what? It just seemed easier to keep my romantic life local.

Plus, while I loved my job, I still loved Provincetown and frequently came home on weekends. Deep inside of me, whenever I went out, I was looking for Richard. The most obvious place to find him was at the Bradford and I got great at driving by slowly while peeking in the large barroom windows. It meant a lot to me to check in with him. We were still supporting each other in our own unusual way.

I found him on one of those weekends, and we sat down at the bar, chatting. I told him of a date I was supposed to have the following night. It was with a Portuguese fisherman I barely knew. I knew his family had deep roots in town and that he must be a hard worker if he was fishing, work I had always respected. Gilberto was supposed to call me in the morning when he was back from his current trip. I told Richard this and asked what he thought of Gilberto.

"Well," Richard answered, "I've seen a lot of things when I've been out fishing. I went on a trip with Gil once, a short trip, just overnight. As we were heading out, he was rummaging through his knapsack in front of me, and I saw a handgun. It creeped me out. There were only four of us on that trip and we all knew each other. You don't have pirates. You might come across some Coasties here and there, but a gun isn't going to help with that, even if they decide to board the boat. The only threat is the ocean itself and a firearm won't stop a rogue wave. What was he planning on doing with a gun, shoot the fish? Threaten them into jumping in the net? I've seen a lot of things while fishing. But that was the only time I ever saw a gun."

That was all Richard had to say about Gilberto. Typical Richard would tell the truth no matter how good, how bad, or how ugly. I was a grown woman, and he knew I needed to make my own decisions. Instead of giving me his opinion, he told me a story and let me figure it out on my own. Taking a handgun on a local trip seemed creepy to me too. I decided that when Gilberto called the next day, I would say I had to leave the Cape early. If he continued to call, I would make up a phantom guy from my work life.

Richard and I sat next to each other, talking some more and drinking our drinks, wine for me, Southern Comfort for him. As he glanced around the bar, the predicted rain arrived, drumming a steady rhythm against the windows on the front of the building. My mind wandered back into the familiar dream. I was not an idiot. I knew the dream was still impossible. Yet it was a comforting place to visit. We could still be that townie couple, the one that would survive all things despite the many couples I saw falling apart all around us. The ones who had married their true loves, stayed in town and had kids. Maybe they couldn't make it, but we were different. If he could get clean, he could make good money as a mechanic, something he loved and was great at. I could go back to my Town of Provincetown job or find another one. With my experience, maybe I would even start at a higher pay grade. Though older, Jesse was still a kid; it wasn't too late for me to start a new relationship with him. And then we could have kids of our own. I loved my career, but not as much as I loved this fantasy. I would give up my current life without a second thought. I could still see the dream as clearly as I did when I first envisioned it.

I knew better, of course. But what's reality when it comes to your heart? The problem wasn't that we didn't know if Richard could get clean. The actual issue was that he had long since lost the desire to try.

As if to reinforce the point, he stood up then. "I've got to go. A buddy of mine was supposed to give me a ride, but it looks like he's blowing me off," he said.

"Richard, if you need a ride somewhere, I'd be happy to take you."

He cocked his head and grinned his grin. "Would you be happy to drive me someplace, wait a few minutes, and then drive me somewhere else?"

The realization that the ride was about scoring coke kicked in. "Uh, no, forget it. I'm not giving you *that* kind of ride."

He laughed and then hugged me. And as more people rushed into the bar to escape the wind and the now heavy rain, he pulled up the hood of his jacket and headed out into the street.

chapter 36
advice

It continued to make me happy when I would bump into Richard. His smile would add a lift to my day, no matter what was going on with me. It would be nice to think that a smile from me benefited him a bit, too, but I'm not so sure. I am ashamed to admit that the one time I remember helping him, I was very cocky about it. We found each other another night when I was home and this time, when I asked how he was, he decided to actually tell me. Usually, he would answer without answering at all, something like "oh, you know," or "same old bullshit, what can I say?" This time, he told me that his latest fight with Patty had erupted to the point where the police were called and they arrested him for domestic assault and battery. He insisted that he never touched her and despite me hearing men in the courthouse saying the same thing constantly, even as their wives and girlfriends appeared before the judge covered in fresh bruises, I believed Richard. But I was angry with him too.

"Was this fight in front of Jesse?" I demanded.

"He was asleep."

"I bet he was. What the hell's the matter with you? That's the last thing he needed to hear."

"We fought, yes, but I never touched her," he insisted.

"I'm sure you didn't, but so fucking what? It's your word against hers. You shouldn't even be with her, and neither of you should expose your kid to this crap!"

Richard thought he needed my help and told me that his attorney was going to subpoena me to tell the judge that he was not violent, had never been violent with me, and that there was no way he could be responsible for this. I was not worried that being subpoenaed for the defense on a domestic abuse case would affect my job. Richard was very important to me. If I was subpoenaed and told the truth, it did not seem likely that there was anything my supervisors could do about it. And there was a huge part of me that wanted to do this for him, to ride to his rescue and save him from the aftermath of the super-destructive and dysfunctional world he chose to live in. But by then I had learned enough about the court system to know that my testifying on his behalf would not happen in this situation. And I told him so, not kindly.

"Richard, you're out of your mind and have a wack job of an attorney if you think that would work. Yes, if subpoenaed, I would be happy to go to court and tell the judge that you were never violent with me, and that you're the least violent person I know. But the judge would never allow it, as it's not relevant. The court doesn't care that you weren't violent with me. It would only help if I was a witness to the event on record and since I wasn't, I'm useless to you."

He looked defeated. I softened some but was still mad that over and over, his life kept bringing him down. He was the only one who could save himself and yet, he couldn't. Or wouldn't. It didn't seem to matter which it was.

"Look," I told him, "Since you don't have any violence on your record, the best thing to do is admit sufficient facts and take a CWOF for six months. It stands for a Continuance Without a Finding and it's like probation. You aren't admitting guilt, but you are saying that the court might have enough to find you guilty and you would rather just resolve the matter quickly. The CWOF will mean you are on a very loose probation, and if there are no other allegations, the case will be dismissed at the end of the six months. You probably won't even have to see a probation officer. You'll likely have a stay away order as a condition of the court, but in your case that would be a good thing."

I threw my big prosecution words at him bitterly—sufficient facts, CWOF, stay away order—further emphasizing how different our worlds had become. He had given me my voice, and I was using that voice to lash out in my frustration. But, as always, we hugged and wished each other well. I told him that if his lawyer thought I was wrong, I would be happy to testify on his behalf. I think I held him even tighter than usual as I realized that he finally had given me some specifics of his life and I had given him attitude.

I never got subpoenaed and, as I advised, he got the CWOF, but for one year instead of six months. After the time was up, the assault and battery charge was dismissed. Unfortunately, however, his record would not remain unblemished.

chapter 37
bouncer

I had heard that he was dating Lisa, the bitchy bartender at the Bradford. I did not like her. She was, after all, a bitch. She clearly hated her job and took it out on the bar patrons when they ordered their drinks, especially the women. But interestingly, aside from the bitch part, she was a lot like me. And not only like me, but also like the wife I only heard about, the woman Richard married and divorced before I ever met him. She was modestly good looking, a brunette, and her life was relatively put together. And she might drink here and there, but she was definitely not into the drug scene. It seemed that this was Richard's drug-free type. That likely meant that Richard was trying to overcome his addiction, and that was a good thing.

It was hard to accept that he was trying to clean himself up with the help of a woman who was not me. I briefly fantasized about him moving with me into my apartment outside Boston. But the reality was there would be nothing for him there. Other than my job and the friends I had made, there was little for me there either. Here was his home, and this is where he would stay. He would be lost and lonely in my new world, and that would make it even harder for him to quit cocaine. These brief escapes from reality still visited me from time to time, but I was used to shaking them off and pulling myself together. Even though it wasn't me, Richard dating Lisa could be a positive step in the right direction. Besides living with her, she had gotten him a job as a bouncer.

Now the Bradford, his anchor as he roamed from sofa to sofa, girlfriend's bed to girlfriend's bed, fishing boat to fishing boat, was also a source of decent income.

I was home for the weekend and I sat at the end of the bar while I waited for my local friends to join me. I saw Richard talking to JB, the regular bouncer, at the emergency exit just by the kitchen. Out of the corner of her eye, Lisa saw she had a new customer and headed over. When she realized it was me sitting there, she frowned. I ordered my usual girly glass of White Zinfandel. As she set it down in front of me, she noticed a group entering the bar.

"Oh great, it's Patty," she said. "First you and now Patty. I've got to deal with both of you."

I don't know what made me say it, why I would want to bond with this difficult woman except that she might be Richard's last chance to escape the grip coke had on him. Without thinking about it too much, I leaned in close and said, "It's alright. I think we can take her."

Lisa smiled slightly and gave me a look that implied we were allies. I still did not like her, but not dealing with her attitude was better than being on the receiving end of it. And a weird part of my being was proud to be included in a grouping with her and Patty. What was with this strange compulsion I had to constantly be reminded by other women that I was an important part of Richard's life? I knew this already. I knew it from Richard himself. So why did I need someone like Lisa to acknowledge it?

Eventually, Richard saw me and came over. As usual, we hugged and chatted and then he asked Lisa to get me another drink on him. She was not happy about it but preferred that it was for me rather than Patty, and so she did. And as Richard went back to checking IDs and clearing the tables nearest the door he was covering, Lisa hung by my side, now wanting to be my friend. That was fine, but I was grateful when my real friends showed up and we grabbed a table by the dance floor. I did not really want

Lisa's friendship. I had my own group and as much as I cared about him, Richard was not my only world. Not even in this town we both loved. I don't think Patty and her posse stayed very long, but I can't be sure. I stopped paying attention to his other girl-friends and had a fun night out, drinking, chatting and dancing. It would be a lie to say that I totally stopped paying attention to Richard. But I definitely stopped focusing on him.

chapter 38
jail

Two years, three moves and one promotion passed, and I still regularly made the two-hour, twenty-minute drive home to hang with family and friends. I had made a ton of good friends at work and loved being part of the team atmosphere. Yet, I still felt more comfortable with the Ptown guys and their hard-partying lifestyle. Drugs were bad, and I hated watching how they were consuming Richard and ruining whatever chances he had to get his act together. But since they could be part of the hometown scene, I could not easily dismiss all those who used as criminal. Lawyers in my office were constantly prosecuting drug offenses, but I had nothing to do with that. I worked on cases involving victims of violence and to me, that was a whole different level of crime. I chose not to tell my coworkers that. But sometimes the lines between my work world and my hometown world were not so clearly divided.

One afternoon in town and hanging out with Heather, her husband Roland brought home a work buddy. His name was Finn, and I casually knew him. He had been a former classmate until his family moved and he went to an Upper Cape school. We had a beer together and hung out for a bit. Roland invited us to stay for dinner and Finn said he would love to. He was short but stocky and good-looking in a rough-edged kind of way. He was flirting with me and I liked the attention. My memories of him back in school were brief, but pleasant. I went with him to the liquor store and the conversation between us flowed nicely. Back at Heather's, we ate, drank and played with the kids, which now included a brand new, adorable baby boy.

During dinner, the topic of what I did for work came up. After explaining my job in the court system, Finn was proud to tell me he was a "cite" in Florida.

"What the hell is a 'cite'?" Roland asked.

Finn explained he had gotten into a bit of legal trouble in Florida and his defense attorney appealed his conviction. He won, and his case was now a law. Thanks to Finn, the people of the sunshine state no longer had to serve conditions of probation if the judge failed to read those conditions out loud during sentencing. My work friends would have been horrified. But buzzed, I found it ironic and amusing.

More drinks followed. As it was the night before Easter, after the kids went to bed, Heather set up their Easter baskets. She had a trash bag full of the collected wrappings and receipts for the candy and gifts she had put in each one, and I volunteered to take the bag with me when I left. Soon Heather and Roland went to bed and Finn and I stayed up on their sofa watching TV and drinking a bit more. Eventually, we fell asleep. I woke up at 2 in the morning, curled up next to Finn. I nudged him awake and told him we needed to leave, quietly, so we would not wake the kids. At my car, Finn kissed me and said he would like to see me the following weekend. I told him I couldn't come down until Saturday because of a work event, but yes, Saturday night, I would enjoy hanging out with him again.

In the morning, Heather called. I had forgotten to take the evidence of the store-bought Easter treats. I felt horrible.

"You totally should," Heather said. "Lucky for you, Ari was the first one up and she was starting to not believe the Easter bunny thing anyway. She brought the bag to me to prove her point, and I was able to grab it from her before her brothers saw it. I had to bribe her with extra candy so she wouldn't fill them in on her find. But thanks to you, I have a smug nine-year-old walking around here like she owns the place and rotting the hell out of her teeth."

The work event the following Friday night was a goodbye party for one of my coworkers at a skanky Chinese restaurant, complete with a fat Elvis impersonator hosting karaoke. That was one aspect where my hometown life and my work life compared— social events for both involved alcohol. I was not driving and per- haps I had a bit too much to drink. So, shocking myself as well as my colleagues, when Elvis held the microphone to my lips for me to sing the "ain't no doubt about it we were doubly blessed" line of Meatloaf's *Paradise by the Dashboard Light*, I sang it. What else could I do? I figured he would get that line out of me and then move on to someone else.

But my singing caused Elvis to grab my hand and bring me up on stage where we sang and danced the whole eight-minute, sexy, angry duet. My coworkers applauded and even though none of them sang with Elvis, I was not embarrassed. Even in the sobriety of the next morning, I smiled, remembering the night. If I hadn't been sure before, I now knew the shy, insecure girl was gone, and I was thrilled to see her go.

I was a little bummed that Finn hadn't called, but I went home anyway. I did not see him, and Roland said he hadn't seen him either. It didn't matter. It had been a fun dinner the week before, but no big deal. I spent time with my family and wasn't back in my apartment an hour that Sunday evening when Finn called. He apologized for not calling before, but swore he had a good reason.

"Actually, it's a little awkward. I was in jail."

"What???"

"My brother and I got into a wicked fight Friday and the police were called. They arrested both of us, but since I had the record, I had to stay. I didn't get bailed until late Saturday and by then I was too embarrassed to call you."

That Finn was in jail for a violent act when he was supposed to be calling me was a little too close for comfort. I wished him well and was vague about when I would be home again. I looked up his case 'cite' and learned the initial crime they had charged him with was cocaine possession—the last thing I needed. Finn was a nice enough guy but was no longer a potential dating prospect and that was ok. There was one consequence from that night, however. The next time I saw Heather's daughter, she whispered to me how she knew the Easter bunny was really just mommy, but I couldn't tell her brothers, or she'd get in trouble.

Finn's history did not shock me. And though I had not seen Richard during my last few visits to town, it wouldn't have shocked me to learn that he was still using as well. So I shouldn't have been surprised at the phone call I received some time later from my friend Shannon. Shannon and I partied together in our high school days, but she gave it up when she married a police officer in my father's department.

"Did you hear about the huge drug bust in town?" she asked.

"No." I responded cluelessly, not knowing where she was going with this.

She read the newspaper article to me, including the list of several town people arrested. I knew most of the names but gasped at one in particular.

"What???" I screamed into the phone. "Did you say Richard? My Richard?"

"Yes, that's why I thought you should know," she answered.

I couldn't believe it. But why not? It was a miracle that he had come this far without being arrested. I should feel lucky that he hadn't become a statistic already, or the victim of the drug-related violence that I so worried about after seeing *New Jack City*. This wasn't a minor incident. He would serve time.

In the weeks that followed, I looked into the circumstances of the bust. Supposedly, many of those arrested had given up fellow users to the undercover cops and thus gotten their felonies dismissed or reduced to misdemeanor. I didn't know if that was true or not, and there was no one I could ask. My dad had not been involved; a drug task force sting operation of the state police completed the bust, keeping the local cops out of it.

In the end, Richard was only charged with possession, but possession of enough to be sentenced to six months. With parole, he was out in less than three. I was proud that he had not given up anyone to get out of his own sentence. That gelled with the good person I knew him to be. He committed the crime. He would own up to it; not screw someone over to save himself.

But in this, I may have also been naïve. Sure, Richard turning in a drug buddy was not his style, but he likely didn't name others solely to be noble. Not only would it be dangerous for him to rat out other users, but it would make things harder for him in the future. No dealer would ever trust him. If he ever wanted to buy again, he needed to keep his mouth shut. I realized I was an idiot if I didn't think that was at least a minor factor in his decision.

The local who took the brunt of the law was Paul, the much older, nice, but sad guy Serena, Lynn and I had come to know. Paul had a tough life, and it did not shock me that cocaine was a part of his coping mechanism. He was the bouncer that had been ready to burst into the ladies' room when he thought I was in trouble years before, and I was always grateful for that. Paul actually served over two years for his part in the bust. Several months after Richard was released, Serena told me she had been writing Paul, and the letters were helping him to keep his spirits up. Feeling a sense of loyalty that diminished possible work conflicts, I started writing to him as well. And on one of my trips home, Serena was going to visit him and talked me into going with her. At first, I was just going to keep her company on the ride. But by the time we reached the county jail, I decided to go in too. Socially visiting an inmate was not in keeping with my work life. It was absurd that I was even considering it, let alone actually going in. I wondered if it was even some type of violation. I could not imagine my bosses understanding what I was doing there, requesting to see an inmate with several more months left in his sentence. I went in though and did not regret it. It cheered Paul up, knowing that a couple of his buddies wanted to encourage him.

The visiting room was how I always pictured it. There was a long table with a plastic divider about 10 inches high down the center. Inmates sat cuffed on one side: visitors un-cuffed on the other. It was noisy as we talked, and I don't remember saying much. I think Serena mostly filled Paul in on the goings on at home. At one point, he put his head down and shook it, saying, "I don't get it. I just don't get it."

"What, Paul?" we asked.

"See that guy at the end, the one with the bushy mustache? He's in here for beating up his girlfriend."

"Ok."

"See the girl trying to hold his hand? That's the girlfriend."

I could have switched to work mode and explained the cycle of violence and the difficulty involved in breaking away from an abusive relationship, but that wasn't my role at the jail. To me, though, the offenses were different, very different. The guy on the end? He was a criminal deserving of the utmost punishment. Paul, Richard, and maybe some of the other guys who had been busted in town, they were dumb guys doing very dumb things, endangering themselves but not others. Hurting others with their bad actions maybe; but not their fists. Still, they all wound up in the same place and that was a place no one should want to be.

After visiting Paul, it surprised me I did not think to go visit Richard when he was locked up. Or why I didn't think to write. I felt bad for Paul, but I loved Richard. Was it simply a matter of being persuaded by Serena that Paul needed cheering up? Would it have cheered Richard up if I had gone to see him? Would it have made a difference?

Many months after his release, we talked about his incarceration. At another one of our bar check-ins, my honest Richard told me how he got caught.

"It was a woman that did it. A hot woman. I never thought they would pull that. But the narc was a woman who was new in town and I just fell for it. Would never have gotten caught if they used a guy."

"Well, did you learn anything from this?" I asked.

"Ya. Never trust a woman...." He smiled at me, being playful.

"I mean, did it help at all? Has it helped you stop this crap?"

He didn't give me an answer, only shrugged.

Which was an answer in itself.

chapter 39
hubcaps

It was Christmastime 2003 in Provincetown and I was picking up last-minute ingredients for the treats I would make later that day. I was a little melancholy. Our family home was rented out, and my mom had made the decision that it was time to sell. The up-keep and needed repairs to the old house had turned overwhelming. At my grandmother's house, I was sleeping on the sofa, while my mother stayed in the guestroom. She was trying to figure out where she wanted to settle and if she wanted to buy something new or just rent. My grandmother and her brother had moved in together after selling their respective, older, large homes. At 84 and 90, they had done this so that they could look after each other in their final years. Downgrading, they had sold most of their belongings and with that, and the general exhaustion that hits the elderly, their new home had few decorations and even less holiday spirit. Drew, now 13, no longer appreciated the magic of Christmas that I so treasured and used to enjoy with him. It was the same with my younger brother and sister, who were also teen-agers. Things in Ptown seemed different and even though I was there, I was more homesick than ever. I was trying to keep my holiday spirit up, but it was getting harder and harder with each snowflake that didn't fall.

Exiting the grocery store, there he was. Richard was just going in and he stopped. We hugged and still, so many years after we had last been together, there was that twinge in my heart; a rush of gladness, excitement, sorrow and love, all combined into one comforting emotion. It didn't matter that he wasn't as dressed for the cold as he should be. Or that the drugs were clearly taking their toll. While still handsome (he would always be handsome to me), he looked older and harsher than his 45 years. Yet it was so good to see him.

He asked how I was, and I told him about my life in Boston. I didn't really live or work in Boston, but in the northwest regions outside of the city. It didn't matter. To us townies, everything north of the bridge was Boston. I asked how he was and, as usual, he did not say much. I did not ask about Jesse. He was a teenager now too, and based on prior conversations, I was worried that he may not have the best relationship with his father.

Richard walked me to my car, and I jokingly showed him proof of the dangerous city life I was living as I pointed out the three missing hubcaps from the tires of my Dodge Neon.

"They've all been stolen," I told him. "Hey, if you want to get me a Christmas present, that's what I need, hubcaps."

He had to know I was joking, but he inspected the naked tires anyway. Then he walked away from me into the parking lot.

"Aren't you even going to say goodbye?" I shouted after him.

"I'll be right back," he answered.

I watched him looking all around as he walked.

"What are you doing?" I called out.

"I'm getting you your Christmas present," he shouted back as he checked out the hubcaps on the other cars in the lot, looking for a match.

I couldn't help myself and burst into laughter.

"Get back here!"

He came back, and we laughed together. We hugged again and said goodbye. Directly to our right, the Provincetown Pilgrim Monument stood grand and decorated right above us, just as it had that Christmas over ten years before. The memory of that day made me smile. As he walked into the store, I thought, *this Christmas, at least I have this. At least I got this brief moment of time with my Richard.*

And that was a lot.

chapter 40
home

I was eight years into my career working with crime victims and I still felt it was what I was meant to do. But I was becoming restless. In the aftermath of the 9/11 terrorist attack that shook the world and deeply affected everyone in the country, I faced a realization. I needed to be home and near the water. If there was only a little bit of time left, where did I want that time to be?

What home, I wasn't sure. Provincetown was drastically changing. The house I grew up in belonged to strangers now and had been torn apart and converted into condominiums. The most expensive of which was the entire third floor that had been our attic. When we lived there, it was dusty, buggy and dangerous, with exposed flooring stuffed with insulation. To walk around, you had to balance carefully on the wooden beams or risk falling through the insulation to the bedrooms below. We knew the attic windows offered a water view; it was just a little tricky to get to it. Now it was high-priced luxury real estate.

Many of my friends had left town. If they had not moved out-of-state altogether, they had at least moved further up Cape, where property was cheaper and the schools offered better opportunities. There were rumors of eventually needing to close Provincetown's high school because of a lack of students. And with so many regulations, rising insurance premiums and lower quotas, the fishing industry had dwindled to only a few working boats.

I desperately wanted to recapture what had been, even if it no longer existed. I started making plans to come back. Even if I couldn't find affordable rent and year-round work in Province-town, at least I could get closer. I understood it would be hard to get the same type of advocacy work I was currently doing on the Cape, and if I did, it wouldn't be very smart. With the closeness of small towns, it was better to be as anonymous as possible in the court system.

When I found an affordable apartment in Orleans, about 30 minutes outside of Ptown, I grabbed it. It was May, and I knew if I could not find a year-round position, I could get two or three seasonal jobs for the summer and take it from there. But luckily I found a full-time, year-round, decent paying job working as an administrative assistant for a doctor. I sacrificed the career I knew I was made for in exchange for being able to live in the place that was meant for me. It felt sad, but right.

When I visited my local friends now, I would simply make a half hour drive home as opposed to crashing on their sofas during a quick weekend visit. Fortunately, the Cape was still the summer hot spot and my court friends were willing to make the long drive to visit me, especially during the summer months. I missed my previous work, but the doctor's office was fine, and I could live vicariously through the stories my friends told after their long days at the courthouse. It pleased me when they called to run case scenarios by me, as if I was still a part of the system, even though I clearly was not. Overall, I was happier on the Cape.

Perhaps part of that happiness came from another angle where I sought the town I grew up in. After attending the funeral of a family friend and being moved to tears by the hymns that were played, I found my way back to the faith that had been instilled in me as a child. Neither of my parents were practicing church goers. But the Catholic faith was very important to both of my grand-mothers and because of this, my parents had made sure I received all of my sacraments. But it hadn't really sunk in. Once I was back in town, however, especially feeling homeless and adrift amidst all the changes, I felt at peace in the church of my childhood. I felt almost as if God was saying this will always be your home. I was spending a lot of time in St. Peter the Apostle parish, the Catholic Church of my hometown, the church nestled just under the base of the monument.

I dated more too, the townie/Ptown connection even more important now that there seemed to be so little of it left. But the townie who made a real difference in my love life wasn't really a townie at all. I met Zack while I was volunteering, serving food at the now annual Portuguese Festival. What had once been a Sunday honoring the fishing fleet, including the sacred blessing of the working fishing boats, had turned into a four-day festival honoring the town's Portuguese fisherman and the heritage that had made up most of those fishing families, my own included. Zachary was a washashore and was exploring the festival with some townies he met through work. From the moment he refused my offer of nice Portuguese bread to go with his seafood feast, I was entranced. After my volunteer duties, I went to the bar, asked around about him, met him and was surprised when he followed me from one bar to another, where the festival partying continued. We talked for a couple of hours, drinking cheap wine on the deck of the Surf Club, a seasonal bar at the foot of the pier. Originally from the Midwest, he had moved to Provincetown the year before for a temporary construction job and had liked it enough to stay. And like all Provincetown connections, I knew his boss, a couple of his coworkers, and some friends he had made. I was committed to several events that weekend and Zack joined me at each one. We fell hard. I didn't realize it, but Zack was a lot like Richard. He was tall and strong, but with longish light brown hair as opposed to Richard's dark hair. Like Richard, he had a wicked playful side that drew me in. As opposed to Richard's famous impish grin, Zack showed his playfulness by making crazy faces and singing silly songs. And also like Richard, he had a very kind heart and a gentle manner. One of my friends called him a gentle giant. My family liked him, and I loved him deeply. In my late thirties, I wasn't so sure there was time to start a family, but knew if I was going to, it would be with Zack. We talked about it and made jokes about what our kids would be like.

We moved in together, eventually renting a small house in Eastham, after only dating a few months. What seemed to work so well was our respect for each other. If we screwed up, neither would have a problem telling the other they were sorry. He was more clever about it, however. One night when I was really furious with him, who knows why, I was holed up in our bedroom watching TV and purposefully ignoring him. He came in and lay on the bed next to me. Then he put his head on my lap and started making pathetic whimpering sounds.

"What the hell are you doing?" I demanded with great attitude.

"I'm being a dog," he replied. "I'm in the doghouse, so I figured I should be a dog."

That, of course, cracked me up. How could you stay mad at someone who resolves a serious disagreement in such a way?

Zack said he was an atheist but was respectful of my faith. Our living together was not conducive to Catholicism, and I struggled with being hypocritical. But I also felt we just fit. I thought I would figure out the details in time and that God would forgive me. Actually, I convinced myself that God had put him in my path. Here was the answer to all of those single nights, broken relationships and bad dates. I had been in love with Richard, dated men I cared for and others I didn't care for so much. But with Zack I felt like finally, I was with the man I was supposed to spend the rest of my life with. Not like with Richard, who I had wanted to spend the rest of my life with and might have, if not for the crucial problem of a lifelong addiction. But with Zack, we were it, soul mates even.

Here I was wrong too. For two years we were together, and I believed happy. But after illness took his mother and then his father became seriously ill, Zack felt guilty that he missed his mom's last year of life and wanted to be nearer to his father. He decided he needed to return to his own hometown. And he did not feel ready to take me with him. I thought we had reached the point of weathering crisis' together, but apparently not. Had he wanted me to, I would have left Massachusetts for him. I had sacrificed a successful career to be near my home, but Zack felt like my future. I would have followed him anywhere. The fact that he didn't want me to, left me reeling.

chapter 41
passing

Nine months had passed since Zack left, and I was in a bad place. Only in my late thirties, I was inexplicably exhausted all the time. Now the exhaustion was out of control, made worse by tension at work. I blamed the unhealthy habits I was using to cope. Never thin, I had gained 15 pounds since Zack left, likely because of the junk and takeout food I existed on. To comfort myself with the weight gain, I started smoking again, an off and on habit since high school. While living with Zack, I had been on birth control and had mostly quit because of the health risks, mooching smokes off of him only in times of extreme stress. In the aftermath of our relationship, I had no reason to be on the pill and in my sad awareness of that fact, I suddenly had a lot of reasons to smoke. I had not received any clinical diagnosis, but I was depressed. I wanted out of that particular state-of-mind but felt way too tired to do much about it.

Thoughts of Richard were far out of my mind. Since Zack left, I had not been out in Ptown very often; the memories were just too upsetting, and the questions and comments too infuriating. Zack was "the one." Since we didn't make it, my emotions were focused on why, what went wrong, how come, how can I fix it, and how long will it take for him to figure things out and come back? For several years, Richard had not been at the forefront of my mind or even my heart. He was a comforting blast from the past and a cherished hug when I saw him. But consumed by my latest failed relationship, I did not think about him; unless it was to remember the time Zack and I saw him while we were out and I introduced the two of them. They greeted each other and shook hands and I got the feeling that Richard approved of him in those brief seconds they spent together. It wouldn't have mattered if he didn't, but Zack was a good guy and I felt that was obvious to Richard. At the time, Richard was looking pretty ragged, but I did not think about it as much as I usually would have. So wrapped up in the man I thought was my future, I paid little attention to this important man from my past.

While I struggled during those cold winter/early spring months, I relied on my faith to help me through. My prayers sustained me through those bleak days. One damp and cloudy Saturday afternoon I was driving to Ptown for the vigil Mass. A boxy, powder blue sedan was behind me on the one-lane highway and it was messing with me. The driver would speed up so that he was only feet from my bumper and then drop back for a while, only to speed up and tailgate me once again. Since I was already easily irritated, I was furious with this car. I couldn't figure it out either. It looked like an older woman's car, similar to the one my grandmother used to drive. But what elderly lady drove this way? As the bad driving continued, I got more annoyed.

The highway opened to two lanes just before an intersection in Wellfleet. As we both approached the traffic light, the car pulled alongside me. I was intent on glaring at the driver to let them know exactly how I felt about their road games. And I did. There was Richard with his huge grin, looking back. Of course it was. It was classic Richard to tease me this way. And of course I smiled back. Just one little smile in what had been months of no smiles at all. I sensed it was his mother's car he was driving. If true, that was a good thing. Whatever was going on in his life, he was in touch with his family enough for his mother to let him borrow her car. It was silly, but the beautiful grin he had first flashed at me

22 years before still brought the same rush of heartwarming adrenaline. The smile stayed on my face the rest of the day.

* * *

It wasn't as though the brief highway greeting completely changed my spirits. But three months later, in early June, with warmer weather, the knowledge that I was going to be 40 *and* that my birthday fell on a Saturday, I felt better. I decided I needed to do something big for this important birthday. I called three of my closest friends from the court job who lived outside Boston and invited them to join me for a weekend in Maine. Ever the ocean girl, that's where I wanted to get away, from one part of the Atlantic coastline to another.

The weather that weekend was gorgeous. We stayed in Portland, where we took the mail boat ferry on a tour of the surrounding islands and visited the local bars. We took a day trip to have lunch and walk along the beachside cliff in Ogunquit. On my birthday itself, we teased each other about Becky's diner, where I insisted we have breakfast as the guidebook said that was where the fishermen all hung out. But once there, one of my friends remarked, "where are all the fishermen, Yvonne? All I see is tourists!"

I replied, "That's because it's 10:30 in the morning—the earliest I could get your lazy butts up! The fishermen were all here at 5:00 a.m. and are probably done hauling their traps by now!"

The dinner that night was in beautiful Cape Elizabeth and we had a great time. Who needed a guy when I was blessed with friends like the ones I so cherished? I was sad to leave the next morning but was thrilled at the new memories I made and at all the times we had laughed over the weekend.

It was on my drive home that I received a text. I should not have looked at it while I was driving, but my Maine companions were driving too and maybe one had broken down somewhere. I picked up my phone and glanced at the screen. The message was from Serena; it simply said, "I'm so sorry about Richard's passing."

I had no idea what she was talking about and it was all I could do to wait the two miles until I saw a rest area and safely pull over. I sat and looked at the message for several minutes, trying to make sense of it. *It means something else besides death. She's heard some sort of ugly rumor. She's talking about another Richard and I am just too stunned to figure out who she really means.*

It took several minutes for me to find the strength, but I called her. And with semis, minivans and motorcycles flying by me at 65 miles per hour, she told me what she knew. Richard had died earlier that morning, the morning after my 40th birthday, after having been very sick for a long time. She apologized for sending the text. She thought I would have heard and if she knew I hadn't, she would have called instead.

But I didn't know. I hadn't even known he was sick. Apparently, he had been ill for a long time, the result of the abuse his body had taken over the years. It made sense then that the last time I had seen him, he might have been in his mother's car. With nowhere else to go, perhaps he had gone home and had been staying with her? That fleeting moment on the highway was the last time I would ever see him. Why didn't we motion to each other to pull over? Why didn't he follow me to tell me he was sick? Maybe I could have helped. Maybe in the last few months when I was emotionally spent, and he was physically depleted, we could have helped each other? When I introduced him to Zack the year before, how did I ignore how thin he was? It was obvious now that he had been dealing with more than the usual effects of drugs—how did I not see it?

I sat in that rest area a long time thinking these thoughts, shedding tears, and wishing I could have that silly moment at a Wellfleet traffic light back again.

chapter 42
match

I collected myself and continued the three-hour drive home. I knew that somehow I would have to prepare myself to go back to work and was glad that when scheduling my long weekend, I thought to take Monday off to rest and catch up on life. But with the news, mostly I spent the day remembering our history. I analyzed whether to send Richard's mother a sympathy note. What could I possibly say? I grabbed a blank card from my desk and sat down to write something, anything. Being so caught up in memories, it didn't take long for the words to come. I wrote I was a better person for having known her son and how I wished I could have helped him like he had helped me. I never mentioned his addiction directly but said that I truly believed he was finally free from the demons that held him captive. Offering my condolences to her and the rest of Richard's family, I wrote about how I would miss his loving soul and his very kind heart. I mailed the card before I could reconsider sending it. Then I waited.

I waited for a response even though I didn't expect one and knew it was selfish to think that in her time of grief, his mother would feel the need to reach out to me. More than anything, I wanted to tell her how her son had changed my life. I was desperate for his family to know that I wasn't just some flighty girl but someone who truly loved him and who had honestly tried to build a drug-free life with him; a healthy, supportive life. I waited to hear about the services and checked the paper every day for an obituary. I asked Serena's boyfriend to ask around as he interacted with Richard's friends in the bar and on the pier.

After two weeks of not hearing anything about him or his death, I went to the Bradford myself and asked the few people I still knew who worked and hung out there. The restaurant manager told me she had heard that Richard wanted to be cremated and to have his ashes scattered from the top of the Pilgrim Monument, the tower that permanently stood over our little town.

"He said he wanted that done so everybody could say 'that damn Richard is all over Ptown,'" she told me.

I could picture him saying it and smiled in agreement. Never being able to save enough for a car, Richard walked everywhere. He walked from wherever he was staying, to his jobs, to the bar, to whichever girl he might be dating, to whichever friend he might be visiting, to whatever dealer he might be buying from. One of the cruelly ironic consequences of his addiction had been that the man who was so good at working on cars hadn't had his own for most of his adult life. So yes, he had been all over town and it would be fitting for him to come up with such a last request. I could picture his playful smirk, even as he lay dying.

She also said that a bunch of folks were inclined to honor his wish, but there was no set plan. I wondered how this would be done as I couldn't imagine such a thing being legal, but I asked her to keep me informed. What did 'legal' matter when it came to saying goodbye?

Another friend said she wanted to take up a collection to put a plaque under the pay phone at the front corner of the bar; the one Richard used all the time. I thought it was a great idea, one that he would have loved, his various phone numbers carved around the plaque. It never happened, though. With the increasing popularity of cell phones, the pay phone was actually removed all together.

Two and a half weeks after his death, an obituary appeared in the paper. It mentioned Richard's sense of humor and his gentle soul. I was happy that they mentioned his sense of humor. I never appreciated how important that was, but it was the essence of him. Never mean or vicious, he loved to tease and was pretty funny about it. The obituary was short and the only thing it said about the arrangements was that there would be a service at a later date.

Soon after the obituary was published, the now married Samantha came up from Florida with Lexi, her two-year-old daughter. Samantha was eager to visit family and friends and to introduce her daughter to the people and places she had grown up with. On one brilliantly blue day of her visit, we walked through town. No proper townie walk would be complete without a stroll down the town's main pier. We were approached by one of the summer harbormasters, who was also our former gym teacher. He was also Richard's brother-in-law, the husband of the sister who had warned my mom about me dating Richard when I was 17. He hugged Samantha and commented on how much Lexi resembled her. I held my breath, wondering if he would say anything to me about his families' recent loss. He chatted some more with Samantha and then greeted me. He thanked me for the beautiful card I had sent his mother-in-law. I smiled and then asked about Richard's life at the end. He told me that the family had been with Richard at the hospital when he died and yes, he told his family about his desire to have his ashes scattered from the monument. He said his mother-in-law was too overwhelmed to schedule a service right then, but they would soon. I told him that Richard had been a dear friend to me and had helped me a lot in life. I longed to tell his family how huge an impact Richard had made on me. How, if not for him, I would never have had the confidence to believe in myself, to find the courage to leave my tiny, safe spot in the world to seek bigger and different things. How, if not for Richard, I would never have learned not only how to speak up for myself but that I had a *right* to speak up for myself.

But he didn't ask me any questions and was needed back at work. I asked him to please let me know when they scheduled something and he promised he would. Then a fellow harbormaster called to him and Samantha and I continued taking turns pushing Lexi's stroller alongside our beautiful waterfront.

Two months went by and I still hadn't heard of any type of memorial at all. I made a point of driving down the pier whenever I came to town looking for Richard's brother-in-law. It was late August by the time I finally saw him again, waving traffic slowly past the passengers disembarking the Boston ferry. He saw me, but his wave was not one of recognition or greeting. It was the look of an official-on-official business, saying please move along. Still, I stopped my car as I passed and asked him if services had been scheduled yet. He seemed blunt when he said, "his mother has decided she doesn't want to hold any services and we need to respect that."

That was that. He insisted I keep moving and so I did, even though I was stunned. Why? Why not hold a formal goodbye? I didn't understand, but maybe it wasn't my place to understand. And what could I do? It seemed a cop out that I couldn't do something; like hold my own service. Buy my own plaque for the vacant space where a pay phone was and insist the damn bar hang it up? Neither Serena nor I heard any more about the bar doing their own tribute or asking the family for some of his ashes to scatter on their own. There should be something I could do, but what? This was a whole life just gone, with no goodbye, at least not from me. My helplessness just seemed to add to the depression and major fatigue I continued to experience. My birthday weekend in Maine had been a fun escape, but it wasn't long before I had fallen back into bad habits, sadness and complete exhaustion.

I had one memorial to attend, however. The previous March, my friend Tweetie had lost her husband, Killer, to a heart attack. Married for less than two years, Killer had been caring for Tweetie after she suffered a brain aneurism. Four weeks after her medical crisis, Killer died suddenly of a heart attack. Through her grief, and still not recovered from her aneurism, Tweetie could not plan any services back then. It was appropriate to hold his memorial in August as they were both beach lovers, having married on the beach and diving into the waves to seal their marital vows. Killer's goodbye was to be held on the beach where they married, and I planned on attending. Killer had been a great guy and another good friend to me.

I arrived at the parking lot a few minutes late and wandered down to the water, searching for Tweetie and her other friends. I wasn't that late. Could I have missed the whole thing? Did I confuse the time? I saw a large group with a bonfire about ¾ of a mile further down the beach. I didn't see any cars I recognized, but the group must be them.

I was a Cape Cod girl and walking on the beach should not have been difficult; yet I was dragging my feet with the effort to reach them. It was a short hike that I should have been used to. But it was way harder than it had ever been before. The one bit of assistance I got on the walk was the strong breeze that was helping to keep me cool and keeping the mosquitoes away. Still, my frustration increased when I finally reached the group and realized I didn't know a single one of them. Tweetie was not among them and neither was her grown son, Brian. I was embarrassed and couldn't think of the words to explain to the ten or twelve people why I had walked up to their bonfire like I had been invited.

I turned and could clearly see a larger group approaching the area where I had originally been. I started rushing back to them as fast as I could, hoping I wouldn't miss the scattering of Killer's ashes. But I wasn't fast enough. By the time I got there, the brief service was over. I tried to explain to Tweetie what had happened, but she was surrounded by other friends consoling her. I saw Brian and tried to explain to him why I had missed everything. In my distress, my words came out jumbled and nonsensical. Brian said that most of the group had gathered at the house before driving to the beach, which was why they all arrived together, just a bit late and probably right after I had started my walk to the group of strangers.

I was empty. I felt spent and useless and overwhelmed and stupid and sad. I walked to the water and collapsed in a heap right at the shoreline. I wanted to be comforted, but the people I knew in this group were there to comfort Tweetie, of course. A cigarette would have to do for fake comfort and so I pulled one out of the pocket of my jeans, thankful that none had broken when I fell to the sand. I'd never bought a lighter, as I planned on quitting as soon as I could shake my depression. I didn't need a lighter if I was going to quit. So with each pack I knew I shouldn't buy, I also grabbed one of the free book of matches on the counter.

I lit one of those matches and the breeze immediately blew it out. I tried again. The same thing happened. I tried to shelter the cigarette as I lit the next match, but each time it went out as soon as I struck the flame. The match sticks were piling up near me in a little heap so that I could remember to throw them away when I left. I was going through them quickly and with each try, I was more and more desperate. It seemed lighting this one smoke was going to save me right then as I listened to the water and felt sorry for myself for missing the scattering of ashes for the one friend who was actually having a memorial service.

Tweetie smoked and likely had a lighter, but I just didn't have the energy to get up right then. I was there to mourn Killer but, in my sorrow, it was another man that I foolishly called out to in the wind.

"Richard, if you ever loved me, you'd light this damn smoke for me!"

I struck the last match. And it stayed lit. It stayed lit while I lit the cigarette and it continued to stay lit as I took my first long drag. It stayed lit until I touched the flame to the softly lapping waves in front of me. As I pulled my hand back from the cool tide, I could see him clearly in my heart and in my mind.

I could see Richard, my Richard, flashing me that classic, playful, beautiful grin

epilogue

I wish I could say that a seemingly miraculous light for a desperate cigarette had been enough of a sign. Enough to get out of my funk, whatever was causing it. Enough for me to feel like things were going to be ok. Enough to feel like maybe Richard was happy and free. Enough to say goodbye.

But life doesn't work like that. We receive signs and they mean so much to us. We know that less-believing people would argue coincidence, but we are sure a loved one long passed has reached out. Then you go back to the banality of your life and question the sign yourself, or at least give it less importance.

After I sat smiling and smoking on the beach that August night, my depression and exhaustion didn't dissipate. When the fatigue became so bad that I was making major mistakes at work, I went to see my doctor. She diagnosed me with a thyroid condition and put me on a prescription. Then, in November, I started having numbness and tingling sensations—first in my feet and then, within a matter of days, the sensations moved up my legs to my abdomen. I did my best to concentrate on life and work while I tried not to think too much about what was going on with my body.

I still wanted to do some sort of formal tribute to my dear friend. A fellowship of some kind? I didn't even know his friends anymore. The best it seemed I could do was to have a Mass said for him. By offering this simple gesture, his name would appear in the church bulletin and be mentioned during the Mass itself. The next date my church had available was on 12/20/09. I remembered that one special Christmas Richard and I had spent together and our last visit in the grocery store parking lot during the Christmas season; the date would work. Worried about his family hearing about this from someone else and feeling like I had overstepped, I wrote to Richard's mother again. In this letter, I explained why I felt the need to have this Mass said and that I thought she should be made aware of it. Then I went back to my work life, Christmas preparations and many doctors' appointments and medical tests.

On December 17, 2009, I was told I had relapsing remitting multiple sclerosis. The phone call that brought the news led me to a new hospital, immediate treatment and grave concerns about my health and future. While I didn't have to stay in the hospital, the following day, Friday the 18th, was an overwhelming blur of emotions. It was all I could do to function in the face of the diagnosis. On the 19th, the fierce winter storm the news channels had been watching was now slated to make a direct hit to my area, Saturday night into Sunday morning. What to do about Richard's Mass?

Church was never cancelled as our priest lived on the property and thus conducted the service no matter the weather, leaving it up to individual parishioners to attend if they could. If the forecasts were true, I would not be able to get there. But this was supposed to be my official goodbye to him. I thought about packing a bag and driving the half hour to this church of our hometown, but even if I stayed with friends or rented a hotel room, I might not get home after. I lived on a private road that wasn't plowed for hours, if not days.

As the snow started late Saturday afternoon, I brought out candles in case I lost power. I knew I couldn't make it to Provincetown that night or in the morning, either. Richard's name would be said and there might not be anyone there who cared. I lit a candle just for him, said a prayer, and then sobbed. Maybe the tears were from exhaustion, or my recent medical news. They might have been for a life lost, or for a relationship that never stood a chance because of an addiction that couldn't be stopped. At the time, though, the tears fell because I felt I had let him down. He had helped me so much. But I couldn't help him fight his demons or support him in court or even show up at a Mass I had requested in his name. The sadness of that was a lot to take.

It occurred to me to try again; to have another Mass said maybe near his birthday or the anniversary date of his death. But I couldn't handle it if I scheduled another one and then had to miss that too. And so I did nothing.

Winter passed, and spring arrived. Then, in a late May church bulletin, I saw his name. Someone else was having a Mass said for him, exactly one year after the day he died. I did not know who had scheduled it, but vowed I would be there.

The anniversary of his death fell during the week, when services were usually much smaller than a regular Sunday service. Running late, I arrived just as Mass was starting. I knew most of the few parishioners that were in attendance, but two women, several pews in front of me, really stood out. I could only see their backs, but I wondered if they might be Richard's mother and one of his sisters. Did they request this Mass in Richard's name? I didn't see anyone else in the church with an obvious connection to him. If it was his family, would they talk to me? I'd never heard from his mother after the card and letter I sent her.

When it was over, the women turned around and I was now very sure that one of them was his mother. Should I go talk to them? I was trying to decide when another parishioner stopped me to chat. I did my best to move away, to be available if Richard's family members wanted to approach me, but somehow I lost sight of them. I gave up, disappointed, only to arrive at the holy water font by the door at the same time as Richard's mother. Our eyes met, and I smiled. She said, "Who are you?" And in the next breath she asked, "Are you Yvonne?"

When I nodded, she came closer and in a rush said how she was glad I saw the notice and that I was there. She said, "I couldn't come in December because of that awful storm and I felt so bad about it. I wanted to explain that to you and am so I'm glad I can tell you that in person."

Teary-eyed, I explained that Richard had been a good friend, that I was glad we were both there, and said again just how much he had helped me in my life. I wanted her to ask me how. What had her addicted son possibly done in his life that could have helped me so much, me with the good education, good background and good reputation? But she didn't. It did not matter. We had both been present and offered prayers for him. We wished each other well and then left the church. I was comforted and relieved by our encounter and was smiling as I drove to work.

Over a year later, MS had forced me to leave my job, and I was trying to make money as a writer. I was published in one edition of *Chicken Soup for the Soul* and was trying to write something for another book in the series. The book they were looking for stories for was "Messages from Heaven" and I had an idea to write about, although today that idea escapes me. As I attempted to put a submission together, all I could think of was Richard. Richard lighting a cigarette for me more than two months after he died was hardly appropriate for a *Chicken Soup for the Soul* book. Yet it was all that would come to me.

To get it out of my head, I wrote an outline of our time together. It was four pages. The next morning, I brought it to my writer's group basically because I didn't have any other writing to contribute. They were silent for several seconds after the reading. Then they asked questions. They encouraged me to go deeper, to delve into the entire story, all the blood and guts of our relationship, the good and the bad.

My group is not your fluffy, sappy writing group. We support each other but also critique each other with honesty, tough and total honesty. Their comments were sincere, and I pondered the idea. Why write this? Who would care? What was the point? My first love had a big impact on me and then died years later; sad, but not terribly unusual. As I thought about him, detailed memories filled my heart. I sat at my laptop and the words poured out of me, demanding to be told. Why, I don't know. I vowed that if I was going to write about this, I wouldn't sugarcoat any of it. There was much about Richard's life I was afraid to know and didn't understand. But I could write about the parts that had touched me in both amazing and heartbreaking ways. And write I did.

Many months later, I was contacted by a woman named Danielle. She and I had worked together in my early 20s and sometimes socialized afterwards. We were friends on Facebook and would periodically comment on each other's posts but weren't in touch very often. There was no way she knew what I was working on when she sent me a private message. She wrote that Richard had appeared to her in a dream and asked her to reach out to me and tell me that he was saying hello and sending his love. It was an incredible message that left me stunned. I asked her how she knew him, and she told me that she didn't. She said I'd introduced them at the bar one night and so she knew who he was, but that she had no other real interaction with him other than that brief introduction more than 20 years earlier. She said that this happens to her; deceased people she barely knows visit in her dreams and ask her to contact their loved ones. She said she didn't know why this happens, but it does and she accepts it. With Danielle's message, I felt even stronger about sharing my experience of the good person I had lost.

Unfortunately, Richard had probably lost himself even before we met, right when he inhaled cocaine for the very first time. But lost or not, he was the world to me.

I've often contemplated visiting a medium to confirm if writing about Richard is a good thing, if that's what he wants me to do. But while my faith doesn't forbid that kind of interaction, it instructs that more than anything we need to believe. When we believe, there is nothing a psychic can tell us we don't already know. And I believe that Richard finally slayed his demons. I believe the good heart of him deserves to be remembered and shared. And in this day of addiction, when so many young people are devoured by a drug too big for them to conquer, I can only hope that the next Richard may have many true friends who love them and who will try to help them through. Friends that will want to tell their stories. Friends who know they are more than their addictions. Friends who believe...

acknowledgements

I am blessed to have much in my life, and the amazing folks who helped shape this manuscript are among the best. My deepest gratitude to my family and to my "chosen family," those dear forever friends who lived this story with me, and who continue to live every story with me, the good, the bad and the humiliating. (Looking at you Serena!)

A special thank you to Jenny, Christine, Peter, Dora and Pon for using their unique talents to help me tell this story of someone they never knew.

Thank you to the real "Jesse" for talking with me, sharing your memories and allowing me to share my own. May your future always be as bright as your smile.

Thank you to the Provincetown Public Library for its gorgeous harbor view that often helped set the mood during the editing process. And thank you to the Snow Library in Orleans for their quiet study room that helped me focus when the drive to my hometown just wasn't in me.

Thank you to my phenomenal writing group- Joan, Carol, Anita, Barbara #1, Barbara #2, Nikole, Iris, Catherine, Jerri and Pat, who encouraged me to tell this story in the first place. When its synopsis came crawling out of my writer's heart in a four-page breakdown, it was this group that insisted it needed to be told completely. For that, I am beyond grateful.

A special thank you to Joan Graham for volunteering to be my first, and excellent, editor. Joan, your deadlines were always exactly where they needed to be, and your slice and dice editing skills were just what I needed. I miss you, my dear friend. I can't help thinking that when you arrived at your final resting place, you met Richard, said "oh, you're the one" and the two of you conspired to make this beautiful memory into an actual book. I believe Joan also sent fellow author Lisa Febre into my world to help sort through pre-production edits in the final manuscript. Lisa, I have zero clue how I would have gotten through this without your help. You are amazing my new friend.

Thank you to Black Rose Writing for liking this story enough to want to publish it. Your entire team is fabulous and I'm so thrilled to work with you!

An extra special thank you to my beta readers for agreeing to take on this project last minute, offering your incredible support and providing such crucial feedback. Mariah Carter Rogers, Dee DiFatta, Suzann Heron, David Mayo, Tammie Orrok, Jan Dowsett Potter, Betty Steele-Jeffers, Brittany Jensen and Kaitelyn Orrok. You are all rocking readers for sure! Also, a shout out and thank you to Marie, Tori, Gail and Laura for their great feedback as well.

Thank you to my dad for being such a character that he made my growing up amusing and filled with stories to make me smile. And most especially, thank you to my mom. Mom, Richard taught me to believe in myself. But you, by your example, your love and your own confident ways, taught me to be independent and strong.

Finally, thank you to the story itself. I'm a better person for having Richard in my life. If he touched any of you, (and I'm sure he did,) please note that these are my memories shared with the best of intentions and in the most honest way I remember them. I hope you find joy in your own memories as well.

If you or someone you love is struggling with addiction, there are resources available. Please contact one of the two agencies below for more information

Substance Abuse and Mental Health Services Administration
(SAMHSA)
800-622-HELP (4357)
English and Spanish
800-487-4889 (TTY)
24/7/365 Hotline

Narcotics Anonymous
na.org

The Pilgrim Monument in Provincetown, MA was completed in 1910 to commemorate the first landing of the Pilgrims to the new world.

It is worth the short climb to the top and has a great museum at its base.

For more information go to pilgrim-monument.org

about the author

Yvonne deSousa was blessed to grow up on Cape Cod, MA where she worked various jobs in the tourist industry. Her interest in true crime blended with her aspiration to serve others, which led to a career outside of Boston. There she met many amazing folks and learned their fascinating stories.

Years later, when the Cape began calling her home, she returned and worked as an office assistant. Then she was diagnosed with MS and began her true calling, writing.

She is the author of *MS Madness! A "Giggle More, Cry Less" Story of Multiple Sclerosis* and her work has appeared in *Chicken Soup for the Soul, Finding My Faith*, 2012, and *Listen to Your Dreams*, 2020.

www.yvonnedesousa.com

note from yvonne desousa

Word-of-mouth is crucial for any author to succeed. If you enjoyed *Shelter of the Monument*, please leave a review online—anywhere you are able. Even if it's just a sentence or two. It would make all the difference and would be very much appreciated.

Thanks!
Yvonne deSousa

We hope you enjoyed reading this title from:

Subscribe to our mailing list – *The Rosevine* – and receive **FREE** books, daily deals, and stay current with news about upcoming releases and our hottest authors.
Scan the QR code below to sign up.

Already a subscriber? Please accept a sincere thank you for being a fan of Black Rose Writing authors.

Printed in the USA
CPSIA information can be obtained
at www.ICGtesting.com
CBHW070948250324
5828CB00012B/54